1177 B.C.

• • • •

TURNING POINTS IN ANCIENT HISTORY

Barry Strauss, Series Editor

Turning Points in Ancient History presents accessible books, by
leading scholars, on crucial events and key moments in the ancient
world. The series aims at fresh interpretations of both famous
subjects and little-known ones that deserve more attention. The
books provide a narrative synthesis that integrates literary and
archaeological evidence.

1177 B.C.

THE YEAR CIVILIZATION COLLAPSED

•••••

Eric H. Cline

PRINCETON UNIVERSITY PRESS

PRINCETON AND OXFORD

Library of Congress Cataloging-in-Publication Data

Cline, Eric H.
  1177 B.C. : the year civilization collapsed / Eric H. Cline.
    pages cm. — (Turning points in ancient history)
  Summary: "In 1177 B.C., marauding groups known only as the "Sea Peoples" invaded Egypt. The
pharaoh's army and navy managed to defeat them, but the victory so weakened Egypt that it soon
slid into decline, as did most of the surrounding civilizations. After centuries of brilliance, the civilized world of the Bronze Age came to an abrupt and cataclysmic end. Kingdoms fell like dominoes
over the course of just a few decades. No more Minoans or Mycenaeans. No more Trojans, Hittites,
or Babylonians. The thriving economy and cultures of the late second millennium B.C., which had
stretched from Greece to Egypt and Mesopotamia, suddenly ceased to exist, along with writing systems, technology, and monumental architecture. But the Sea Peoples alone could not have caused
such widespread breakdown. How did it happen? In this major new account of the causes of this
"First Dark Ages," Eric Cline tells the gripping story of how the end was brought about by multiple
interconnected failures, ranging from invasion and revolt to earthquakes, drought, and the cutting
of international trade routes. Bringing to life the vibrant multicultural world of these great civilizations, he draws a sweeping panorama of the empires and globalized peoples of the Late Bronze Age
and shows that it was their very interdependence that hastened their dramatic collapse and ushered
in a dark age that lasted centuries. A compelling combination of narrative and the latest scholarship, 1177 B.C. sheds new light on the complex ties that gave rise to, and ultimately destroyed, the
flourishing civilizations of the Late Bronze Age—and that set the stage for the emergence of classical Greece"— Provided by publisher.
  Includes bibliographical references and index.
  ISBN 978-0-691-14089-6 (hardback)
  1. Bronze age—Mediterranean Region. 2. Mediterranean Region—Civilization. 3. Mediterranean Region—History—To 476. 4. Sea Peoples. I. Title.
  GN778.25.C55 2014
  930.1'56—dc23
  2013032059

British Library Cataloging-in-Publication Data is available

This book has been composed in Minion Pro

Printed on acid-free paper. ∞

Printed in the United States of America

7 9 10 8

Dedicated to James D. Muhly,

who has been debating these issues,

and introducing them to his students,

for nearly half a century

• • • •

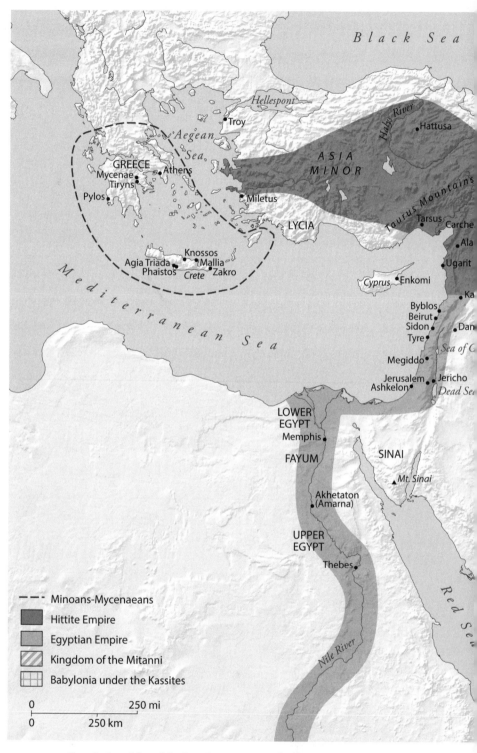

Frontispiece. Map of the Late Bronze Age civilizations in the Aegean and Eastern Mediterranean.

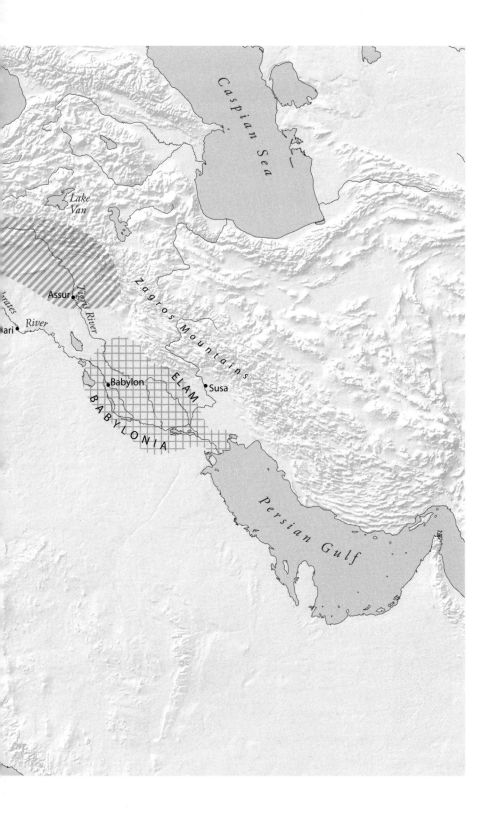

·❯ CONTENTS ❮·

··❧ ILLUSTRATIONS ❧··

FIGURES

TABLES

This volume is part of a series called Turning Points in Ancient History. Each book in the series looks at a crucial event or key moment in the ancient world. Always volatile and frequently dramatic, these were points at which history took a new direction. Whether famous or forgotten, they are moments that matter. Our focus is on why and how, as well as on when. Series authors are scholars who know how to tell a story and narrators who have the latest research at their command.

Turning Points in Ancient History reflects wide-ranging trends in the study of the ancient world. Each book integrates archaeology and classic texts; that is, it combines the evidence of material and literary culture. Books look both at the elite and at ordinary lives. The series does not confine itself strictly to the Greco-Roman world, though that certainly is at its core. We examine as well neighboring peoples of Greece and Rome, the non-Greco-Roman people of Greco-Roman lands, and civilizations and peoples of the wider ancient world, both East and West.

This is an exciting time for ancient history. Now more than ever, we realize that understanding the ancient past is essential to our understanding of the present and just plain fascinating.

Few events had a bigger impact on the evolution of the ancient world than the end of the Bronze Age. It was then that the great kingdoms and city-states of prehistory fell. They left behind stirring monuments like the Pyramids and dimly remembered tales such as the ones that were eventually reshaped into the Trojan War saga. To those who lived through it, the calamity seemed to be the end of the world. Yet the end of the massive palatial states of the Bronze Age opened the door for the growth of a new world on a more human scale, the world of the first millennium BC, a world in which we are still at home today.

1177 B.C.: The Year Civilization Collapsed begins with the invasion of Egypt by the Sea Peoples in 1177 and moves outward and backward. It takes us to the Late Bronze Age in the glory days of the fifteenth century BC and surveys a range of civilizations from Mesopotamia to Greece, and from Israel to the Hittites. Then it proceeds over the centuries to the processes, people, and events that brought down a world. Throughout there is a fingertip feel for the evidence. The scale of detail is as grand as the sack of the Syrian port city of Ugarit around 1190 BC, and as intimate as a CT scan of King Tut's skeleton and the infection after a broken leg that probably killed him.

With verve, wit, and a sense of drama, Eric Cline explores the echoes between the Late Bronze Age and our own time, from economic crisis and climate change to war in the Middle East. The year 1177 BC might not be a household word, but it deserves to be.

Barry Strauss

The economy of Greece is in shambles. Internal rebellions have engulfed Libya, Syria, and Egypt, with outsiders and foreign warriors fanning the flames. Turkey fears it will become involved, as does Israel. Jordan is crowded with refugees. Iran is bellicose and threatening, while Iraq is in turmoil. AD 2013? Yes. But it was also the situation in 1177 BC, more than three thousand years ago, when the Bronze Age Mediterranean civilizations collapsed one after the other, changing forever the course and the future of the Western world. It was a pivotal moment in history—a turning point for the ancient world.

The Bronze Age in the Aegean, Egypt, and the Near East lasted nearly two thousand years, from approximately 3000 BC to just after 1200 BC. When the end came, as it did after centuries of cultural and technological evolution, most of the civilized and international world of the Mediterranean regions came to a dramatic halt in a vast area stretching from Greece and Italy in the west to Egypt, Canaan, and Mesopotamia in the east. Large empires and small kingdoms, which had taken centuries to evolve, collapsed rapidly. With their end came a period of transition, once regarded by scholars as the world's first Dark Age. It was not until centuries later that a new cultural renaissance emerged in Greece and the other affected areas, setting the stage for the evolution of Western society as we know it today.

Although this book is primarily concerned with the collapse of Bronze Age civilizations and the factors that led to that collapse more than three millennia ago, it may contain lessons relevant to our globalized and transnationalized societies today. Some might assume that there is no valid comparison to be made between the world of the Late Bronze Age and our current technology-driven culture. However, there are enough similarities between the two—including diplomatic embassies and economic trade embargoes; kidnappings and ransoms; murders and royal assassinations; magnificent marriages and unpleasant divorces; international intrigues and deliberate military disinformation; climate change and drought; and even a shipwreck or two—that taking a closer look at the events, peoples, and places of an era that existed more than three millennia ago is more than merely an academic exercise in studying ancient history.[1] In the current global economy, and in a world recently wracked by earthquakes and tsunamis in Japan and the "Arab Spring" democratic revolutions in Egypt, Tunisia, Libya, Syria, and Yemen, the fortunes and investments of the United States and Europe are inextricably intertwined within an international system that also involves East Asia and the oil-producing nations of the Middle East. Thus, there is potentially much to be gleaned from an examination of the shattered remains of similarly intertwined civilizations that collapsed more than three thousand years ago.

Discussing "collapses" and comparing the rise and fall of empires is not a new idea; scholars have been doing it since at least the 1700s, when Edward Gibbon wrote about the fall of the Roman Empire. A more recent example is Jared Diamond's book *Collapse*.[2] However, these authors were considering how a single empire or a single civilization came to an end—the Romans, the Maya, the Mongols, and so forth. Here, we are considering a globalized world system with multiple civilizations all interacting and at least partially dependent upon each other. There are only a few instances in history of such globalized world systems; the one in place during the Late Bronze Age and the one in place today are two of the most obvious examples, and the parallels—comparisons might be a better word—between them are sometimes intriguing.

To give just one illustration, Carol Bell, a British academician, has recently observed that "the strategic importance of tin in the LBA [Late Bronze Age] . . . was probably not far different from that of crude oil today."[3] At that time, tin was available in quantity only from specific mines in the Badakhshan region of Afghanistan and had to be brought overland all the way to sites in Mesopotamia (modern Iraq) and north Syria, from where it was distributed to points farther north, south, or west, including onward across the sea to the Aegean. Bell continues, "The availability of enough tin to produce . . . weapons grade bronze must have exercised the minds of the Great King in Hattusa and the

Pharaoh in Thebes in the same way that supplying gasoline to the American SUV driver at reasonable cost preoccupies an American President today!"[4]

Susan Sherratt, an archaeologist formerly at the Ashmolean Museum in Oxford and now at the University of Sheffield, began arguing for such a comparison a decade ago. As she noted, there are some "genuinely useful analogies" between the world of 1200 BC and that of today, including an increase in political, social, and economic fragmentation, as well as the conducting of direct exchange at "unprecedented social levels and over unprecedented distances." Most relevant is her observation that the situation at the end of the Late Bronze Age provides an analogy for our own "increasingly homogenous yet uncontrollable global economy and culture, in which . . . political uncertainties on one side of the world can drastically affect the economies of regions thousands of miles away."[5]

The historian Fernand Braudel once said, "The story of the Bronze Age could easily be written in dramatic form: it is replete with invasions, wars, pillage, political disasters and long-lasting economic collapses, 'the first clashes between peoples.'" He also suggested that the history of the Bronze Age can be written "not only as a saga of drama and violence, but as a story of more benign contacts: commercial, diplomatic (even at this time), and above all cultural."[6] Braudel's suggestions have been taken to heart, and so here I present the story (or rather, stories) of the Late Bronze Age as a play in four acts, with appropriate narrative and flashbacks to provide proper contexts for the introduction of some of the major players, as they first appeared on the world stage and then made their exits: from Tudhaliya of the Hittites and Tushratta of Mitanni to Amenhotep III of Egypt and Assur-uballit of Assyria (a glossary, "Dramatis Personae," has been provided at the back of the book, for those wishing to keep the names and dates straight).

However, our narrative will also be something of a detective story, with twists and turns, false leads, and significant clues. To quote Hercule Poirot, the legendary Belgian detective created by Agatha Christie, who was herself married to an archaeologist,[7] we will need to use our "little grey cells" in order to weave together the various strands of evidence at the end of our chronicle, as we attempt to answer the question of why a stable international system suddenly collapsed after flourishing for centuries.

Moreover, in order to truly understand what collapsed in 1177 BC and why it was such a decisive moment in ancient history, we must begin earlier, just as one might wish to go back to the eighteenth century AD and begin with the culmination of the Enlightenment period, the Industrial Revolution, and the founding of the United States, in order to really understand the origins of today's globalized world. Although I am primarily interested in examining the possible causes of the collapse of the Bronze Age civilizations in this area, I also raise the question of what it was that the world lost at this pivotal moment, when the empires and kingdoms of the second millennium BC came crashing down, and the extent to which civilization in this part of the world was set back, in some places for centuries, and altered irrevocably. The magnitude of the catastrophe was enormous; it was a loss such as the world would not see again until the Roman Empire collapsed more than fifteen hundred years later.

··✈ ACKNOWLEDGMENTS ✈··

I have been wanting to write a book like this for a long time, and so, first and foremost, my heartfelt thanks go to Rob Tempio, who got this project going and then actively helped to shepherd the manuscript through the usual growing pains and into press. He also exhibited tremendous patience in waiting for the final manuscript to be submitted, somewhat past the original anticipated deadline. I am very pleased to have it chosen as the first book in the new Turning Points in Ancient History series published by Princeton University Press, under the direction of Barry Strauss and Rob Tempio.

I am also indebted to the University Facilitating Fund of The George Washington University for summer stipend money, and to numerous friends and colleagues, including Assaf Yasur-Landau, Israel Finkelstein, David Ussishkin, Mario Liverani, Kevin McGeough, Reinhard Jung, Cemal Pulak, Shirly Ben-Dor Evian, Sarah Parcak, Ellen Morris, and Jeffrey Blomster, with whom I have had rewarding conversations about relevant topics. I would also like specifically to thank Carol Bell, Reinhard Jung, Kevin McGeough, Jana Mynářová, Gareth Roberts, Kim Shelton, Neil Silberman, and Assaf Yasur-Landau for sending materials upon request or providing detailed answers to specific questions, and Randy Helm, Louise Hitchcock, Amanda Podany, Barry Strauss, Jim West, and two anonymous reviewers for reading and commenting upon the entire manuscript. Thanks also go to the National Geographic Society, the Oriental Institute of the University of Chicago, the Metropolitan Museum of Art, and the Egypt Exploration Society for permission to reproduce some of the figures that appear in this book.

Much of the material in this book represents an up-to-date and accessible rendition of my research and publications on international relations during the Late Bronze Age that have appeared over the course of the past two decades or more, in addition to presenting, of course, the research and conclusions of many other scholars. Grateful thanks therefore also go to the editors and publishers of the various journals and edited volumes in which some of my previous relevant articles and publications have appeared, for their permission to reproduce that material here, albeit usually altered and updated. These include especially David Davison of Tempus Reparatum/Archaeopress, as well as Jack Meinhardt and *Archaeology Odyssey* magazine; James R. Mathieu and *Expedition* magazine; Virginia Webb and the *Annual of the British School at Athens*; Mark Cohen and CDL Press; Tom Palaima and *Minos*; Robert Laffineur and the Aegaeum series; Ed White and Recorded Books/Modern Scholar; Garrett Brown and the National Geographic Society; and Angelos Chaniotis and Mark Chavalas, among others. I have made every attempt to clearly document within the endnotes and bibliography the publications in which my previous discussions of the data presented here may be found. Any phrasing or other borrowing, from either my own previous publications or those by any other scholar, that remains unattributed is purely unintentional and will be rectified in future editions, as necessary.

And last, but certainly not least, I would like to thank my wife, Diane, for many stimulating conversations about aspects of this material. Among other contributions, she introduced me to the topics of social network analysis and complexity theory, and created some of the images used here. I would also like to thank both her and our children for their patience while I worked on this book. As always, the text has benefited from the firm editing and critical feedback of my father, Martin J. Cline.

1177 B.C.

·•••·

THE COLLAPSE OF CIVILIZATIONS:
1177 BC

The warriors entered the world scene and moved rapidly, leaving death and destruction in their wake. Modern scholars refer to them collectively as the "Sea Peoples," but the Egyptians who recorded their attack on Egypt never used that term, instead identifying them as separate groups working together: the Peleset, Tjekker, Shekelesh, Shardana, Danuna, and Weshesh—foreign-sounding names for foreign-looking people.[1]

We know little about them, beyond what the Egyptian records tell us. We are not certain where the Sea Peoples originated: perhaps in Sicily, Sardinia, and Italy, according to one scenario, perhaps in the Aegean or western Anatolia, or possibly even Cyprus or the Eastern Mediterranean.[2] No ancient site has ever been identified as their origin or departure point. We think of them as moving relentlessly from site to site, overrunning countries and kingdoms as they went. According to the Egyptian texts, they set up camp in Syria before proceeding down the coast of Canaan (including parts of modern Syria, Lebanon, and Israel) and into the Nile delta of Egypt.

The year was 1177 BC. It was the eighth year of Pharaoh Ramses III's reign.[3] According to the ancient Egyptians, and to more recent archaeological evidence, some of the Sea Peoples came by land, others by sea.[4] There were no uniforms, no polished outfits. Ancient images portray one group with feathered headdresses, while another faction sported skullcaps; still others had horned helmets or went bareheaded. Some had short pointed beards and dressed in short kilts, either bare-chested or with a tunic; others had no facial hair and wore longer garments, almost like skirts. These observations suggest that the Sea Peoples comprised diverse groups from different geographies and different cultures. Armed with sharp bronze swords, wooden spears with gleaming metal tips, and bows and arrows, they came on boats, wagons, oxcarts, and chariots. Although I have taken 1177 BC as a pivotal date, we know that the invaders

Fig. 1. Sea Peoples portrayed as captives at Medinet Habu (after *Medinet Habu*, vol. 1, pl. 44; courtesy of the Oriental Institute of the University of Chicago).

came in waves over a considerable period of time. Sometimes the warriors came alone, and sometimes their families accompanied them.

··҂ ҂··

According to Ramses's inscriptions, no country was able to oppose this invading mass of humanity. Resistance was futile. The great powers of the day—the Hittites, the Mycenaeans, the Canaanites, the Cypriots, and others—fell one by one. Some of the survivors fled the carnage; others huddled in the ruins of their once-proud cities; still others joined the invaders, swelling their ranks and adding to the apparent complexities of the mob of invaders. Each group of the Sea Peoples was on the move, each apparently motivated by individual reasons. Perhaps it was the desire for spoils or slaves that spurred some; others may have been compelled by population pressures to migrate eastward from their own lands in the West.

On the walls of his mortuary temple at Medinet Habu, near the Valley of the Kings, Ramses said concisely:

> The foreign countries made a conspiracy in their islands. All at once the lands were removed and scattered in the fray. No land could stand before their arms, from Khatte, Qode, Carchemish, Arzawa, and Alashiya on,

being cut off at [one time]. A camp [was set up] in one place in Amurru. They desolated its people, and its land was like that which has never come into being. They were coming forward toward Egypt, while the flame was prepared before them. Their confederation was the Peleset, Tjekker, Shekelesh, Danuna, and Weshesh, lands united. They laid their hands upon the lands as far as the circuit of the earth, their hearts confident and trusting.[5]

We know these places that were reportedly overrun by the invaders, for they were famous in antiquity. Khatte is the land of the Hittites, with its heartland located on the inland plateau of Anatolia (the ancient name for Turkey) near modern Ankara and its empire stretching from the Aegean coast in the west to the lands of northern Syria in the east. Qode is probably located in what is now southeastern Turkey (possibly the region of ancient Kizzuwadna). Carchemish is a well-known archaeological site first excavated almost a century ago by a team of archaeologists that included Sir Leonard Woolley, perhaps better known for his excavation of Abraham's "Ur of the Chaldees" in Iraq, and T. E. Lawrence, who was trained as a classical archaeologist at Oxford before his exploits in World War I ultimately transformed him into Hollywood's "Lawrence of Arabia." Arzawa was a land familiar to the Hittites, located within their grasp in western Anatolia. Alashiya may have been what we know today as the island of Cyprus, a metal-rich island famous for its copper ore. Amurru was located on the coast of northern Syria. We shall visit all of these places again, in the pages and stories that follow.

The six individual groups who made up the Sea Peoples during this wave of invasion—the five mentioned above by Ramses in the Medinet Habu inscription and a sixth group, named the Shardana, mentioned in another relevant inscription—are far more shadowy than the lands that they reportedly overran. They left no inscriptions of their own and are therefore known textually almost entirely from Egyptian inscriptions.[6]

Most of these groups are also difficult to detect in the archaeological record, although archaeologists and philologists have been making a valiant attempt for much of the past century, first by playing linguistic games and then, more recently, by looking at pottery and other archaeological remains. For instance, the Danuna were long ago identified with Homer's Danaans, from the Bronze Age Aegean. The Shekelesh are often hypothesized to have come from what is now Sicily and the Shardana from Sardinia, based in part on the consonantal similarities in each case and the fact that Ramses refers to these "foreign countries" as making a conspiracy "in their islands," for the Shardana in particular were labeled in Ramses's inscriptions as being "of the sea."[7]

However, not all scholars accept these suggestions, and there is an entire school of thought which suggests that the Shekelesh and the Shardana did not come from the Western Mediterranean, but rather were from areas in the Eastern Mediterranean and only fled to the regions of Sicily and Sardinia, and gave their name to these regions, after having been defeated by the Egyptians. In favor of such a possibility is the fact that the Shardana are known to have been fighting both for and against the Egyptians long before the advent of the Sea Peoples. Against the possibility is the fact that we are later told, by Ramses III, that he settled the survivors of the attacking forces in Egypt itself.[8]

Of all the foreign groups active in this arena at this time, only one has been firmly identified. The Peleset of the Sea Peoples are generally accepted as none other than the Philistines, who are identified in the Bible as coming from Crete.[9] The linguistic identification was apparently so obvious that Jean-François Champollion, the decipherer of Egyptian hieroglyphics, had already suggested it before 1836, and the identification of specific pottery styles, architecture, and other material remains as "Philistine" was begun as early as 1899 by biblical archaeologists working at Tell es-Safi, identified as biblical Gath.[10]

While we do not know with any precision either the origins or the motivation of the invaders, we do know what they look like—we can view their names and faces carved on the walls of Ramses III's mortuary temple at Medinet Habu. This ancient site is rich in both pictures and stately rows of hieroglyphic text. The invaders' armor, weapons, clothing, boats, and ox-carts loaded with possessions are all clearly visible in the representations, so detailed that scholars have published analyses of the individual people and even the different boats shown in the scenes.[11] Other panoramas are more graphic. One of these shows foreigners and Egyptians engaged in a chaotic naval battle; some are floating upside down and are clearly dead, while others are still fighting fiercely from their boats.

Since the 1920s, the inscriptions and scenes at Medinet Habu have been studied and exactingly copied by Egyptologists from the Oriental Institute at the University of Chicago. The institute was and still is one of

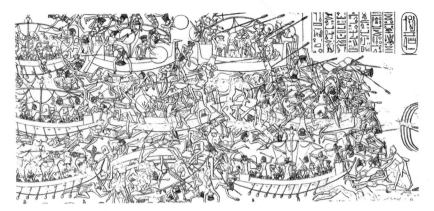

Fig. 2. Naval battle with Sea Peoples at Medinet Habu (after *Medinet Habu*, vol. 1, pl. 37; courtesy of the Oriental Institute of the University of Chicago).

the preeminent centers in the world for the study of ancient civilizations in Egypt and the Near East. James Henry Breasted founded it upon his return from an epic journey through the Near East in 1919 and 1920, with fifty thousand dollars in seed money from John D. Rockefeller, Jr. Archaeologists from the OI (as it is generally called) have excavated all over the Near East, from Iran to Egypt and beyond.

Much has been written about Breasted and the OI projects that began under his direction, including the excavations at Megiddo (biblical Armageddon) in Israel, which lasted from 1925 to 1939.[12] Among the most important were the epigraphic surveys that were conducted in Egypt, during which the Egyptologists painstakingly copied the hieroglyphic texts and scenes left by the pharaohs on their temples and palaces throughout Egypt. It is a tremendously tedious job to copy the hieroglyphics carved into stone walls and monuments. It involves hours of work, and transcribers are usually perched on ladders or scaffolding in the hot sun, peering at deteriorated symbols inscribed on gates, temples, and columns. Suffice it to say, the results are invaluable, especially since many of the inscriptions have suffered greatly as a result of erosion, damage by tourists, or other injuries. Were these inscriptions not transcribed, they would eventually become undecipherable to future generations. The results of the transcriptions from Medinet Habu were published in a series of volumes, the first of which appeared in 1930, with subsequent and related volumes appearing in the 1940s and 1950s.

Although scholarly debate continues, most experts agree that the land and sea battles depicted on the walls at Medinet Habu were probably fought nearly simultaneously in the Egyptian delta or nearby. It is possible that they represent a single extended battle that occurred both on land and at sea, and some scholars have suggested that both represent ambushes of the Sea Peoples' forces, in which the Egyptians caught them by surprise.[13] In any event, the end result is not in question, for at Medinet Habu the Egyptian pharaoh quite clearly states:

> Those who reached my frontier, their seed is not, their heart and soul are finished forever and ever. Those who came forward together on the sea, the full flame was in front of them at the river-mouths, while a stockade of lances surrounded them on the shore. They were dragged in, enclosed, and prostrated on the beach, killed, and made into heaps from tail to head. Their ships and their goods were as if fallen into the water. I have made the lands turn back from (even) mentioning Egypt: for when they pronounce my name in their land, then they are burned up.[14]

Ramses then continues, in a famous document known as the Papyrus Harris, again naming his defeated enemies:

> I overthrew those who invaded them from their lands. I slew the Danuna [who are] in their isles, the Tjekker and the Peleset were made ashes. The Shardana and the Weshesh of the sea, they were made as those that exist not, taken captive at one time, brought as captives to Egypt, like the sand of the shore. I settled them in strongholds bound in my name. Numerous were their classes like hundred-thousands. I taxed them all, in clothing and grain from the store-houses and granaries each year.[15]

·· ·

This was not the first time that the Egyptians fought against a collective force of "Sea Peoples." Thirty years earlier, in 1207 BC, during the fifth year of Pharaoh Merneptah's reign, a similar coalition of these shadowy groups had attacked Egypt.

Merneptah is perhaps best known to students of the ancient Near East as the Egyptian pharaoh who first uses the term "Israel," in an inscription dating to this same year (1207 BC). This inscription is the earliest occurrence of the name *Israel* outside the Bible. In the Pharaonic inscription, the name—written with a special sign to indicate that it is a people rather than just a place—appears in a brief description of a campaign to the region of Canaan, where the people whom he calls "Israel" were located.[16] The sentences are found within the context of a long inscription that is otherwise concerned with Merneptah's ongoing battles with the Libyans, located just to the west of Egypt proper. It is the Libyans and the Sea Peoples who occupied most of Merneptah's attention during this year, rather than the Israelites.

For example, in a text found at the site of Heliopolis, dated to "Year 5, second month of the third season (tenth month)," we are told, "The wretched chief of Libya has invaded [with] Shekelesh and every foreign country, which is with him, to violate the borders of Egypt."[17] The same wording is repeated on another inscription, known as the "Cairo Column."[18]

In a longer inscription found at Karnak (modern-day Luxor), we are given additional details about this earlier wave of incursions by the Sea Peoples. The names of the individual groups are included:

[Beginning of the victory that his majesty achieved in the land of Libya] Eqwesh, Teresh, Lukka, Shardana, Shekelesh, Northerners coming from all lands. . . . the third season, saying: The wretched, fallen chief of Libya . . . has fallen upon the country of Tehenu with his bowmen—Shardana, Shekelesh, Eqwesh, Lukka, Teresh, taking the best of every warrior and every man of war of his country . . .

List of the captives carried off from this land of Libya and the countries which he brought with him . . .

> Sherden, Shekelesh, Eqwesh of the countries of the sea, who had no
>   foreskins:
> Shekelesh 222 men
> Making 250 hands
> Teresh 742 men
> Making 790 hands
> Shardana—
> [Making]—
> [Ek]wesh who had no foreskins, slain, whose hands were carried off,
>   (for) they
> had no [foreskins]—
> Shekelesh and Teresh who came as enemies of Libya—
> Kehek, and Libyans, carried off as living prisoners 218 men.[19]

Several things are apparent in this inscription. First there are five groups, rather than six, who made up this earlier wave of Sea Peoples: the Shardana (or Sherden), Shekelesh, Eqwesh, Lukka, and Teresh. The Shardana and Shekelesh are present in both this invasion and the later one during the time of Ramses III, but the other three groups are different. Second, the Shardana, Shekelesh, and Eqwesh are specifically identified as being "of the countries of the sea," while the five groups are together described as "Northerners coming from all lands." The latter is not too surprising, for most lands with which the New Kingdom Egyptians were in contact (except for Nubia and Libya) lay to the north of Egypt. The identification of the Shardana and the Shekelesh as "countries of the sea" reinforces the suggestion that they are to be linked with Sardinia and Sicily, respectively.

The description of the Eqwesh as being from "the countries of the sea" has led some scholars to suggest that they are Homer's Achaeans, that is, the Mycenaeans of the Bronze Age Greek mainland, whom Ramses III would perhaps identify as the Danuna in his Sea Peoples inscriptions two decades later. As for the final two names, scholars generally accept Lukka as a reference to peoples from southwestern Turkey, in the region later known during the classical era as Lycia. The origin of the Teresh is uncertain but might be linked to the Etruscans in Italy.[20]

We are told little else in the inscriptions, and have no more than a very general idea where the battle or battles were fought. Merneptah says only that the victory was "achieved in the land of Libya," which he further identifies as "the country of Tehenu." However, Merneptah clearly claims victory, for he lists the killed and captured enemy combatants, both men and "hands." The general practice of the day was to cut off the hand of a dead enemy and bring it back as proof, in order to get credit and reward for the kill. Gruesome evidence of this practice has just been found from the Hyksos period in Egypt, some four hundred years before Merneptah's time, in the form of sixteen right hands buried in four pits at the Hyksos palace at Avaris in the Nile delta.[21] In any event, we do not know whether all of the Sea Peoples were killed or some survived, but we can probably assume the latter, since several of the groups returned in the second invasion thirty years later.

··❧ ❧··

In 1177 BC, as previously in 1207 BC, the Egyptians were victorious. The Sea Peoples would not return to Egypt a third time. Ramses boasted that the enemy were "capsized and overwhelmed in their places." "Their hearts," he wrote, "are taken away; their soul is flown away. Their weapons are scattered in the sea."[22] However, it was a Pyrrhic victory. Although Egypt under Ramses III was the only major power to successfully resist the onslaught of the Sea Peoples, New Kingdom Egypt was never the same again afterward, most likely because of the other problems faced by the entire Mediterranean region during this period, as we shall see below. The succeeding pharaohs, for the rest of the second millennium BC, were content to rule over a country much diminished in influence and power. Egypt became a second-rate empire; a mere shadow of what it had once been. It was not until the days of Pharaoh Shoshenq, a Libyan who founded the Twenty-Second Dynasty ca. 945 BC—and who is probably to be identified as Pharaoh Shishak of the Hebrew Bible[23]—that Egypt rose to a semblance of prominence again.

Beyond Egypt, almost all of the other countries and powers of the second millennium BC in the Aegean and Near East—those that had been present during the golden years of what we now call the Late Bronze Age—withered and disappeared, either immediately or within less than a century. In the end, it was as if civilization itself had been wiped away in much of this region. Many, if not all, of the advances of the previous centuries vanished across great swaths of territory, from Greece to Mesopotamia. A new transitional era began: an age that was to last for at least one century and perhaps as many as three in some areas.

There seems little doubt that terror must have prevailed throughout the lands in the final days of these kingdoms. A specific example can be seen on a clay tablet, inscribed with a letter from the king of Ugarit in northern Syria, addressed to the higher-ranking king on the island of Cyprus:

> My father, now the ships of the enemy have come. They have been setting fire to my cities and have done harm to the land. Doesn't my father know that all of my infantry and [chariotry] are stationed in Khatte, and that all of my ships are stationed in the land of Lukka? They have not arrived back yet, so the land is thus prostrate. May my father be aware of

this matter. Now the seven ships of the enemy which have been coming have done harm to us. Now if other ships of the enemy turn up, send me a report somehow, so that I will know.[24]

There is some dispute about whether the tablet ever reached the intended recipient on Cyprus. The original excavators who found the tablet thought the letter might never have been sent. It was originally reported to have been found in a kiln, along with more than seventy other tablets, where it had apparently been placed for baking—the better to survive the rough journey to Cyprus.[25] These excavators and other scholars initially surmised that the enemy ships had returned and sacked the city before the urgent request for assistance could be dispatched. This is the story that has since been repeated in textbooks for a generation of students, but scholars have now shown that the tablet was not found in a kiln and, as we shall see, was probably a copy of a letter that had been dispatched to Cyprus after all.

·⋅ঌ ঌ⋅·

There was a tendency on the part of earlier scholars to attribute any destruction from this period to the Sea Peoples.[26] However, it may be presumptuous to lay the blame for the end of the Bronze Age in the Aegean and Eastern Mediterranean entirely at their feet. It probably gives them too much credit, for we have no clear evidence, apart from the Egyptian texts and inscriptions, which give conflicting impressions. Did the Sea Peoples approach the Eastern Mediterranean as a relatively organized army, like one of the more disciplined Crusades intent on capturing the Holy Land during the Middle Ages? Were they a loosely or poorly organized group of marauders, like the Vikings of a later age? Or were they refugees fleeing a disaster and seeking new lands? For all we know, the truth could involve a combination of all or none of the above.

A wealth of new data available in the past few decades now needs to be considered within the equation.[27] We are no longer certain that all of the sites with evidence of destruction were razed by the Sea Peoples. We can tell from the archaeological evidence that a site was destroyed, but not always by what or by whom. Moreover, the sites were not all destroyed simultaneously, or even necessarily within the same decade. As we shall see, their cumulative demise spans several decades and perhaps as much as a century.

Moreover, while we do not know for certain the cause, or all the causes, of the collapse of the Bronze Age world in Greece, Egypt, and the Near East, the weight of contemporary evidence suggests that it was probably not the Sea Peoples alone who were to blame. It now seems likely that they were as much the victims as they were the aggressors in the collapse of civilizations.[28] One hypothesis suggests that they were forced out of their homes by a series of unfortunate events and migrated eastward where they encountered kingdoms and empires already in decline. It is also quite possible that they were able to attack and ultimately vanquish many of the kingdoms of the region precisely because those monarchies were already in decline and in a weakened state. In this context, the Sea Peoples might perhaps be considered simply opportunistic, as one scholar has called them, and might have settled down in the Eastern Mediterranean much more peacefully than has previously been assumed. We shall consider these possibilities in greater detail below.

Nevertheless, for decades of scholarly research the Sea Peoples were a convenient scapegoat, taking the fall for a situation that may have been far more complex and not of their own making. The tide is now turning, for several scholars have recently pointed out that the "story" of the Sea Peoples' catastrophic wave of wanton destruction and/or migration had been created by scholars such as Gaston Maspero, the famous French Egyptologist, as early as the 1860s and 1870s, and was solidified by 1901. However, it was a theory based solely upon the epigraphic evidence of the inscriptions, long before any of the destroyed sites had actually been excavated. In fact, even those scholars who followed Maspero's lead were divided as to the direction followed by the Sea Peoples, for some thought that they ended up in the Western Mediterranean after being defeated by the Egyptians, rather than starting there.[29]

In our current view, as we shall see below, the Sea Peoples may well have been responsible for some of the destruction that occurred at the end of the Late Bronze Age, but it is much more likely that a concatenation of events, both human and natural—including climate change and drought, seismic disasters known as earthquake storms, internal rebellions, and "systems collapse"—coalesced to create a "perfect storm" that brought this age to an end. However, in order to understand the enormity of the events that took place around 1177 BC, we have to begin three centuries earlier.

Table 1.

Late Bronze Age Egyptian and Near Eastern kings mentioned in the text, listed by country/kingdom and chronology

Century	Egyptian	Hittite	Assyrian	Babylonian	Mitanni	Ugarit	Other
18th		Hattusili I		Hammurabi			Zimri-Lim (Mari)
17th		Mursili I					
16th	Seknenre Kahmose Ahmose I Thutmose I Thutmose II						Khyan (Hyksos) Apophis (Hyksos)
15th	Hatshepsut Thutmose III	Tudhaliya I/II			Saushtatar		Kukkuli (Assuwa)
14th	Amenhotep III Akhenaten Tutankhamen Ay	Suppiluliuma I Mursili II	Adad-nirari I Assur-uballit	Kurigalzu I Kadashman-Enlil I Burna-Buriash II Kurigalzu II	Shuttarna II Tushratta Shattiwaza	Ammistamru I Niqmaddu II Niqmepa	Tarkhundaradu (Arzawa)
13th	Ramses II Merneptah	Mursili II (cont'd) Muwattalli II Hattusili III Tudhaliya IV Suppiluliuma II	Tukulti-Ninurta I	Kashtiliashu		Niqmepa (cont'd) Ammistamru II Niqmaddu III Ammurapi	Shaushgamuwa (Amurru)
12th	Ramses III	Suppiluliuma II (cont'd)				Ammurapi (cont'd)	Shutruk-Nahhunte (Elam)

Table 2.
Modern areas and their probable Late Bronze Age names

Area	Ancient name #1	Ancient name #2	Ancient name #3
Cyprus	*Alashiya*		
Mainland Greece	*Tanaja*	*Ahhiyawa*	*Hiyawa*
Crete	*Keftiu*	*Caphtor (Kaptaru)*	
Troy/Troad	*Assuwa (?)*	*Isy (?)*	*Wilusa*
Canaan	*Pa-ka-na-na*	*Retenu*	
Egypt	*Misraim*		

CHAPTER ONE

ACT I
· · · ·

OF ARMS AND THE MAN:

THE FIFTEENTH CENTURY BC

In about the year 1477 BC, in the city of Peru-nefer in the Nile delta of Lower Egypt, quite close to the Mediterranean Sea, Pharaoh Thutmose III ordered the construction of a grand palace with elaborate frescoes. Minoan artists from distant Crete, located far to the west across the Great Green (as the Mediterranean Sea was known to the Egyptians), were hired to create these frescoes. They painted pictures never seen before in Egypt—strange scenes of men leaping over bulls—with the paint applied to the plaster while it was still wet, in an *al fresco* style so that the colors became part of the wall itself. It was a technique, and a scene, that they had learned on Crete in the Aegean. The unique images created in this manner were now in vogue not only in Egypt but also at palaces up and down the coast, from northern Canaan to the Egyptian delta at sites now known as Kabri in Israel, Alalakh in Turkey, Qatna in Syria, and Dab'a in Egypt.[1]

Peru-nefer, the city in the delta, has now been identified with modern Tell ed-Dab'a. It is a site that has been excavated by the Austrian archaeologist Manfred Bietak and his team since 1966. The city had also previously been known as Avaris, capital city of the Hyksos, the hated invaders of Egypt who ruled much of the country from ca. 1720 to 1550 BC. Avaris was transformed into Peru-nefer, a valued Egyptian metropolis, after its capture by Thutmose's ancestor the Egyptian pharaoh Kamose around the year 1550 BC.

In uncovering a formerly wealthy city now buried under meters of sand and debris, Bietak brought both the Hyksos capital city and the later Egyptian metropolis back to life over the course of four decades.

He also recovered the amazing fresco paintings created by Minoans, or possibly local artisans trained by the Minoans, which date to the early Eighteenth Dynasty (about 1450 BC).[2] These serve as a good example of the internationalized world that began to coalesce in the Eastern Mediterranean and Aegean after the expulsion of the Hyksos from Egypt.

HARKENING BACK TO THE HYKSOS

The Hyksos had first invaded Egypt in about the year 1720 BC, a quarter of a millennium before the time of Thutmose III. They stayed for nearly two hundred years, until 1550 BC. At the time that the Hyksos overran the country, Egypt was one of the established powers in the ancient Near East. The pyramids of Giza were already nearly a thousand years old by that point, having been built during the Fourth Dynasty, in the Old Kingdom period. Manetho, an Egyptian priest who lived and wrote during the much-later Hellenistic period in the third century BC, identified the Hyksos as "Shepherd Kings"—a mistranslation of the Egyptian phrase *hekau khasut*, which actually means "chieftains of foreign lands." And foreigners they were, for the Hyksos were Semites who migrated into Egypt from the region of Canaan, that is, modern-day Israel, Lebanon, Syria, and Jordan. We see representations of such Semites in Egypt as early as the nineteenth century BC—for example, a wall painting within an Egyptian tomb at Beni Hasan, where we are shown "Asiatic" merchants and traders bringing their goods into the country.[3]

The Hyksos invasion of Egypt brought the Middle Kingdom period (ca. 2134–1720 BC) to an end. Their success was quite possibly the result of an advantage in weapons technology and first-strike capability, for they possessed composite bows that could shoot arrows much farther than a traditional bow of the time. They also had horse-drawn chariots, the likes of which had not previously been seen in Egypt.

After their conquest, the Hyksos then ruled over Egypt, primarily from their capital city of Avaris in the Nile delta, during the so-called Second Intermediate period (Dynasties Fifteen–Seventeen) for nearly two hundred years, from 1720 to 1550 BC.[4] It is one of the only times during the period from 3000 to 1200 BC when Egypt was ruled by foreigners.

Fig. 3. "Asiatics" at Beni Hasan (after Newberry 1893, pls. xxx/xxxi; courtesy of the Egypt Exploration Society).

Stories and inscriptions dating to near the end of this period, about 1550 BC, record some of the battles that flared up between the Egyptians and the Hyksos. In particular, we have one story that records a disagreement between two rulers, *The Quarrel of Apophis and Seknenre*. In this tale—quite possibly apocryphal—the Hyksos king Apophis complains that he is being kept awake at night by the noise from hippopotami kept in a pond by the Egyptian king Seknenre, who was ruling simultaneously elsewhere in Egypt. The complaint is preposterous because several hundred miles separated the two royal courts; one was located in Upper Egypt and the other in Lower Egypt. The Hyksos king could not possibly have heard the hippos, no matter how loudly they were bellowing.[5] However, the mummy of Seknenre has been recovered by archaeologists, and it is clear from wounds on his skull—made by a battle-ax—that he died violently in battle. Was the battle with the Hyksos? We do not know for certain; however, it is possible that Apophis and Seknenre fought each other, whether or not it was over hippopotami.

We also have an inscription left to us by the pharaoh Kamose, last king of the Seventeenth Dynasty of Egypt. At the time, Kamose was ruling from his home in Thebes, in Upper Egypt. He gives details about the final victorious battle against the Hyksos, whom he refers to as "Asiatics," writing as follows in about 1550 BC:

> I sailed north in my might to repel the Asiatics . . . with my brave army before me like a flame of fire and the . . . archers atop our fighting-tops to destroy their places. . . . I passed the night in my ship, my heart happy; and when day dawned I was upon him as if it were a hawk. When breakfast time came, I overthrew him having destroyed his walls and slaughtered his people, and made his wife descend to the riverbank. My army acted like lions with their spoil . . . chattles, cattle, fat, honey . . . dividing their things, their hearts joyful.

Kamose also tells us about the fate of Avaris itself:

> As for Avaris on the Two Rivers, I laid it waste without inhabitants; I destroyed their towns and burned their homes to reddened ruin-heaps forever, because of the destruction they had wrought in the midst of Egypt: they who had allowed themselves to hearken to the call of the Asiatics, (who) had forsaken Egypt their mistress![6]

And, with that, the Egyptians expelled the Hyksos from the land. They fled back to *Retenu* (one of the ancient Egyptian names for modern-day Israel and Syria, the same general area also known to the Egyptians as *Pa-ka-na-na*, or Canaan). The Egyptians, meanwhile, established the Eighteenth Dynasty, begun by Kamose's brother Ahmose, which initiated what we now call the New Kingdom period in Egypt.

Avaris and the rest of Egypt were rebuilt during this period, and Avaris itself was renamed. By the time of Hatshepsut and Thutmose III some sixty years later, ca. 1500 BC, it was once again a flourishing city, this time known as Peru-nefer, with palaces decorated with Minoan-style frescoes depicting bull-leaping and other scenes more clearly at home on Crete in the Aegean than in Egypt proper. One archaeologist has speculated that there may even have been a royal marriage between an Egyptian ruler and a Minoan princess.[7] There are certainly a number of later Eighteenth and Nineteenth Dynasty Egyptian pharaohs who married foreign princesses, primarily to cement diplomatic bonds or a treaty with a foreign power, as we shall see below, but it is not necessary to invoke politically instigated marriages to explain the occurrence of

Minoan wall paintings in Egypt, since there is other independent evidence for contacts between the Eastern Mediterranean, Egypt, and, in this case, the Aegean.

FLASHBACK: MESOPOTAMIA AND THE MINOANS

It is clear, from a multitude of data, including archaeological artifacts, and textual and pictorial evidence, that the Minoans of Crete had already been in contact with several areas in the ancient Near East long before their interactions with the New Kingdom Egyptian pharaohs. For example, we know of Minoan-manufactured objects that had been transported across the Aegean Sea and the Eastern Mediterranean all the way to Mesopotamia, the land between the two rivers—the Tigris and Euphrates—by the eighteenth century BC, nearly four thousand years ago.

Documentation of this ancient trade comes from the ancient site of Mari, on the western side of the Euphrates River in what is now modern Syria, where French archaeologists excavated a treasure trove of more than twenty thousand inscribed clay tablets during the 1930s. They had been summoned to the site by locals who had accidentally uncovered what they thought at first was a headless man—which turned out to be a stone statue, one of many, including one with an inscription identifying him as a king of the ancient city.[8] The tablets, inscribed with texts written in ancient Akkadian, came from an archive of royal correspondence and other more mundane records belonging to the kings of Mari, including one named Zimri-Lim who ruled ca. 1750 BC. They record all sorts of information pertinent to the administration of the palace and the organization of his kingdom, as well as aspects of daily life at the time.

One tablet, for instance, is concerned with the ice that Zimri-Lim was using in his summer drinks, which included wine, beer, and fermented barley-based drinks flavored with either pomegranate juice or licorice-like aniseed. We know that he had ordered an icehouse to be built on the bank of the Euphrates, which was to be used specifically to hold ice collected from the snowy mountains during the winter until it was needed during the hot summer months. He claimed that no previous king had ever built such an icehouse, and that may well have been the case, but the use of ice in drinks was not new to the region, even though one king had to remind his son to have the servants clean the ice before actually putting it in the drinks: "Make them collect the ice! Let them wash it free of twigs and dung and dirt."[9]

The archives included records of trade and contact with other areas of the Mediterranean and Near East, with specific mention of unusual items that were received. We also know from these tablets that gifts were frequently exchanged between the rulers of Mari and those of other cities and kingdoms, and that the kings requested the services of physicians, artisans, weavers, musicians, and singers from one another.[10]

Included among the exotic imported objects recorded in the tablets at Mari were a dagger and other weapons made of gold and inlaid with precious lapis lazuli, as well as clothing and textiles "made in the Caphtorian manner."[11] *Caphtor* (or *Kaptaru*) was the Mesopotamian and Canaanite name for Crete, just as the Egyptians later called it *Keftiu*. The items had traveled a long way from Crete, acquiring what is now known as "distance value," in addition to the inherent value that they already held because of the workmanship and the materials from which they were made.

We also have a tablet that records an unusual situation, when Zimri-Lim, the king of Mari, sent a pair of Minoan shoes from Crete as a gift to King Hammurabi of Babylon. The text says simply, "One pair of leather shoes in the Caphtorian style, which to the palace of Hammurabi, King of Babylon, Bahdi-Lim (an official) carried, but which were returned."[12] It does not give the reason why the shoes were returned. Perhaps they simply didn't fit. Hammurabi's law code, which is the first to contain the saying "an eye for an eye, a tooth for a tooth" later made famous by the Hebrew Bible, does not mention any penalties for returning items such as shoes.

It is a bit surprising that Hammurabi rejected the leather shoes, regardless of whether or not they fit, because they probably would have been both rare and unusual in his lands at the time, given the distance lying between Crete and Mesopotamia, that is, between what is now modern Greece and Syria/Iraq. Such a journey would not have been undertaken lightly and would likely have been made in stages, with different traders or merchants transporting the items for separate segments of the trip. On the other hand, such gift giving between kings of equal rank was a practice quite well known in the ancient Near East during the second millennium BC.[13] In these cases, the items in question were brought directly by emissaries of one king, in what we would call today a diplomatic embassy.

DISCOVERY AND OVERVIEW OF THE MINOANS

From the foregoing, it is clear that the Minoans of Crete were in contact with several areas in the ancient Near East during the Middle and Late Bronze Ages, from at least 1800 BC on. There is even mention in the Mari letters of Minoans, and a possible Minoan interpreter (or an interpreter *for* the Minoans), present at the site of Ugarit in north Syria during the early eighteenth century BC, where they were receiving tin that had been sent westward from Mari.[14] However, there seems to have been a special relationship with Egypt beginning in the fifteenth century, during the time of Hatshepsut and then Thutmose III, which is why our tale begins at this point in time.

It is interesting to note that the Minoan civilization was given its name by the British archaeologist Sir Arthur Evans in the early 1900s. We don't actually know what they called themselves, although we do know that the Egyptians, Canaanites, and Mesopotamians each had a name for them. Furthermore, we do not know where they came from, although our suspicion points to Anatolia/Turkey as most likely.

We do know that they established a civilization on Crete during the third millennium BC that lasted until ca. 1200 BC. Partway through this period, in about 1700 BC, the island was hit by a devastating earthquake that required the rebuilding of the palaces at Knossos and elsewhere on the island. However, the Minoans recovered quickly and flourished as an independent civilization until Mycenaeans from the Greek mainland invaded the island later in the second millennium, after which time the island continued under Mycenaean rule until everything collapsed ca. 1200 BC.

Sir Arthur Evans began excavating on Crete after tracking down the source of so-called milk stones that he found for sale in the marketplace of Athens. Greek women who had given birth or were about to give birth wore these "milk stones." The stones had symbols engraved upon them that Evans had never seen before, but which he recognized as writing. He traced them back to a buried site at Knossos (Kephala Hill) near the major modern city of Heraklion on Crete—a site that Heinrich Schliemann, the excavator of Troy, had tried to purchase and excavate, but to no avail. Evans, however, was able to purchase the land and began excavating in March 1900. He continued to dig for the next several decades, sinking most of his personal fortune into the project, and eventually publishing his findings in a massive multivolume work entitled *The Palace of Minos at Knossos.*[15]

Aided by his trusted Scottish assistant Duncan Mackenzie,[16] Evans soon uncovered what appeared to be a royal palace. He promptly named the newly discovered civilization "Minoan," after King Minos of Greek legend, who it was said ruled Crete during ancient times, complete with a Minotaur (half man, half bull) in the labyrinthine subterranean extensions of the palace. Evans found numerous clay tablets, and other objects, with writing on them—in both Linear A (still undeciphered) and Linear B (an early form of Greek probably brought to Crete by the Mycenaeans). However, he never did discover the real name of these people, and, as mentioned, it remains unknown to this day—despite more than a century of continuous excavation not only at Knossos but at numerous other sites on Crete as well.[17]

Evans uncovered numerous imports from Egypt and the Near East at Knossos, including an alabaster lid inscribed in hieroglyphs with "the good god, Seweserenre, son of Re, Khyan."[18] Khyan, one of the best-known Hyksos kings, ruled during the early years of the sixteenth century BC. His objects have been found across the ancient Near East, but how this lid got to Crete is still a mystery.

Of additional interest is an Egyptian alabaster vase found many years later during another archaeologist's excavation in a tomb at the site of Katsamba on Crete, one of the port cities on the north coast related to Knossos. It is inscribed with the royal name of Pharaoh Thutmose III: "the good god Men-kheper-Re, son of Re, Thutmose perfect in transformations." It is one of the only objects bearing his name to be found in the Aegean.[19]

The fifth-century Greek historian Thucydides claimed that the Minoans had a navy and ruled the seas during this period: "And the first person known to us by tradition as having established a navy is Minos. He made himself master of what is now called the Hellenic sea" (Thucydides, *History of the Peloponnesian War*, 1.3–8). To earlier scholars, this became known as the "Minoan Thalassocracy," from *kratia* meaning power and *thalassos* meaning sea. Although this supposed Minoan naval supremacy has now been called into question, there are mentions of "*Keftiu*-boats" in the Egyptian records—*Keftiu* being the Egyptian term for Crete at that time—although it is unclear whether these were boats from Crete, going to Crete, or built in a Minoan manner.[20]

Evans's successor at the site, John Devitt Stringfellow Pendlebury, was extremely interested in the possible connections between Egypt and Crete; he excavated at the Egyptian site of Amarna (Akhenaten's capital city, of which we will speak more below) as well as at Knossos. Pendlebury even published a monograph on the topic, entitled *Aegyptiaca*, in which he collected and cataloged all of the Egyptian imports found at Knossos and elsewhere on the island, before being shot to death by German paratroopers when they invaded Crete in 1941.[21]

Evans and Pendlebury found additional imported objects at Knossos, and it has become clear over the ensuing decades that the Minoans seem to have been in both the import and the export business, industriously networking with a number of foreign areas in addition to Egypt. For instance, cylinder seals from Mesopotamia and storage jars from Canaan have been found at various sites on Crete in Middle and Late Bronze Age contexts, while Minoan pottery and other finished objects, or at least mentions of them, have been found in countries stretching from Egypt, Israel, Jordan, and Cyprus to Syria and Iraq.

BACK TO EGYPT

We must keep in mind that the goods mentioned above represent only a tiny portion of those that once crossed the Mediterranean Sea, for many of the goods traded during the Late Bronze Age were perishable and would be unlikely to leave much in the way of identifiable remains today. Grain, wine, spices, perfumes, wood, and textiles almost certainly have long since disappeared. Raw materials such as ivory, precious stones like lapis lazuli, agate, and carnelian, and metals such as gold, copper, and tin will also have been locally converted long ago into other objects such as weapons and jewelry. Thus, the most abundant signposts of the trade routes and of international contacts may have perished, disintegrated, or otherwise disappeared in antiquity. However, the existence of perishable trade goods can sometimes be identified in written texts or by depiction in wall paintings that have survived to the present. Such paintings, inscriptions, and literary references can serve as less ambiguous guides to contacts between peoples, provided that they are interpreted correctly. Thus, the representations of foreign peoples in a number of painted Egyptian tombs dating to the reigns of New Kingdom pharaohs, from Hatshepsut through Amenhotep III, are invaluable as concrete attestations to diplomatic, commercial, and transportation networks functioning during the fifteenth and fourteenth centuries BC.[22]

It is during Hatshepsut's reign, in the fifteenth century BC, that the first of the tombs was built in which Aegean peoples are actually shown in wall paintings. In these tombs, we frequently see Minoans depicted, often with their goods and with inscriptions that identify them in unequivocal terms as coming from the island of Crete. For instance, in the tomb of Senenmut, Hatshepsut's architect, adviser, and perhaps paramour, an embassy from the Aegean is pictured, with six men carrying metal vases of general Aegean manufacture.[23]

In another painting, within the tomb of Rekhmire, vizier to Thutmose III (ca. 1450 BC), we see men dressed in typical Aegean-style kilts and carrying specifically Aegean objects. Next to them is written (in part), "Coming in peace by the chiefs of Keftiu and 'Islands in the Midst of the Sea,' bowing down and bending the head to the might of his Majesty the King of Upper and Lower Egypt."[24] This is clearly a representation of an Aegean delegation to Egypt, one of several depicted in Egyptian tombs from this period.

The Aegean peoples are not the only ones shown in Rekhmire's tomb; in other registers both above and below are shown emissaries from Punt, Nubia, and Syria, with inscriptions next to each. Although unproven, it seems likely that we are looking here at a depiction of some major event that took place during Thutmose III's reign, and that the delegates or merchants from the Aegean are just one part of the multinational crowd that has gathered or been summoned. If so, this would most likely be the Sed (or Jubilee) festival, first celebrated by a pharaoh after thirty years of rule and then irregularly thereafter; in Thutmose III's case, we know that he held at least three such festivals, which is not surprising since he ruled for fifty-four years.[25]

Fig. 4. Rekhmire's tomb, with Aegean peoples depicted (after Davies 1943, pl. xx;
courtesy of the Metropolitan Museum of Art).

In all, there are about fourteen tombs dating from Hatshepsut's reign and/or that of Thutmose III, all belonging to high-ranking officials and advisers, that depict delegations of foreigners visiting Egypt, including Aegean peoples, Nubians, and Canaanites, all carrying foreign products.[26] In the nine tombs dating specifically to the time of Thutmose III, we often see depictions of foreigners presenting diplomatic gifts, delivering annual dues, or participating in a royally commissioned expedition that Thutmose III sent to Lebanon in order to acquire cedar.[27]

Keftiu, *Keftiu*-men, and *Keftiu*-boats are mentioned in a variety of other contexts in Egypt from this period, including inscriptions on temples and notations on papyri. Among the most interesting of these is a papyrus from Thutmose III's thirtieth year (about 1450 BC) that mentions several "*Keftiu*-ships" in the context of the importation of materials for the Egyptian navy: "Given to craftsman [man's name], this sheathing-timber for the *Keftiu*-ship"; "Today given to craftsman Tity for the other *Keftiu*-ship on his commission"; and "Given to craftsman

Ina for the other . . . *Keftiu*-ship."[28] Similarly, an inscription on a wall of the Temple of Amun at Karnak from Thutmose III's thirty-fourth year also mentions *Keftiu*-ships.[29]

Although it is still unclear whether these ships are from *Keftiu* (that is, Minoan ships) or are capable of going to *Keftiu* (that is, Egyptian ships), it is clear that there was contact, and probably direct contact, between Minoan Crete and New Kingdom Egypt during the time of Thutmose III. Because of the prevailing winds, a sailing vessel—whether today or thirty-four hundred years ago—can travel with relative ease from the southern shores of Crete to Marsa Matruh on the northern coast of Egypt and thence to the Nile delta. The return journey by sail is not easy, given the winds and currents, but is possible at certain times of the year. It was also possible to go in a counterclockwise motion from Egypt to Canaan and Cyprus, thence to Anatolia and Rhodes, and from there to Crete, the Cycladic islands, and the Greek mainland, then back to Crete and south to Egypt.

It is clear from the painting and inscription in the tomb of Menkheperreseneb, first prophet of Amun,[30] that the Egyptians knew about Minoan royalty and understood them to be on a par with those from other foreign areas. On the walls of the tomb we can see the "Prince of *Keftiu*" (Crete) in the company of the Prince of the Hittites (from Anatolia), the Prince of Tunip (probably in Syria), and the Prince of Qadesh (in Syria). The title used to identify the figures, *wr*, meaning "Prince" or "Chief," is the same in each case.[31] The picture presented seems to indicate that such royalty visited Egypt upon occasion, including perhaps a very special occasion. Did they all come at the same time (possibly a different perspective on the same event depicted in Rekhmire's tomb?) or on separate occasions? We cannot be certain, but it is interesting to consider the possibility of the principal figures of the Late Bronze Age gathering together for some great event in Egypt, much as dignitaries gather today for a British royal wedding or a G-8 conference.

The same term, *wr* (Prince or Chief), is also used elsewhere by Thutmose III, in the entry for the forty-second year of his Annals, where he mentions the "Prince of Tanaja," the Egyptian designation for mainland Greece. Here he lists objects from the Aegean, including a silver vessel in *Keftiuan* workmanship and four bowls with handles of silver. Interestingly, he calls them *inw*, a term usually translated as "tribute," but which more likely means "gift" in this context.[32] Engaging in "regular" trade may have been considered beneath the dignity of the king, whereas exchanging "gifts" with equals (or near equals) was perfectly acceptable. We will discuss this further in the next chapter, in the context of international trade conducted in the guise of gift giving during the fourteenth century BC.

HATSHEPSUT AND THUTMOSE III

Hatshepsut's reign, just prior to that of Thutmose III, saw interactions not only with the Aegean but also with other areas of the ancient Near East. It was she who essentially started the Eighteenth Dynasty on its road to international contacts and global prestige, using diplomacy rather than war. She was of fully royal blood, the daughter of Pharaoh Thutmose I and Queen Ahmose—though it should be noted that her father had achieved royal status only by marrying into the family.

Hatshepsut married her own half brother, Thutmose II, in an arrangement meant to help out the young man since he was only half-royal, for his mother was a minor royal wife rather than the actual queen. Being married to Hatshepsut gave him more legitimacy than he would otherwise have had. Their union produced a daughter but no son, which could have been a disaster for the dynasty. However, he did father a son with a harem girl, who was raised as Thutmose III, destined to follow his father on the throne. Unfortunately, when Thutmose II died unexpectedly, the young son was not yet old enough to rule on his own. Hatshepsut, therefore, stepped in to rule temporarily as regent on his behalf. But when it came time to hand the throne over to him, she refused to do so. She ruled for more than twenty years, while Thutmose III waited—probably impatiently—in the background.[33]

During those two decades, Hatshepsut began to wear the traditional Pharaonic false beard and other accoutrements of office, and men's clothing with body armor to conceal her breasts and other female attributes, as can be seen in statues created at Deir el-Bahari, her mortuary temple. She also changed her name, giving it a masculine rather than a feminine ending, and became "His Majesty, Hatshepsu."[34] In other words, she ruled as a man, a male pharaoh, not simply as regent. As a result, she is now considered to be one of the most illustrious women from ancient Egypt, along with Nefertiti and Cleopatra. Hatshepsut apparently never remarried after Thutmose II died, but may have taken her architect and chief steward, Senenmut, as a lover; an image of him was carved, perhaps secretly, on Hatshepsut's funerary temple at Deir el-Bahari, whose construction he oversaw.[35]

This intriguing ruler is associated with peaceful trading expeditions that she sent to Phoenicia (modern Lebanon) in search of wood, and to the Sinai in search of copper and turquoise,[36] but the most famous delegation was one that she sent to the land of Punt during her ninth regnal year, the record of which is inscribed on the walls at Deir el-Bahari. The exact location of Punt is now lost to scholars and is still a matter of dispute. Most authorities place it somewhere in the region of Sudan, Eritrea, or Ethiopia, but others look elsewhere, most usually along the shores of the Red Sea, including the area of modern-day Yemen.[37]

Hatshepsut's expedition was not the first sent from Egypt to Punt, nor would it be the last. Several had been sent during the Middle Kingdom period, and later, during the mid-fourteenth century BC, Amenhotep III sent a delegation. However, it is only in Hatshepsut's record that the queen of Punt—named "Eti" according to the accompanying inscription—is depicted. The illustration of the foreign queen has engendered much comment because of her short stature, curved spine, rolls of fat, and large posterior, usually resulting in modern descriptions of the queen as steatopygous (i.e., having a fleshy abdomen and massive—usually protruding—thighs and buttocks). There are also palm trees, exotic animals, and other details showing the distant locale, and depictions of the ships that transported the Egyptians to and from Punt, complete down to the masts and rigging.

In the thirty-third year of his rule, sometime after 1450 BC, Thutmose III sent his own trade delegation to the land of Punt. This is duly recorded in his Annals, as is another expedition to the same area, sent in Year 38.[38] These are some of the few instances, along with the expeditions he sent to Lebanon to acquire cedar, where we can actually point to ongoing trade between Egypt and a foreign area during Thutmose III's reign, though we suspect that much of the "tribute" (inw) depicted in the tomb scenes of the nobles from his reign is actually traded goods.

Among the far-flung areas with which Egypt under Thutmose III was apparently trading, and from which he recorded receiving *inw* on three separate occasions, was a region known to the Egyptians as *Isy*, most likely to be identified with the coalition of city-states in northwest Anatolia (modern Turkey) known as Assuwa, or with Alashiya, the name by which Cyprus was known during the Bronze Age. Thutmose's scribes mention *Isy* at least four times in various inscriptions, including alongside *Keftiu* in his "Poetic Stele/Hymn of Victory": "I have come to let You smite the West, *Keftiu* and *Isy* being in awe, and I let them see Your Majesty as a young bull, firm of heart, sharp of horns, whom one cannot approach."[39] In the Annals of his ninth campaign, in Year 34 (1445 BC), the "Chief of *Isy*" is said to have brought *inw* consisting of raw materials: pure copper, blocks of lead, lapis lazuli, an ivory tusk, and wood. Similarly, in the record for his thirteenth campaign, in Year 38 (1441 BC), we learn that the "Prince of *Isy*" brought *inw* consisting of copper and horses, and in the description of his fifteenth campaign, in Year 40 (1439 BC), we are told that the "Chief of *Isy*" brought *inw* consisting of forty bricks of copper, one brick of lead, and two tusks of ivory. Most were typical of items found in high-level gift exchanges across the Bronze Age Near East.[40]

Egypt and Canaan at the Battle of Megiddo, 1479 BC

Hatshepsut's mummy may have finally been identified in recent years, located in a tomb known as KV 60 (for "Kings Valley, Tomb 60"), rather than in her own tomb (KV 20), which lies elsewhere in the Valley of the Kings. She was one of the few women ever to be buried in this elite valley, usually reserved for the male kings of Egypt. If the identified mummy is indeed that of Hatshepsut, then she suffered in her old age from obesity, dental problems, and cancer.[41] When she finally died, in about 1480 BC, Thutmose III, who is sometimes suspected of having had a hand in her death, wasted no time in assuming power and marching off to battle in his first year of solo rule. He also attempted to erase Hatshepsut's name from history, ordering her monuments desecrated and her name chiseled out of inscriptions wherever possible.

When Thutmose III began his first campaign—the first of seventeen that he instigated over the next twenty or so years—he managed to put

himself into the history books, quite literally, for the itinerary and details of his journey and conquests in 1479 BC were transferred from the
daily journals kept along the way and inscribed for posterity on the wall
of the Temple of Amun at Karnak in Egypt. The battle that he fought
at Megiddo (later to become better known as biblical Armageddon)
against local rebellious Canaanite chiefs during the campaign is the first
battle that we know of whose details were written down and made accessible for the edification of those who were not present.

The inscribed account indicates that Thutmose III marched his men
up from Egypt for ten days, as far north as the site of Yehem. There he
stopped to hold a war council and decide how best to proceed against
the fortified city of Megiddo and the surrounding temporary camps of
the local Canaanite rulers who had initiated a rebellion against Egyptian
rule upon his ascension to the throne. From Yehem, there were three
ways to get to Megiddo: a northern route, which emerged in the Jezreel
Valley in the vicinity of Yokneam; a southern route, which opened into
the Jezreel Valley near Ta'anach; and a central route, which ended right
at Megiddo.[42]

His generals, according to the written account, suggested that they
take either the northern or the southern route because these were wider
and less susceptible to an ambush. Thutmose replied that such tactics
were exactly what the Canaanites would be expecting; they would never
believe him to be so stupid as to go up the central route since it was so
narrow and vulnerable to an ambush. And yet, precisely because that
was their thinking, he would indeed march with the army up the central route, hoping to catch the Canaanites by surprise, and that is exactly what transpired. It took the Egyptians nearly twelve hours to get
through the central pass (known, at various times throughout history,
as the Wadi Ara, the Nahal Iron, and/or the Musmus Pass) from the
first man to the last, but they got through without a scratch and found
nobody guarding either Megiddo or the temporary enemy camps surrounding it. The Canaanite forces were all at Yokneam to the north and
Ta'anach to the south, just as Thutmose III had predicted. The only mis-
take that Thutmose III made was in allowing his men to stop to loot and
plunder the enemy camps before actually capturing the city. This was
an error that allowed the few defenders of Megiddo—mostly old men,
women, and children—time to close the city gates. This in turn resulted

in a prolonged siege lasting seven more months before the Egyptians were able to capture the city.

Some thirty-four hundred years later, General Edmund Allenby tried the same tactics as Thutmose III, in September 1918 during World War I, with the same successful results. He won the battle at Megiddo and took prisoner hundreds of German and Turkish soldiers, without any loss of life except for a few of his horses. He later admitted that he had read James Breasted's English translation of Thutmose III's account, leading Allenby to decide to replicate history. George Santayana once reportedly said that those who do not study history are doomed to repeat it, but Allenby proved that the opposite could be true as well—those who study history can successfully repeat it, if they choose to do so.[43]

Egypt and Mitanni

Thutmose III also led campaigns to northern Syria, against the Mitannian kingdom that had come into existence in this area by 1500 BC, when his ancestor Thutmose I had earlier campaigned against it.[44] The Mitannian kingdom kept growing and assimilating other nearby areas, such as the Hurrian kingdom of Hanigalbat. Consequently, it was known by several names, depending upon the time period and who was writing or talking about it. In general, the Egyptians called it "Naharin" or "Naharina"; the Hittites called it "the land of Hurri"; the Assyrians called it "Hanigalbat"; while the Mitannian kings themselves referred to it as the kingdom of "Mitanni." Its capital city, Washukanni, has never been found. It is one of the very few such ancient Near Eastern capitals that has so far eluded archaeologists, despite tantalizing clues in the archaeological record and in ancient texts. Some think that it may be located in the mound of Tell al-Fakhariyeh in Syria, to the east of the Euphrates River; this has never been confirmed, though not for lack of trying.[45]

According to various texts, the population of this kingdom was about 90 percent local Hurrians, as they were called, ruled over by the remaining 10 percent; these were the Mitannian overlords, seemingly of Indo-European stock. This small group, who had apparently moved in from elsewhere to take over the indigenous Hurrian population and create the Mitannian kingdom, had a military elite known as the *maryannu* ("chariot-warriors") who were known for their use of chariots and prowess in training horses. One text found at Hattusa, the capital city of the Hittites in Anatolia, contains a treatise written about 1350 BC by Kikkuli, a master Mitannian horse-trainer, giving instructions on how to train horses over a period of 214 days. It is an elaborate text, stretching over four clay tablets, but begins simply, "Thus (speaks) Kikkuli, the horse-trainer from the land of Mitanni."[46]

In his eighth campaign, during his Year 33 (ca. 1446 BC), Thutmose III, like his grandfather before him, launched both a land and a naval assault against the kingdom of Mitanni. He reportedly sailed his forces up the Euphrates River, despite the difficulties in going against both the wind and the current, perhaps in retaliation for Mitanni's suspected involvement in the Canaanite rebellion during his first year of rule.[47] He defeated the Mitanni forces and ordered an inscribed stele to be placed north of Carchemish on the east bank of the Euphrates, to commemorate his victory.

However, Mitanni did not remain vanquished for long. Within fifteen or twenty years, the Mitannian king Saushtatar began greatly expanding the kingdom once again. He attacked the city of Assur, capital city of the Assyrians, taking as booty a door of precious gold and silver that he used to adorn his palace in Washukanni—as we know from a later text in the Hittite archives at Hattusa—and may even have faced off against the Hittites.[48] In less than a century, by the time of Pharaoh Amenhotep III in the mid-fourteenth century BC, relations between Egypt and Mitanni were so cordial that Amenhotep married not one but two Mitannian princesses.

Mitanni, Assyria, Egyptians. The world was already growing more interconnected, even if sometimes only in war.

THE ASSUWA REBELLION IN ANATOLIA

It is intriguing that Thutmose III was in contact, and perhaps involved in active commercial exchange, with distant areas, including areas located to the north and west of Egypt. It is possible that contact with Assuwa (assuming that is the proper identification for *Isy*) was initiated by Assuwa rather than by Egypt. About 1430 BC, Assuwa launched a rebellion against the Hittites of central Anatolia, and one must consider the possibility that Assuwa was actively searching for diplomatic contacts with other major powers during the decade leading up to the rebellion.[49]

The Assuwa Rebellion, which had previously been of interest to only a few scholars, came to the forefront in 1991, when a bulldozer operator was digging the blade of his machine into the shoulder of a road by the ancient site of Hattusa, capital city of the Hittites—now a two-hour car ride (208 kilometers) east of modern Ankara. The blade struck something metallic. Hopping down from his seat on the cab and reaching into the loosened dirt, he pulled out a long, thin, and surprisingly heavy green-colored object. It looked and felt like an ancient sword, an identification that was confirmed when it was cleaned up in the local museum by the resident archaeologists.

However, it wasn't a typical Hittite sword but rather was a type not seen previously in the region. In addition, it had an inscription incised into the blade. It initially proved easier to read the inscription than to identify the make of the sword, and so the translation was done first. Written in Akkadian—the diplomatic language of the Bronze Age in the ancient Near East—using cuneiform (wedge-shaped) signs, the inscription reads as follows: *i-nu-ma* ᵐ*Du-ut-ha-li-ya* LUGAL.GAL KUR ᵁᴿᵁ*A-as-su-wa u-hal-liq* GIR*ᴴᴵᴬ an-nu-tim a-na* ᴰ*Iskur be-li-su u-se-li.* For those few readers not conversant with Akkadian, the English translation is: "As Duthaliya the Great King shattered the Assuwa country, he dedicated these swords to the storm-god, his lord."[50]

The inscription refers to the so-called Assuwa Rebellion, which the Hittite king Tudhaliya I/II put down in approximately 1430 BC (he is referred to as "I/II" because we are not certain whether he was the first or the second king with that name). The revolt was already well known to scholars who study the Hittite Empire because of a number of other texts, all written in cuneiform on clay tablets, that had been found by German archaeologists excavating at Hattusa earlier in the century. However, the sword was the first weapon—and the first artifact of any kind, for that matter—that could be associated with the revolt. It is clear from the inscription that there are likely more swords remaining to be found. However, before we proceed further, we shall spend some time among the Hittites, locating Assuwa, and examining the rebellion. We shall consider why this is evidence of early "internationalism" and—potentially—evidence that the Trojan War was fought two hundred years earlier and for different reasons from those Homer adduced.

EXCURSUS: DISCOVERY AND OVERVIEW OF THE HITTITES

We should first note that the Hittites, despite ruling a large empire from their homelands in central Anatolia for much of the second millennium BC, were lost to history, at least geographically, until only about two hundred years ago.[51]

The Hittites were known to biblical scholars because of their mention in the Hebrew Bible, where they are listed as one of the many peoples ending in "*-ite*" (Hittites, Hivites, Amorites, Jebusites, and so on) who lived in Canaan during the late second millennium BC, interacting with and eventually succumbing to the Hebrews/Israelites. We are told, for instance, that Abraham bought a burial plot for his wife Sarah from Ephron the Hittite (Gen. 23:3–20), that King David's wife Bathsheba was first married to Uriah the Hittite (2 Sam. 11: 2–27), and that King Solomon had "Hittite women" among his wives (1 Kings 11:1). However, early efforts to find the Hittites in the biblical lands were unsuccessful, despite the specific geographical location pinpointed in the declaration made to Moses from the burning bush: "I have come down to deliver them [the Israelites] from the Egyptians, and to bring them up out of that land to a good and broad land, a land flowing with milk and honey, to the country of the Canaanites, the Hittites, the Amorites, the Perizzites, the Hivites, and the Jebusites" (Exod. 3:7).[52]

In the meantime, early nineteenth-century explorers, like Johann Ludwig Burckhardt, a Swiss gentleman with a penchant for dressing in local Middle Eastern garb (and calling himself "Sheik Ibrahim") in order to facilitate his explorations, were discovering the remains of a previously unknown Bronze Age civilization, especially on Turkey's central plateau. Eventually, the connection was made. In 1879, at a conference in London, the respected Assyriologist A. H. Sayce announced that the Hittites were located not in Canaan but rather in Anatolia; that is, in Turkey rather than in Israel/Lebanon/Syria/Jordan. His announcement was generally accepted, and the equation is still accepted today, but one has to wonder how the Bible could have gotten it so wrong.

The answer is actually fairly logical. Much as the British Empire stretched far from England proper, so too did the Hittite Empire stretch west in Turkey and south into Syria. And just as some former parts of the British Empire continue to play cricket and drink afternoon tea, long after the original empire vanished, so too some of the former parts of the Hittite Empire in northern Syria retained portions of Hittite culture, language, and religion—so much so that we now refer to them as the Neo-Hittites, who flourished during the early first millennium BC. By the time the Bible was written down, sometime between the ninth and the seventh centuries BC according to authorities, the original Hittites were long gone, but their successors—the Neo-Hittites—were firmly established in the northern part of Canaan. There they no doubt interacted with the Israelites and other peoples of the Levant, ensuring their mention in the biblical accounts and unintentionally creating confusion for later explorers seeking the original Hittites.[53]

Moreover, as archaeologists began to excavate Hittite sites and eventually to translate the numerous clay tablets found at these sites, it became clear that they had not called themselves Hittites. Their name for themselves was actually something close to "Neshites" or "Neshians," after the city of Nesha (now known and excavated as Kultepe Kanesh in the Cappadocian region of Turkey). This city flourished for some two hundred years as the seat of a local Indo-European dynasty, before a king named Hattusili I (meaning "the man of Hattusa") sometime around 1650 BC established his capital city farther to the east, at a new site with that name, Hattusa. We still call them Hittites today only because that name became firmly ensconced in the scholarly literature before the tablets giving their true name were translated.[54]

The location of the new capital city, Hattusa, was carefully chosen. It was so well fortified and so well situated geographically, with a narrow valley providing the sole access up to the city, that it was captured only twice during its five-hundred-year occupation—probably both times by a neighboring group called the Kashka. The site has yielded thousands of clay tablets during excavations conducted since 1906 by German archaeologists such as Hugo Winckler, Kurt Bittel, Peter Neve, and Jürgen Seeher. Included among these tablets are letters and documents from what must have been the official state archives, as well as poems, stories, histories, religious rituals, and all kinds of other written documents. Together they allow us to piece together not only the history of the Hittite rulers and their interactions with other peoples and kingdoms, but also that of the ordinary people, including their daily life and society, belief systems, and law codes—one of which contains the rather intriguing ruling "If anyone bites off the nose of a free person, he shall pay 40 shekels of silver"[55] (one wonders just how frequently that happened).

We are told at one point that a Hittite king named Mursili I, grandson and successor of the above-named Hattusili I, marched his army all the way to Mesopotamia, a journey of over one thousand miles, and attacked the city of Babylon in 1595 BC, burning it to the ground and bringing to an end the two-hundred-year-old dynasty made famous by Hammurabi "the Law-Giver." Then, instead of occupying the city, he simply turned the Hittite army around and headed for home, thus effectively conducting the longest drive-by shooting in history. As an unintended consequence of his action, a previously unknown group called the Kassites was able to occupy the city of Babylon and then ruled over it for the next several centuries.

While the first half of Hittite history is known as the Old Kingdom and is justifiably famous because of exploits by kings like Mursili, it is the second half with which we are more concerned here. Known during this period as the Hittite Empire, it flourished and rose to even greater heights during the Late Bronze Age—beginning in the fifteenth century BC and lasting until the early decades of the twelfth century BC. Among its most famous kings is a man named Suppiluliuma I, whom we will meet in the next chapter and who led the Hittites to a preeminent position in the ancient Near East by conquering a great deal of territory and dealing as an equal with the pharaohs of New Kingdom Egypt. One recently widowed Egyptian queen even asked Suppiluliuma to send her one of his sons as a husband, declaring that he would rule over Egypt with her. It's not clear which queen it was, or whose widow she was, but some well-informed scholars favor Ankhsenamen as the queen and King Tut as the dead ruler of Egypt, as we shall see.

THE ASSUWA REBELLION AND THE AHHIYAWA QUESTION

Let us return now to approximately the year 1430 BC, when the Hittites and their king Tudhaliya I/II were dealing with a coalition of renegade states. These states were collectively known as Assuwa. They were located in northwestern Turkey, just inland from the Dardanelles where the battle of Gallipoli was fought during World War I. The Hittite tablets give us the names of all twenty-two of these allied states that rose up in rebellion against the Hittites. Most of these names do not mean much to us anymore and cannot be identified with a specific locale, except for the last two on the list: *Wilusiya* and *Taruisa*, which are most likely references to Troy and its surrounding area.[56]

The rebellion apparently began as Tudhaliya I/II and his army were returning from a military campaign in west Anatolia. Upon hearing the news, the Hittite army simply turned around and headed northwest to Assuwa, to put down the rebellion. We are told in the Hittite account that Tudhaliya personally led the army and defeated the Assuwan confederacy. The records indicate that ten thousand Assuwan soldiers, six hundred teams of horses and their Assuwan charioteers, and "the conquered population, oxen, sheep, [and] the possessions of the land" were taken back to Hattusa as prisoners and booty.[57] Included among these were the Assuwan king and his son Kukkuli, along with a few other members of the Assuwan royalty and their families. Eventually, Tudhaliya appointed Kukkuli as king of Assuwa and reestablished Assuwa as a vassal state to the Hittite kingdom. However, Kukkuli then promptly rebelled, only to be defeated again by the Hittites. Kukkuli was put to death, and the coalition of Assuwa was destroyed and vanished from the face of the earth. Its legacy lives on primarily in the modern name "Asia," but also possibly in the story of the Trojan War, for the names *Wilusiya* and *Taruisa* bear a strong resemblance, according to scholars, to the Bronze Age names for the city of Troy—also known as Ilios—and its surrounding area, the Troad.

And it is here that the sword found at Hattusa, with the inscription left by Tudhaliya I/II, comes into play, for, as mentioned above, this is not a sword of local manufacture. The sword is of a type used primarily on mainland Greece during the fifteenth century BC. It is a Mycenaean sword (or a very good imitation of one). Why such a sword was being used in the Assuwa Rebellion is a good question whose answer we do not know; was it wielded by an Assuwan soldier, or a Mycenaean mercenary, or someone else entirely?

There are five other Hittite tablets that mention Assuwa and/or the rebellion, besides the primary one with the longest account. One, for instance, confirms the entire event, beginning with the simple statement

"Thus speaks . . . Tudhaliya, the Great King: When I had destroyed Assuwa and returned to Hattusa . . ."[58] The most interesting is a fragmentary letter that is tantalizingly incomplete but which manages to mention the king of Assuwa twice and Tudhaliya once, refers also to a military campaign, and mentions as well the land of Ahhiyawa, the king of Ahhiyawa, and islands belonging to the king of Ahhiyawa. The letter is damaged and incomplete, so it is dangerous to read too much into the occurrence of both Assuwa and Ahhiyawa within the same text, but it seems to indicate that Assuwa and Ahhiyawa were associated in some manner at this time.[59]

The letter—known as KUB XXVI 91 from its initial German publication—was long thought to have been sent by the Hittite king to the king of Ahhiyawa, but it has recently been suggested that it was actually sent *to* the Hittite king *from* the king of Ahhiyawa, which would make it the only such letter found anywhere sent from that area and that king.[60] But what area and king is it? Where is Ahhiyawa? That question has bedeviled academic scholarship for much of the past century, but most scholars now agree that it is mainland Greece and the Mycenaeans, probably based at the city of Mycenae. The attribution is made on the basis of some twenty-five tablets in the Hittite archive at Hattusa that mention Ahhiyawa in some context or another over the course of nearly three hundred years (from the fifteenth to the end of the thirteenth century BC), and which, when analyzed exhaustively, can only be referring to mainland Greece and the Mycenaeans.[61] Again, we must make a brief excursus, this time to meet the Mycenaeans, before continuing the story.

DISCOVERY AND OVERVIEW OF THE MYCENAEANS

The Mycenaean civilization first came to the attention of the general public nearly 150 years ago, in the mid- to late eighteenth century, courtesy of Heinrich Schliemann—the so-called Father of Mycenaean Archaeology. He is the man whom modern archaeologists love to hate, in part because of his primitive digging methods and in part because it's never clear how much he and his reports can be trusted. Following his excavations in the early 1870s at Hisarlik in northwest Anatolia, which he identified as Troy, Schliemann decided that, since he had found the Trojan side of the Trojan War (as we shall discuss), it was only fitting that he now find the Mycenaean side.

He had a decidedly easier time finding Mycenae on mainland Greece than he had had in finding Troy in Anatolia, for portions of the ancient site of Mycenae were still protruding from the ground, including the top of the famous Lion Gate, which had already been discovered and partially reconstructed several decades before. The locals in the nearby village of Mykenai readily led Schliemann to the site when he arrived to begin excavating in the mid-1870s. He didn't have an excavation permit, but that had never stopped him before, and it didn't stop him now. Soon he unearthed a number of shaft graves filled with skeletons, weapons, and gold beyond his greatest dreams. He broke the news by sending a telegram to the king of Greece, reportedly declaring that he "had gazed upon the face of Agamemnon."[62]

Of course, Schliemann—who was dramatically wrong even when he was right—had misdated the graves and remains. We now know that these shaft graves (of which there are two great circles at Mycenae) date to near the beginning of the city's and the civilization's greatness, from 1650–1500 BC, rather than from the time of Agamemnon and Achilles (ca. 1250 BC). He may have been off by four centuries, but at least he was digging at the correct city. Schliemann was by no means the only archaeologist to be investigating these Bronze Age remains—other scholars, such as Christos Tsountas and James Manatt, were also busy excavating and were doing better work than Schliemann—but he was the one who had the attention of the public because of his previous announcements regarding Troy and the Trojan War, as we shall see below.[63]

Schliemann dug at Mycenae, and at the nearby site of Tiryns and elsewhere as well, for a few more seasons before returning to Troy to conduct additional excavations in 1878 and in the 1880s. He also attempted to dig at Knossos on Crete, but without success. It was left to others, fortunately for the field of archaeology, to continue the investigations of the Mycenaeans. Two of the greatest were an American from the University of Cincinnati named Carl Blegen and an Englishman from Cambridge named Alan Wace. They eventually joined forces to lay out the groundwork for defining the civilization and its growth from beginning to end.

Wace was in charge of the British excavations at Mycenae for several decades, beginning in the 1920s, while Blegen not only excavated at Troy from 1932 to 1938 but also dug at Pylos in southern Greece. At Pylos, on the very first day of excavations in 1939, Blegen and his team found the first few clay tablets from what would turn out to be a huge archive containing texts written in Linear B.[64] The onset of World War II temporarily halted their work at the site, but following the war, excavations resumed in 1952. That same year, an English architect named Michael Ventris definitively proved that Linear B was in fact an early version of Greek.

The subsequent translation of Linear B texts found at sites such as Pylos, Mycenae, Tiryns, and Thebes, as well as Knossos, continues to the present day and has provided an additional window into the world of the Mycenaeans. The textual evidence has added to the details already known from excavations and has allowed archaeologists to reconstruct the world of Bronze Age Greece, just as their colleagues working at sites in Egypt and the Near East have been able to do in those countries, as a consequence of translating texts written in Egyptian, Hittite, and Akkadian. Simply put, archaeological remains combined with textual inscriptions have allowed modern scholars to reconstruct ancient history.

We now know that the Mycenaean civilization essentially began in the seventeenth century BC, at approximately the same time as the Minoans on Crete were recovering from the dramatic earthquake that marks (according to archaeological terminology) the transition from the First to the Second Palatial period on the island. Wace and Blegen christened the chronological periods belonging to the Mycenaeans as the Late Helladic period, with Late Helladic I and II dating to the seventeenth through fifteenth centuries BC and Late Helladic III divided into three sections: IIIA to the fourteenth century, IIIB to the thirteenth century, and IIIC to the twelfth century BC.[65]

The reasons underlying the rise of the Mycenaean civilization are still a matter of discussion among archaeologists. One early suggestion was that they helped the Egyptians oust the Hyksos from Egypt, but this is not a commonly accepted view today. If objects found in the Shaft Graves at Mycenae are any indication, then some of the earliest influences at Mycenae came from Crete. In fact, Evans thought that the Minoans had invaded the Greek mainland, but Wace and Blegen later reversed this argument; all scholars accept their position today. It is now clear that when the Mycenaeans took over Crete, they also took over the international trade routes to Egypt and the Near East. They (relatively) suddenly became players in the cosmopolitan world—a role that they would continue to exploit for the next several centuries, until the end of the Late Bronze Age.

The Egyptians apparently knew the Mycenaeans as *Tanaja*, while the Hittites called them *Ahhiyawa*, and the Canaanites (if the texts at Ugarit a bit farther north in Syria are any indication) similarly called them *Hiyawa*—or so we think, for those toponyms fit nobody but the Mycenaeans. If those references are not to the Mycenaeans, then these peoples are unknown in the texts of the Egyptians and the other great powers of the Late Bronze Age in the Near East, but this seems unlikely given the quantities of Mycenaean vases and vessels found in those regions in contexts dating from the fourteenth to the twelfth century BC.[66]

AN EARLY TROJAN WAR?

If Ahhiyawa represents both mainland Greece and the Mycenaeans, and if the letter known as KUB XXVI 91 found at Hattusa shows that Ahhiyawa was involved somehow with Assuwa during its rebellion against the Hittites, then what can we conclude? The letter itself, and all of those relating to the Assuwa Rebellion, date to 1430 BC, some two hundred years before the generally accepted date for the Trojan War (usually placed between 1250 BC and 1175 BC). All of the data presented above, including the Mycenaean sword with the Akkadian inscription found at Hattusa, might be simply a series of unrelated phenomena. However, they may possibly be interpreted as indicating that warriors from the Bronze Age Aegean were involved in the Assuwa Rebellion against the Hittites. If so, it might be proposed that it was this aid that was chronicled in contemporary Hittite records and remembered rather more indistinctly in the literary traditions of later archaic and classical Greece—not as the Trojan War, but as the pre–Trojan War battles and raids in Anatolia that were also remembered and attributed to Achilles and other legendary Achaean heroes.[67]

Scholars are now agreed that even within Homer's *Iliad* there are accounts of warriors and events from the centuries predating the traditional setting of the Trojan War in 1250 BC. These include the tower shield of the warrior Ajax, a shield type that had been replaced long before the thirteenth century BC. There are also the "silver-studded" swords (*phasganon arguwelon* or *xiphos arguroelon*) of various heroes, an expensive type of weapon that had gone out of use long before the Trojan War. And there is the story of Bellerophon, recounted in book 6 of the *Iliad* (lines 178–240), who is a Greek hero almost certainly of pre–Trojan War date. Proteus, king of Tiryns, sent Bellerophon from Tiryns on mainland Greece to Lycia in Anatolia. After completing three tasks and overcoming numerous additional obstacles, he was eventually awarded a kingdom in Anatolia.[68]

In addition, the *Iliad* records that long before the time of Achilles, Agamemnon, Helen, and Hector—in fact during the time of Priam's father Laomedon—the Greek hero Heracles sacked Troy. He needed only six ships (*Iliad*, book 5, lines 638–42):

> Of other sort, men say, was mighty Heracles, my father, staunch in fight, the lion-hearted, who on a time came hither [to Troy] by reason of the mares of Laomedon with but six ships and a scantier host, yet sacked the city of Ilios and made waste her streets.[69]

As I have said elsewhere, if one were to search for a historical event with which to link pre-Homeric traditions of Achaean warriors fighting on the Anatolian mainland, the Assuwa Rebellion, ca. 1430 BC, would stand out as one of the largest military events within northwestern Anatolia prior to the Trojan War, and as one of the few events to which the Mycenaeans (Ahhiyawans) might tentatively be linked via textual evidence such as the Hittite letter KUB XXVI 91 mentioned above. We might well wonder, therefore, whether it was this incident that was the historical basis for the contemporary Hittite tales of Mycenaean (Ahhiyawan) warriors or mercenaries fighting in Anatolia, and which generated the stories of earlier, pre–Trojan War, military endeavors of the Achaeans on the Anatolian mainland.[70] We might also wonder whether it was this impending rebellion, which the Assuwans had probably been planning for some time, that lay behind their possible overtures to Thutmose III in the late 1440s and early 1430s BC.

Concluding Remarks

The well-respected art historian Helene Kantor once said: "The evidence preserved to us by the passage of time constitutes but a small fraction of that which must have once existed. Each imported vessel . . . represents scores of others that have perished."[71] In fact, most of the goods sent back and forth were most likely either perishable—and have since disappeared—or were raw materials that were immediately converted into other objects, such as weapons and jewelry, as noted. Thus, we should probably understand that the trade between the Aegean, Egypt, and the Near East during the Bronze Age took place on a scale many times larger than the picture that we currently see through the lens of archaeological excavation.

It is perhaps in this context that we should understand the Minoan-style paintings that Manfred Bietak uncovered in Thutmose III's palace at Tell ed-Dab'a in the Egyptian delta. While they may not necessarily have been painted at the whim of a Minoan princess, they are certainly evidence of the extent to which international contact, trade, and influences flowed around the ancient Mediterranean world during the fifteenth century BC, even as far abroad as Minoan Crete and back again.

We may sum up this century as a period that saw the rise of international connections on a sustained basis throughout the ancient Mediterranean world, from the Aegean to Mesopotamia. By this time, the Minoans and Mycenaeans of the Bronze Age Aegean were well established, as were the Hittites in Anatolia. The Hyksos had been evicted from Egypt, and the Egyptians had begun what we now call the Eighteenth Dynasty and the New Kingdom period.

However, as we shall see next, this was only the beginning of what would become a "Golden Age" of internationalism and globalization during the following fourteenth century BC. For instance, the combination of Thutmose III's numerous years of campaigning and diplomacy, hard on the heels of Hatshepsut's peaceful trading expeditions and military exploits of her own,[72] took Egypt to a pinnacle of international power and prosperity that had rarely, if ever, been seen before in the country. As a result, Egypt established itself as one of the great powers for the rest of the Late Bronze Age, along with the Hittites, Assyrians, and Kassites/Babylonians, in addition to assorted other players such as the Mitannians, Minoans, Mycenaeans, and Cypriots, more of whom we shall meet in the next chapter and following.

CHAPTER TWO

ACT II
· · · ·

AN (AEGEAN) AFFAIR TO REMEMBER:

THE FOURTEENTH CENTURY BC

Towering more than sixty feet high and destined to stand guard for the next thirty-four hundred years, even as the mortuary temple that stood behind them was looted for its magnificent stone blocks and slowly crumbled into dust, the two huge statues standing at the entrance to Amenhotep III's mortuary temple at Kom el-Hetan were, and still are, erroneously called the Colossi of Memnon as a result of a mistaken identification with Memnon, a mythological Ethiopian prince killed at Troy by Achilles. Each statue depicts a seated Amenhotep III, pharaoh of Egypt from 1391 to 1353 BC. In part because of this erroneous identification, the Colossi were already famous two thousand years ago, visited by ancient Greek and Roman tourists familiar with Homer's *Iliad* and *Odyssey*, who carved graffiti on the legs. One of the Colossi—after being damaged by an earthquake in the first century BC—was known for giving off an eerie whistling sound at dawn, as the stone contracted and expanded with the cold of night and heat of day. Unfortunately for the ancient tourist trade, restoration work during the Roman period in the second century AD finally put an end to the daily "cries of the god."[1]

However, fascinating as they are, it is not the two Colossi that are critical to our story of important events in the fourteenth century BC, but rather the fifth of five statue bases standing in a north–south row within the boundaries of where the mortuary temple once stood. The temple was located on the west bank of the Nile, near what is now known as the Valley of the Kings, across from the modern city of Luxor. The five bases each held a larger-than-life-sized statue of the king, although they were not nearly as tall as the Colossi placed at the entrance to the temple. The court in which they stood contained almost forty such statues and bases in all.

THE AEGEAN LIST OF AMENHOTEP III

Each of the five bases, as well as many of the others, is inscribed with a series of topographical names carved into the stone within what the Egyptians called a "fortified oval"—an elongated oval carved standing upright, with a series of small protrusions all along its perimeter. This was meant to depict a fortified city, complete with defensive towers (hence the protrusions). Each fortified oval was placed on, or rather replaced, the lower body of a bound prisoner, portrayed with his arms behind his back and bound together at the elbow, sometimes with a rope tied around his neck attaching him to other prisoners in front of and behind him. This was a traditional New Kingdom Egyptian method of representing foreign cities and countries; even if the Egyptians didn't actually control these foreign places or were not even close to conquering them, they still wrote the names within such "fortified ovals" as an artistic and political convention, perhaps as symbolic domination.

Together the names on these statue bases formed a series of geographical lists that designated the world known to the Egyptians of Amenhotep III's time, in the early fourteenth century BC. Some of the most important peoples and places in the Near East at that time were named on the lists, including the Hittites in the north, the Nubians in the south, and the Assyrians and Babylonians to the east. Taken as a whole, the lists were unique in the history of Egypt.

But what immediately strikes us is that the list carved by the stonemason on the fifth statue base contained names never before mentioned in Egyptian inscriptions. They were the names of cities and places located to the west of Egypt—strange names, such as Mycenae, Nauplion, Knossos, Kydonia, and Kythera, written on the left front and left side of the base, and with two more names written separately on the right front side of the base, as if they were titles placed at the head of the list: Keftiu and Tanaja.

What was the meaning of this list and what did the names represent? For the past forty years, modern archaeologists and Egyptologists have been debating the significance of the fifteen names found on this statue base, now commonly referred to as the "Aegean List."

Fig. 5a–b. Colossi and Aegean List of Amenhotep III (photographs by
E. H. Cline and J. Strange).

German archaeologists originally excavated the statue base, and its companions, in the 1960s, but sometime in the 1970s it was accidentally destroyed. According to one unverified story, members of a local Bedouin tribe built a fire under the base and poured cold water onto it in an attempt to crack off the inscribed panels, in order to sell them on the antiquities market. The official version is that wildfires in the area caused the damage. Whoever, or whatever, the culprit, the entire base was shattered into nearly a thousand pieces. Until recently, only a few color photographs of the original base were left for archaeologists, which was most unfortunate, for the names on the list are so distinctive that thirteen of the fifteen had never previously been seen in Egypt . . . and never would be again.

What modern tourists to the site now see (usually as they are passing by the ruins in an air-conditioned bus on their way to the nearby Valley of the Kings) are the statue bases, and the statues upon them, being reassembled once again, to stand beneath the sun-drenched skies for the first time in more than three thousand years. In 1998, a multinational team led by Egyptologist Hourig Sourouzian and her husband Rainer Stadelmann, the former director of the German Archaeological Institute in Cairo, reopened the excavations at Kom el-Hetan. They have been excavating there every year since and have recovered the fragments of the destroyed Aegean List statue base, as well as those of its neighbors. They are now in the process of reconstructing and restoring them. The eight hundred pieces from the Aegean List alone took more than five years to piece together.[2]

Only two of the names on the Aegean List were already familiar to the Egyptian scribes and to modern Egyptologists—the two that seem to be the names used as titles at the top of the list: *Keftiu*, which was the Egyptian word for the island of Crete, and *Tanaja*, which seems to have been the Egyptian word for mainland Greece. These two names began to appear in Egyptian texts during the time of Hatshepsut and Thutmose III, nearly a century earlier, but never in the company of specific toponyms of individual cities and areas in the Aegean.

The other names on this statue base list were so unusual, and yet almost instantly recognizable, that the first Egyptologist to publish them in English, the eminent professor Kenneth Kitchen of the University of Liverpool, was initially hesitant to suggest a translation for them, for fear of scholarly ridicule. In his first short note on the statue base inscription, which was only a few pages long in the 1965 issue of the scholarly journal *Orientalia*, Kitchen remarked cautiously: "I hardly like to put the following idea on record; readers may ignore it if they wish. The two names 'Amnisa and Kunusa look uncomfortably like Amniso(s) and . . . Knossos, famous ancient settlements on the north coast of Crete."[3]

In the years since then, a number of scholars have worked on deciphering the names on the list and the meaning behind their appearance. The German scholar Elmar Edel published the first thorough consideration of all five statue base lists in 1966; a second edition, updated and with revisions and emendations, was published just a few years ago, forty years later, in 2005. In that interval, many other scholars devoted much thought and ink to the possible interpretations of the list.[4]

First on the list, after the headnames of Keftiu (Crete) and Tanaja (mainland Greece) come a few names of important Minoan sites on Crete, including Knossos and its port city of Amnisos, followed by Phaistos and Kydonia, listed in an order that goes from east to west. All of these either had Minoan palaces or, in the case of Amnisos, functioned as a port for a nearby Minoan palace. Next on the list comes the island of Kythera, positioned midway between Crete and mainland Greece, and then important Mycenaean sites and regions on mainland Greece, including Mycenae and its port city of Nauplion, the region of Messenia, and perhaps the city of Thebes in Boeotia. Last on the list are more names from Minoan Crete, this time in order from west to east and including Amnisos again.

The list looks suspiciously like an itinerary of a round-trip voyage from Egypt to the Aegean and back again. According to the order of the names, the voyagers from Egypt went first to Crete, perhaps to visit the Minoan royalty and merchants with whom, by this point, the Egyptians had been familiar for almost a century. They then continued, via Kythera, to mainland Greece to visit the Mycenaeans—the new power on the scene, who were taking over the trade routes to Egypt and the Near East from the Minoans about this time. And then they returned to Egypt via Crete as the fastest and most direct route, calling at Amnisos for water and food as one of the last stops on the homeward journey, just as they had made that port their first stop shortly after setting out.

The lists on the statue bases as a whole catalog the world known to the Egyptians of Amenhotep III's time. Most of the names were already known from other documents and treaties; among these familiar names were the Hittites and the Kassites/Babylonians (about whom more below), as well as cities in Canaan. The Aegean place-names, however, were (and still are) exceptional and were carved in a particular order. Some were even specifically recarved, for the first three names were recut (to their present values) at some point before or while the list was on display.[5]

Some scholars believe that this list is merely propaganda, idle boasting by a pharaoh who had heard of faraway places and yearned to conquer them or wished to convince people that he had. Others believe that the list is not mendacious self-aggrandizement, but is based on factual knowledge and actual contacts in that long-ago time. This latter explanation seems more likely, for we know, from the numerous other depictions in tombs of nobles dating to the time of Hatshepsut and Thutmose III in the fifteenth century BC, that there were multiple contacts with the Aegean during that earlier time, including instances in which diplomatic ambassadors and/or merchants came to Egypt bearing gifts. It is probable that such contacts continued into the next century, during the reign of Amenhotep III. If so, we may have here the earliest written record of a round-trip voyage from Egypt to the Aegean, a voyage undertaken more than thirty-four centuries ago, a few decades before the boy king Tut ruled the eternal land.

The suggestion that we are looking at the documentation of an early fourteenth-century BC voyage from Egypt to the Aegean, rather than a record of Mycenaeans and Minoans coming to Egypt, seems plausible for the following fascinating reason. There are a number of objects with the cartouche (royal name) of either Amenhotep III or his wife Queen Tiyi carved upon them that have been found by archaeologists at six sites scattered around the Aegean area—on Crete, mainland Greece, and Rhodes. There is a correlation between the Aegean find-spots of these objects and the sites named on the Aegean List, for four of the six sites are included among the names carved on it.

Some of these inscribed objects are simply scarabs and small stamp seals, but one is a vase; all have the cartouche of either the pharaoh or his wife. Most important are the numerous fragments of double-sided plaques made of faience, a material halfway between pottery and glass, which were found at Mycenae, probably the leading city in fourteenth-century BC Greece. These fragments, of which there are at least twelve, come from a total of nine or more original plaques, each measuring about six to eight inches in length, about four inches wide, and less than an inch thick. All had Amenhotep III's titles baked onto them in black paint, reading on both sides of each plaque, "the good god, Neb-Ma'at-Re, son of Re, Amenhotep, prince of Thebes, given life."[6]

Egyptologists refer to these as foundation deposit plaques. They are normally found, at least in Egypt, placed in specific deposits under temples or, sometimes, statues of the king.[7] They function much as time capsules do in our present culture, and as such deposits have done since the Early Bronze Age in Mesopotamia. Their presumed purpose was to ensure that the gods and future generations would know the identity and generosity of the donor/builder, and the date when the building, statue, or other construction was completed.

What makes these plaques at Mycenae unique is simply that—they are unique in the Aegean. Actually, they are exclusive to Mycenae, out of all the places in the entire ancient Mediterranean world, for such faience plaques with Amenhotep III's name on them have never been found anywhere else outside of Egypt. The first fragments at Mycenae were found and published by Greek archaeologists back in the late 1800s and early 1900s, when they were thought to be made out of "porcelain," and Amenhotep's name was not yet clearly recognized or deciphered. More were discovered over the years, including some by the eminent British archaeologist Lord William Taylor within the Cult Center at Mycenae. The most recent fragment was discovered just a few years ago, discarded deep within a well at Mycenae, by UC Berkeley archaeologist Kim Shelton.

None of the fragments have been found in their original context at Mycenae. In other words, we have no idea how they were originally used at the site. But the mere fact that they are at Mycenae, and nowhere else in the world, indicates that there is probably a special relationship between this site and Egypt during the time of Amenhotep III, especially since it is at Mycenae that the vase of Amenhotep III was also found, as well as two scarabs of his wife Queen Tiyi. Considering that this region was on the fringes—the very periphery—of the known and civilized region with which Egypt was in contact during this period, the correlation of these objects with the names on the Aegean List suggests that

Fig. 6. Faience plaque of Amenhotep III, found at Mycenae (photograph by
E. H. Cline).

something unusual in terms of international contact had probably taken
place during Amenhotep III's reign.

The imported Egyptian and Near Eastern objects found in the Aegean
form an interesting pattern, perhaps related to the Aegean List. Minoan
Crete apparently continued to be the principal destination within the
Aegean of the trade routes from Egypt and the Near East during at least
the early part of the fourteenth century BC. However, since objects from
Egypt, Canaan, and Cyprus are found in approximately equal quantities
on Crete, it may be that goods from Egypt were no longer the dominant
cargo being carried by the merchants and traders sailing between Crete
and the Eastern Mediterranean, as had been the case during the previous centuries. If Egyptian and Minoan envoys and traders dominated
the routes to the Aegean during the earlier periods, they were now most
likely either joined, or even replaced, by others from Canaan and Cyprus.

This more complex international situation continued throughout the next two centuries, but there is a shift in the importation of foreign goods into the Aegean as early as the end of the fourteenth century BC. At the same time that there is a sudden drop in the number of imports on Crete, there is a large increase on the Greek mainland. If this shift in the magnitude of importation—from Crete to mainland Greece—is real, it seems possible (although decidedly conjectural) that the decrease and ultimate cessation of Orientalia arriving in Crete might be linked to the destruction of Knossos in about 1350 BC, and to a Mycenaean takeover of the trade routes to Egypt and the Near East soon thereafter.[8]

Amenhotep III's Aegean List possibly records such a situation, for the sites listed on the statue base include both Minoan sites on Crete and Mycenaean sites on the Greek mainland. If an Egyptian embassy had been sent to the Aegean during the reign of Amenhotep III, it might have had a dual mission: to affirm connections with an old and valued trading partner (the Minoans) and to establish relations with a new rising power (the Mycenaeans).[9]

THE AMARNA ARCHIVES

We should probably not be surprised at the existence of the Aegean List, or the other lists also in the temple, which together catalog the world as known to the Egyptians in the fourteenth century BC, for we know from other evidence that Amenhotep III recognized the importance of creating relationships with external powers, particularly with the kings of the lands of diplomatic and mercantile importance to Egypt. He concluded treaties with many of these kings, and married several of their daughters to cement those treaties. We know this from his correspondence with these kings—left to us as an archive inscribed on clay tablets that was first found in 1887.

The generally accepted story concerning the discovery of this archive is that it was found by a peasant woman who had been gathering either fuel or soil at the modern site of Tell el-Amarna, which contains the ruins of the city once called Akhetaten (meaning "Horizon of the Solar Disk").[10] Amenhotep III's heretic son, Amenhotep IV, better known to the world as Akhenaten, had built it in the mid-fourteenth century BC as a new capital city.

Akhenaten was Amenhotep III's successor, probably serving as co-ruler with his father for a few years before Amenhotep died in 1353 BC. Soon after assuming sole power, Akhenaten implemented what is now called the "Amarna Revolution." He closed down the temples belonging to Ra, Amun, and other major deities, seized their vast treasuries, and generated for himself unrivaled power, as the head of the government, military, and religion. He condemned the worship of every Egyptian deity except Aten, the disk of the sun, whom he—and he alone—was allowed to worship directly.

This is sometimes seen as the first attempt at monotheism, since seemingly only one god was worshipped, but in fact the matter is quite debatable (and has been the subject of numerous scholarly discussions). For the ordinary Egyptians, there were essentially two gods: Aten and Akhenaten, for the people were allowed to pray only to Akhenaten; he then prayed to Aten on their behalf. Akhenaten may have been a religious heretic, and perhaps even a fanatic to a certain degree, but he was also calculating and a powermonger rather than a zealot. His religious revolution may actually have been a shrewd political and diplomatic move, designed to restore the power of the king: power that had slowly been lost to the priests during the reigns of previous pharaohs.

But Akhenaten did not undo everything that his ancestors had put into place. In particular, he recognized the importance of maintaining international relationships, especially with the kings of the lands surrounding Egypt. Akhenaten carried on his father's tradition of diplomatic negotiations and trade partnerships with foreign powers, both high and low, including those with Suppiluliuma and the Hittites.[11] He kept an archive of the correspondence with these kings and governors in his capital city, Akhetaten. These are the so-called Amarna Letters, inscribed on clay tablets, which the peasant woman accidentally uncovered in 1887.

The archive was originally housed in the "records office" of the city. It is a treasure trove of correspondence with kings and governors with whom both Amenhotep and his son Akhenaten had diplomatic relationships, including Cypriot and Hittite rulers, and Babylonian and Assyrian kings. There are also letters to and from the local Canaanite rulers, including Abdi-Hepa of Jerusalem and Biridiya of Megiddo. The letters from these local rulers, who were usually vassals of the Egyptians, are full of requests for Egyptian help, but those sent between the rulers of the Great Powers (Egypt, Assyria, Babylon, Mitanni, and the Hittites) are more frequently filled with requests and mentions of gifts made on a much higher diplomatic level. This Amarna archive, along with that found at Mari from the eighteenth century BC, is among the first in the history of the world to document the substantial and sustained international relations of the Bronze Age in Egypt and the Eastern Mediterranean.[12]

The letters were written in Akkadian, the diplomatic lingua franca of the day used in international relations, on nearly four hundred clay tablets. Having been sold on the antiquities market at the time of their discovery, the tablets are now dispersed among museums in England, Egypt, the United States, and Europe, including the British Museum in London, the Cairo Museum in Egypt, the Louvre in Paris, the Oriental Museum at the University of Chicago, the Pushkin Museum in Russia, and the Vorderasiatisches Museum in Berlin (which has almost two-thirds of the tablets).[13]

GREETING-GIFTS AND FAMILY RELATIONS

These letters, including copies of those sent to the foreign rulers and replies from those rulers, provide us with insights into trading and international connections in the time of Amenhotep III and Akhenaten during the mid-fourteenth century BC. It is apparent that much of the contact involved "gift giving" conducted at the very highest levels—from one king to another. For instance, one Amarna Letter, sent to Amenhotep III by Tushratta, the king of Mitanni in northern Syria who came to the throne about 1385 BC, opens with a paragraph containing traditional greetings and then goes on to discuss the gifts that he has sent, brought by his messengers:

> Say to Nibmuareya [Amenhotep III], the king of Egypt, my brother: Thus [says] Tushratta, the king of Mitanni, your brother. For me, all goes well. For you, may all go well. For Kelu-Hepa [your wife], may all go well. For your household, for your wives, for your sons, for your magnates [chief men], for your warriors, for your horses, for your chariots, and in your country, may all go very well . . .

I herewith send you 1 chariot, 2 horses, 1 male attendant, 1 female attendant, from the booty from the land of Hatti. As the greeting-gift of my
brother, I send you 5 chariots, 5 teams of horses. And as the greeting-gift
of Kelu-Hepa, my sister, I send her 1 set of gold toggle-pins, 1 set of gold
earrings, 1 gold *mašu*-ring, and a scent container that is full of "sweet oil."

I herewith send Keliya, my chief minister, and Tunip-ibri. May my
brother let them go promptly so they can report back to me promptly,
and I hear the greeting of my brother and rejoice. May my brother seek
friendship with me, and may my brother send his messengers to me that
they may bring my brother's greetings to me and I hear them.[14]

Another royal letter, from Akhenaten to Burna-Buriash II, the Kassite king of Babylon, includes a detailed list of the gifts that he has sent.
The itemization of the gifts takes up more than three hundred lines of
writing on the tablet. Included are objects of gold, copper, silver, and
bronze, containers of perfume and sweet oil, finger-rings, foot-bracelets,
necklaces, thrones, mirrors, linen cloth, stone bowls, and ebony boxes.[15]
Similar detailed letters with comparable long lists of objects, sometimes
sent as part of a dowry accompanying a daughter and sometimes just
sent as gifts, come from other kings, such as Tushratta of Mitanni.[16] We
should also note that the "messengers" referred to in these, and other,
letters were often ministers, essentially sent as ambassadors, but were
frequently also merchants, apparently serving double duty for both
themselves and the king.

In these letters, the kings involved often referred to each other as rela-
tives, calling one another "brother" or "father/son," even though usually
they were not actually related, thereby creating "trade partnerships."[17]
Anthropologists have noted that such efforts to create imaginary family relationships happen most frequently in preindustrial societies,
specifically to solve the problem of trading when there are no kinship
ties or state-supervised markets.[18] Thus, a king of Amurru wrote to the
neighboring king of Ugarit (both areas were located in coastal northern
Syria): "My brother, look: I and you, we are brothers. Sons of a single
man, we are brothers. Why should we not be on good terms with each
other? Whatever desire you will write to me, I will satisfy it; and you will
satisfy my desires. We form a unit."[19]

It should be emphasized that these two kings (of Amurru and Ugarit)
were not necessarily related at all, even by marriage. Not all were, and

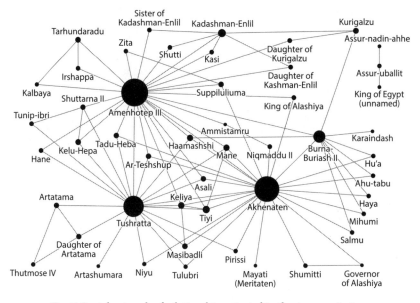

Fig. 7. Social network of relationships attested in the Amarna Letters
(created by D. H. Cline).

not all appreciated this shortcut approach to diplomatic relations. The Hittites of Anatolia seem to have been especially prickly in this regard, for one Hittite king wrote to another king: "Why should I write to you in terms of brotherhood? Are we sons of the same mother?"[20]

It is not always clear what relationship merits use of the term "brother," as opposed to "father" and "son," but it usually seems to indicate equality in status or in age, with "father/son" being reserved to show respect. The Hittite kings, for instance, use "father" and "son" more frequently in their correspondence than do the rulers of any other major Near Eastern power, while the Amarna Letters employ almost entirely the term "brother," whether for the mighty king of Assyria or the less-powerful king of Cyprus. It seems that the Egyptian pharaohs regarded the other Near Eastern kings, their trade partners, as members of an international brotherhood, regardless of age or years on the throne.[21]

In some cases, however, the two kings were actually related by marriage. For instance, in letters from Tushratta of Mitanni to Amenhotep III, Tushratta refers to Amenhotep III's wife Kelu-Hepa as his sister, which she actually was (his father had given her in marriage to

Amenhotep III). Similarly, Tushratta also gave his own daughter, Tadu-Hepa, to Amenhotep III in another arranged marriage, which made Tushratta both brother-in-law ("brother") and father-in-law ("father") to Amenhotep. Thus, one of his letters legitimately starts with "Say to . . . the king of Egypt, my brother, my son-in-law . . . Thus speaks Tushratta, the king of the land of Mitanni, your father-in-law."[22] After Amenhotep III's death, Akhenaten seems to have taken (or inherited) Tadu-Hepu as one of his wives, which gave Tushratta the right to call himself father-in-law to both Amenhotep III and Akhenaten in different Amarna Letters.[23]

In each case, the royal marriage was arranged to cement relations and treaties between the two powers, and specifically between the two individual kings. This also therefore gave Tushratta the right to call Amenhotep III his "brother" (though, technically, he was his brother-in-law) and to expect better relations with Egypt than he might otherwise have had. The marriages were accompanied by elaborate dowries, which are recorded in several of the Amarna Letters. For instance, one letter from Tushratta to Amenhotep III, which is only partially intact and not entirely legible, still lists 241 lines of gifts, of which he himself says: "It is all of these wedding-gifts, of every sort, that Tushratta, the king of Mitanni, gave to Nimmureya [Amenhotep III], the king of Egypt, his brother and his son-in-law. He gave them at the same time that he gave Tadu-Hepa, his daughter, to Egypt and to Nimmureya to be his wife."[24]

Amenhotep III seems to have utilized this diplomatic angle of dynastic marriage to a greater extent than did any other king of his time, for we know that he married, and had in his harem, the daughters of the Kassite kings Kurigalzu I and Kadashman-Enlil I of Babylon, Kings Shuttarna II and Tushratta of Mitanni, and King Tarkhundaradu of Arzawa (located in southwestern Anatolia).[25] Each marriage undoubtedly cemented yet another diplomatic treaty and allowed the kings in question to practice diplomatic relations as if between family members.

Some kings attempted to take advantage of the link between dynastic marriage and gift giving right away, forgoing the other niceties. For instance, one Amarna Letter, probably from the Kassite king Kadashman-Enlil of Babylon to Amenhotep III, directly combines the two, when Kadashman-Enlil writes:

Moreover, you, my brother . . . as to the gold I wrote you about, send me whatever is on hand, as much as possible, before your messenger [comes] to me, right now, in all haste . . . If during this summer, during the months of Tammuz or Ab, you send the gold I wrote you about, I will give you my daughter.[26]

For this cavalier attitude toward his own daughter, Amenhotep III admonished Kadashman-Enlil in another letter: "It is a fine thing that you give your daughters in order to acquire a nugget of gold from your neighbors!"[27] And yet, at some point during his reign, the transaction did take place, for we know from three other Amarna Letters that Amenhotep III did marry a daughter of Kadashman-Enlil, although we do not know her name.[28]

Gold, Fool's Gold, and High-Level Trade

Egypt in particular was sought after as a trading partner by the kings of other countries. This was not only because Egypt was among the Great Powers of the time, but also because of the gold that the Egyptians commanded, courtesy of the mines in Nubia. More than one king wrote to Amenhotep III and Akhenaten, requesting shipments of gold while acting as if it were nothing out of the ordinary—the refrain "gold is like dust in your land," and similar phrases, are seen again and again in the Amarna Letters. In one letter, Tushratta of Mitanni invokes the family relationship and asks Amenhotep III to "send me much more gold than he [you] did to my father," for, as he says, "in my brother's country, gold is as plentiful as dirt."[29]

But it seems that the gold wasn't always gold, as the Babylonian kings in particular complained. In one letter sent by Kadashman-Enlil to Amenhotep III, he said, "You have sent me as my greeting-gift, the only thing in six years, 30 minas of gold that looked like silver."[30] His successor in Babylon, the Kassite king Burna-Buriash II, similarly wrote in one letter to Amenhotep III's successor, Akhenaten: "Certainly my brother [the king of Egypt] did not check the earlier (shipment of) gold that my brother sent to me. When I put the 40 minas of gold that were brought to me into a kiln, not (even) 10 minas, I swear, appeared." In another letter, he said: "The 20 minas of gold that were brought here were not all there. When they put it into the kiln, not 5 minas of gold appeared. The (part) that did appear, on cooling off looked like ashes. Was the gold ever identified (as gold)?"[31]

On the one hand, one might ask why the Babylonian kings were putting the gold sent by the Egyptian king into a kiln and melting it down. It must have been scrap metal sent for its value only rather than nice finished pieces being given as gifts, much as today one sees advertisements on late-night television urging the viewer to sell old and broken jewelry for cash, with the clear implication that it will be melted down immediately. They must have needed it to pay their artisans, architects, and other professionals, as indeed some of the letters state.

On the other hand, we also have to ask whether the Egyptian king knew that the shipments he was sending were not actually gold, and if the action was deliberate, or whether the real gold was swapped out en route by unscrupulous merchants and emissaries. Burna-Buriash suspected the latter in the case of the forty minas of gold mentioned above, or at least offered Akhenaten a diplomatic way out of the uneasy situation, and wrote: "The gold that my brother sends me, my brother should not turn over to the charge of any deputy. My brother should make a [personal] check [of the gold], then my brother should seal and send it to me. Certainly my brother did not check the earlier (shipment of) gold that my brother sent to me. It was only a deputy of my brother who sealed and sent it to me."[32]

It also seems that the caravans loaded with gifts and sent between the two kings were frequently robbed en route. Burna-Buriash writes of two caravans belonging to Salmu, his messenger (and probably diplomatic representative), that he knows have been robbed. He even knows whom to blame: a man named Biriyawaza was responsible for the first heist, and a man supposedly named Pamahu (possibly a place-name mistaken for a personal name) perpetrated the second. Burna-Buriash asks when Akhenaten is going to prosecute the latter case, since it is within his jurisdiction, but he received no reply, at least as far as we know.[33]

Moreover, we should not forget that these high-level gift exchanges were probably the tip of the iceberg of commercial interaction. An analogous, relatively modern, situation may be the following. In the 1920s, the anthropologist Bronisław Malinowski studied the Trobriand Islanders who were participating in the so-called Kula Ring in the South

Pacific. In this system, the chiefs of each island exchanged armbands and necklaces made of shells, with armbands always traveling one way around the ring and necklaces circulating in the other direction. The value of each object increased and decreased depending upon its lineage and past history of ownership (now referred to by archaeologists as an object's "biography"). Malinowski discovered that while the chiefs were in the ceremonial centers exchanging armbands and necklaces according to traditional pomp and circumstance, the men who served as crew on the canoes that transported the chiefs were busy trading with the locals on the beach for food, water, and other necessary staples of life.[34] Such mundane commercial transactions were the real economic motives underlying the ceremonial gift exchanges of the Trobriand chiefs, but they would never admit to that fact.

Similarly, we should not underestimate the importance of the messengers, merchants, and sailors who were transporting the royal gifts and other items across the deserts of the ancient Near East, and probably overseas to the Aegean as well. It is clear that there was much contact between Egypt, the Near East, and the Aegean during the Late Bronze Age, and undoubtedly ideas and innovations were occasionally transported along with the actual objects. Such transfers of ideas undoubtedly took place not only at the upper levels of society, but also at the inns and bars of the ports and cities along the trade routes in Greece, Egypt, and the Eastern Mediterranean. Where else would a sailor or crew member while away the time waiting for the wind to shift to the proper quarter or for a diplomatic mission to conclude its sensitive negotiations, swapping myths, legends, and tall tales? Such events may perhaps have contributed to cultural influences spreading between Egypt and the rest of the Near East, and even across the Aegean. Such an exchange between cultures could possibly explain the similarities between the *Epic of Gilgamesh* and Homer's later *Iliad* and *Odyssey,* and between the Hittite *Myth of Kumarbi* and Hesiod's later *Theogony.*[35]

We should also note that gift exchanges between Near Eastern rulers during the Late Bronze Age frequently included physicians, sculptors, masons, and skilled laborers, who were sent between the various royal courts. It is little wonder that there are certain similarities between architectural structures in Egypt, Anatolia, Canaan, and even the Aegean, if the same architects, sculptors, and stonemasons were working in each area. The recent finds of Aegean-style wall paintings and painted floors at Tell ed-Dab'a in Egypt, mentioned in the previous chapter, as well as at Tel Kabri in Israel, Alalakh in Turkey, and Qatna in Syria, indicate that Aegean artisans may have made their way to Egypt and the Near East as early as the seventeenth century and perhaps as late as the thirteenth century BC.[36]

RISE OF ALASHIYA AND ASSYRIA

From the Amarna Letters that date specifically to the time of Akhenaten, we know that Egypt's international contacts expanded during his reign to include the rising power of Assyria, under its king Assur-uballit I, who had come to the throne in the decade before Amenhotep III died. There are also eight letters to and from the king of the island of Cyprus, known to the Egyptians and others of the ancient world as *Alashiya*,[37] which provide confirmation of contact with Egypt.

These letters sent to and from Cyprus, which probably date to the time of Akhenaten rather than Amenhotep III, are of great interest, in part of because of the staggering amount of raw copper mentioned in one of the letters. Cyprus was the primary source of copper for most of the major Aegean and Eastern Mediterranean powers during the Late Bronze Age, as is made clear by the discussions found in the letters, including that in which the king of Alashiya apologizes for sending *only* five hundred talents of copper because of an illness that is ravaging his island.[38] It is currently thought that such raw copper was probably shipped in the shape of oxhide ingots, such as those that have been found on the Uluburun shipwreck discussed in the next section. Each of the oxhide ingots on board the ship weighs about sixty pounds, meaning that this one consignment mentioned in the Amarna Letter would have consisted of some thirty thousand pounds of copper—an amount for which the Cypriot king is (ironically?) apologetic because it is so small!

As for Assyria, there are two letters in the Amarna archive from Assur-uballit I, who ruled that kingdom from ca. 1365 to 1330 BC. It is not clear to which Egyptian pharaoh these two letters were addressed, for one simply begins, "Say to the King of Egypt," while the name given

in the other is unclear and the reading is uncertain. Previous transla-
tors have suggested that they were probably sent to Akhenaten, but at
least one scholar proposes that the second one might be addressed to Ay,
who came to the throne after the death of Tutankhamen.[39] This seems
unlikely, given the late date for Ay's accession to the throne (ca. 1325
BC), and, in fact, the letters are much more likely to have been sent to
Amenhotep III or Akhenaten, as were the vast majority of letters from
other rulers.

The first of these letters is simply a message of greeting and includes
a brief list of gifts, such as "a beautiful chariot, 2 horses, [and] 1 date-
stone of genuine lapis lazuli."[40] The second is longer and contains the
by-now-standard request for gold, with the usual disclaimer: "Gold in
your country is dirt; one simply gathers it up." However, it also contains
an interesting comparison to the king of Hanigalbat, that is, Mitanni, in
which the new king of Assyria states that he is "the equal of the king of
Hanigalbat"—an obvious reference to his position in the pecking order
of the so-called Great Powers of the day, of which Assyria and its king
strongly wished to be a part.[41]

It seems that Assur-uballit was not idly boasting, for he was more
than an equal to the then-current Mitannian king, Shuttarna II. Assur-
uballit defeated Shuttarna in battle, probably about 1360 BC, and ended
the Mitannian domination of Assyria that had begun a little more than
a century earlier, when the earlier Mitannian king Saushtatar had stolen
the gold and silver door from the Assyrian capital and taken it to the
Mitannian capital of Washukanni.

Thus began Assyria's rise to greatness, primarily at the expense of
Mitanni. Assur-uballit quickly became one of the major players in the
international world of realpolitik. He arranged for a royal marriage between his daughter and Burna-Buriash II, the Kassite king of Babylon,
only to invade the city of Babylon itself some years later, after his grandson was assassinated in 1333 BC, and place a puppet king named Kurigalzu II on the throne.[42]

Thus, the two last major players of the Late Bronze Age in the ancient Near East, Assyria and Cyprus, finally appear on stage. We now
have a full cast of characters: Hittites, Egyptians, Mitannians, Kassites/
Babylonians, Assyrians, Cypriots, Canaanites, Minoans, and Mycenaeans, all present and accounted for. They all interacted, both positively

and negatively, during the coming centuries, though some, such as Mitanni, vanished from the stage long before the others.

NEFERTITI AND KING TUT

Soon after his death, the reforms of Akhenaten were reversed, and an attempt was made to erase his name and his memory from the monuments and records of Egypt. The attempt almost succeeded, but through the efforts of archaeologists and epigraphers, we now know a great deal about Akhenaten's reign, as well as his capital city of Akhetaten and even his royal tomb. We also know about his family, including his beautiful wife Nefertiti, and their daughters, who are portrayed on a number of inscriptions and monuments.

The well-known bust of Nefertiti was found by Ludwig Borchardt, the German excavator of Amarna (Akhetaten), in 1912 and shipped back to Germany a few months later. But it was not unveiled to the public until 1924 at the Egyptian Museum of Berlin. The statue is still in Berlin today, despite many requests by the Egyptian government for its return, since it reportedly left Egypt under less than ideal circumstances. The story is told, but not confirmed, that the German excavators and the Egyptian government had an agreement to split the finds from the excavation equally, with the Egyptians getting first choice. The Germans knew this but wanted the bust of Nefertiti for themselves. So they reportedly kept the bust uncleaned and placed it deliberately at the end of a long line of objects. When the Egyptian authorities passed on the filthy-looking head, the Germans promptly shipped it to Berlin. When it was finally put on display in 1924, the Egyptians were furious and demanded its return, but it remains in Berlin.[43]

We also know now about Akhenaten's son, Tutankhaten, who changed his name and ruled using the name by which we know him today, Tutankhamen, or King Tut. He was not born in Arizona, contrary to what Steve Martin once said on *Saturday Night Live*, nor did he ever move to Babylonia.[44] He did, however, come to the throne of Egypt at an early age, when he was about eight years old—approximately the same age at which Thutmose III came to the throne almost 150 years earlier. Fortunately for Tut, there was no Hatshepsut around to rule on his behalf.

Tut therefore was able to reign for approximately ten years before his premature death.

The vast majority of the details surrounding Tut's short life are not immediately relevant to our study of the international world in which he lived. However, his death is relevant, in part because the discovery of his tomb in 1922 launched a modern worldwide obsession with ancient Egypt (known as Egyptomania) and established him as the most recognized king of all those who ruled during the Late Bronze Age, and because of the strong possibility that it may have been his widow who wrote to the Hittite king Suppiluliuma I, asking for a husband after Tut died.

The cause of Tut's death has been long debated—including the possibility that he might have been murdered by a blow to the back of his head—but recent scientific studies, including a CT scan of his skeleton, point to a broken leg followed by an infection as the most likely culprit.[45] Whether he broke his leg by falling off a chariot, as is suspected, may never be proven, but it is now clear that he suffered from malaria as well and had congenital deformations, including a club foot. It has also been suggested that he may have been born of an incestuous brother-sister relationship.[46]

Tut was buried in a tomb within the Valley of the Kings. The tomb might not have originally been meant for him, as was the case for many of the dazzling objects found buried with him, since he died so suddenly and unexpectedly. It also proved remarkably hard for modern Egyptologists to locate, but Howard Carter finally discovered it in 1922.

The Earl of Carnarvon had hired Carter for the express purpose of finding Tut's tomb. Carnarvon, like some other members of the British aristocracy, was looking for something to do while wintering in Egypt. Unlike some of his compatriots, Carnarvon was under his doctor's orders to be in Egypt each year, for he had been involved in a car accident in Germany in 1901—having rolled his car while doing the unheard-of speed of twenty miles per hour—and had punctured a lung, leading his doctor to fear that he would not survive a winter in England. So he had to spend winters in Egypt and promptly began playing amateur archaeologist, by hiring a pet Egyptologist.[47]

Carter had been inspector-general of monuments of Upper Egypt and then held an even more prestigious post at Saqqara. However, he had resigned after refusing to apologize to a group of French tourists who created a problem at the site in 1905. He was therefore most amenable to being hired by Carnarvon, as he was unemployed at the time and was working as an artist painting watercolor scenes for the tourists. The two men began working together in 1907.[48]

After a decade of successful excavations at a variety of sites, the two men were able to begin work in the Valley of the Kings in 1917. They were looking specifically for Tut's tomb, which they knew must be somewhere in the valley. Carter then dug for six seasons, for several months each year, until Carnarvon's funding, and perhaps interest as well, were about to run out. Carter pleaded for one last season, offering to pay for it himself, because there was one place in the valley that he hadn't yet excavated. Carnarvon relented and Carter returned to the Valley of the Kings, beginning work on November 1, 1922.[49] Carter realized that he had been pitching his camp in the same place every season, so now he moved his headquarters and dug where the camp had originally been positioned . . . and three days later, a member of his team found the first steps leading down into the tomb. As it turned out, one of the reasons why the tomb had lain undiscovered for thousands of years was that the entrance had been buried under dirt tossed by later diggers creating the nearby tomb of Ramses VI, who died almost a century after Tut.

Since Carter had discovered the entrance to the tomb while Carnarvon was still in England, he sent a telegram immediately and then had to wait until Carnarvon was able to sail to Egypt. He also alerted the media. By the time Carnarvon arrived and they were ready to open the tomb on November 26, 1922, journalists surrounded them, as photographs from that day show.

As an opening was chiseled in the door, Carter was able to peer through the hole and into the entrance corridor of the tomb, with the antechamber beyond. Carnarvon tugged on Carter's jacket and asked him what he saw. Carter reportedly replied, "I see wonderful things," or words to that effect, and indeed he later reported that he could see gold, everywhere the glint of gold.[50]

Undoubtedly, relief was evident in his voice, for during the long wait for Carnarvon, Carter had been plagued by worries that the tomb had been looted at least once, if not twice, to judge by the replastering at the tomb's entrance, with the stamps of the necropolis on it.[51] The penalty for tomb robbing in ancient Egypt was death by impalement on a stick stuck in the ground, but this does not seem to have fazed many grave robbers.

When Carter and Carnarvon did eventually get into the tomb, it became clear that it had indeed been robbed, to judge by the messy condition of the objects in the antechamber, tossed about like goods in a modern apartment or house that has been ransacked by burglars, and by the golden rings wrapped in a handkerchief and dropped in the entrance corridor, most likely by the robbers either in their haste to get out of the tomb or as they were being caught by the necropolis guards. However, the sheer quantity of goods remaining in the tomb was astounding—it took Carter and his associates most of the next ten years to completely excavate and catalog everything in the tomb, even though Carnarvon himself died of blood poisoning only eight days after the tomb was opened, thereby giving rise to the story of the "mummy's curse."

The huge number of burial goods in Tut's tomb led some Egyptologists to wonder what might once have been in the tomb of one of the pharaohs who had ruled much longer, such as Ramses III or even Amenhotep III, but all of those tombs had been robbed long ago. It is more likely, though, that the amazing goods in Tut's tomb were unique and may have been the result of gifts from the Egyptian priests, who were grateful because he had reversed his father's reforms and given power back to the priests of Amun and others. Until another unlooted royal Egyptian tomb is found, however, we have nothing with which to compare Tut's tomb.

When Tut died, he left widowed his young queen Ankhsenamen who was also his sister. And this is where we come to the saga of the Hittite king Suppiluliuma I and the Zannanza Affair, one of the most unusual diplomatic episodes of the fourteenth century BC.

Suppiluliuma and the Zannanza Affair

After Tudhaliya I/II, the Hittites of Anatolia/Turkey had languished for a while under comparatively weak rulers. Their fortunes began to rise again about 1350 BC, under a new king named Suppiluliuma I, briefly mentioned earlier in relation to Akhenaten's correspondence and archives.

As a young prince acting on the orders of his father, Suppiluliuma I had helped the Hittites to regain control of Anatolia.[52] The reemergence of the Hittites at this time posed a threat to Amenhotep III and his empire, so it is not surprising that the treaties negotiated by Amenhotep III, and the dynastic marriages that he arranged, were initiated with the rulers of virtually all the lands surrounding the Hittite homelands, from Ugarit on the coast of north Syria to Babylon in Mesopotamia to the east and Arzawa in Anatolia to the west. They were most likely sought in an attempt at first to take advantage of the relative weakness of the Hittites during the early part of Suppiluliuma I's reign, and subsequently, as the Hittites began to rise again under his leadership, to limit the extent of their activities.[53]

We know a lot about Suppiluliuma from the Hittite records, especially one set of tablets written by his son and eventual successor, Mursili II, containing what are known as the *Plague Prayers*. It seems that Suppiluliuma died, after a reign of about thirty years, of a plague that had been brought back to the Hittite homelands via Egyptian prisoners of war who had been captured during a war fought in northern Syria. The plague ravaged the Hittite populace. Many members of the royal family died, including Suppiluliuma.

Mursili saw the deaths, and especially that of his father, as divine retribution for a murder that had been committed at the beginning of Suppiluliuma's reign, and for which he had never asked forgiveness from the gods. It was Suppiluliuma's own brother who had been murdered: a Hittite prince named Tudhaliya the Younger. It is not clear whether Suppiluliuma was directly involved in the murder, but he certainly benefited, for Tudhaliya had been intended for the Hittite throne instead of Suppiluliuma, despite all of the great military victories that Suppiluliuma had accomplished on behalf of his father. Mursili writes:

> But now you, O gods, have eventually taken vengeance on my father for this affair of Tudhaliya the Younger. My father [died] because of the blood of Tudhaliya, and the princes, the noblemen, the commanders of the thousands, and the officers who went over to my father, they also died because of that affair. This same affair also came upon the Land of Hatti, and the population of the Land of Hatti began to perish because of this affair.[54]

We do not know any more details about Suppiluliuma's power grab, except that it obviously worked. However, we are then told about additional important events from his reign, courtesy of a lengthy document entitled the *Deeds of Suppiluliuma*, also written by his son and successor, Mursili II. The details of Suppiluliuma's reign could take up an entire book, which will undoubtedly be written at some point. Here it will have to suffice to say simply that Suppiluliuma was able to bring most of Anatolia back under Hittite control, through almost continual warfare and shrewd diplomacy. He also expanded Hittite influence, and the empire's borders, down into northern Syria, where he may have destroyed the city of Alalakh, capital city of the kingdom of Mukish.[55] His numerous campaigns to the south and east eventually brought him into conflict with the Egyptians, although not until the time of Akhenaten. These also brought him into conflict with Mitanni, farther to the east, during the reign of its king Tushratta. Suppiluliuma eventually defeated and subjugated the kingdom of Mitanni, but only after a number of attempts—including the so-called Great Syrian War, when Suppiluliuma sacked and plundered the Mitanni capital Washukanni.[56]

Among the other towns that Suppiluliuma attacked and destroyed within the Mitanni lands was the site of ancient Qatna—modern Tell Mishrife—that is today being excavated by Italian, German, and Syrian archaeologists. Tremendous finds have been made just in the past decade, including an unlooted royal tomb, Aegean-style wall paintings with pictures of turtles and dolphins, a piece of clay with the throne name of Akhenaten (probably used to seal a jar or originally attached to a letter), and dozens of tablets from the royal archive, all located within or underneath the palace. In among these tablets is a letter dating to about 1340 BC from Hanutti, the commander in chief of the Hittite army under Suppiluliuma, telling King Idadda of Qatna to prepare for war. The letter was found in the burned remains of the king's palace, evidence that the Hittites had attacked and been victorious.[57]

Suppiluliuma was no stranger to diplomacy, for that went hand in hand with warfare in those days. He even seems to have married a Babylonian princess, probably after banishing his primary wife (and mother of his sons) overseas to Ahhiyawa for an unnamed transgression.[58] He also married off one of his daughters to Shattiwaza, the son of Tushratta, whom he placed on the throne of Mitanni as a vassal king after sending a Hittite army with him to win his father's throne. However, the most interesting marriage linked to Suppiluliuma's reign is one that never happened. It is known today as the "Zannanza Affair."

We learn of the Zannanza Affair in the *Deeds of Suppiluliuma*, as written by his son Mursili II, the same son who was responsible for writing the *Plague Prayers*. Apparently a letter was received at the Hittite court one day, purportedly from the queen of Egypt. The letter was regarded with suspicion because it contained an offer that had never before been made by a ruler of Egypt. It was a request so surprising that Suppiluliuma immediately doubted the letter's authenticity. It read, simply:

> My husband is dead. I have no son. But they say that you have many sons. If you would give me one of your sons, he would become my husband. I will never take a servant of mine and make him my husband![59]

The *Deeds* record that the sender of the letter was a woman named "Dahamunzu." However, this is simply a Hittite word meaning "the wife of the king." In other words, the letter was supposedly from the queen of Egypt. But this made no sense, because Egyptian royalty did not marry foreigners. In all of his treaty negotiations, for instance, Amenhotep III had never once given away a member of his family in marriage to a foreign ruler, despite being asked on more than one occasion to do so. Now, the queen of Egypt was offering not only to marry Suppiluliuma's son but to immediately make him pharaoh of Egypt. Such an offer was unbelievable, and so Suppiluliuma's response is understandable. He sent a trusted messenger named Hattusa-ziti to Egypt, to ask whether the queen had indeed sent the letter, and whether she was serious about her offer.

Hattusa-ziti traveled to Egypt, as instructed, and returned not only with an additional letter from the queen but also with her special envoy, a man named Hani. The letter was written in Akkadian, rather than in either Egyptian or Hittite. It still survives today in a fragmentary form after its discovery at Hattusa, within the Hittite archives, and reflects the queen's anger at being doubted. As quoted in the *Deeds*, it reads as follows:

> Had I a son, would I have written about my own and my country's shame to a foreign land? You did not believe me, and you even spoke thus to me! He who was my husband is dead. I have no son! Never shall I take a servant of mine and make him my husband! I have written to no other

country. Only to you have I written. They say you have many sons; so give me one son of yours. To me he will be husband. In Egypt he will be king![60]

Since Suppiluliuma was still skeptical, the Egyptian envoy Hani spoke next, saying:

Oh my Lord! This is our country's shame! If we had a son of the king at all, would we have come to a foreign country and kept asking for a lord for ourselves? Niphururiya [the Egyptian king] is dead. He has no sons! Our Lord's wife is solitary. We are seeking a son of our Lord [i.e. Suppiluliuma] for the kingship in Egypt. And for the woman, our Lady, we seek him as her husband! Furthermore, we went to no other country, only here did we come! Now, oh our Lord, give us a son of yours![61]

According to the *Deeds*, Suppiluliuma was finally persuaded by this speech and decided to send one of his sons, named Zannanza, to Egypt. He was not risking much, for Zannanza was the fourth of his five sons. The older three were already serving him in various capacities, so he could spare Zannanza. If things went well, his son would become king of Egypt; if things did not go well, he still had four other sons.

As it turned out, things did not go well. After several weeks, a messenger arrived and informed Suppiluliuma that the party traveling to Egypt had been ambushed en route and Zannanza had been killed. Those responsible had escaped and had still not been identified. Suppiluliuma was furious; he had no doubt that the Egyptians were somehow responsible for this . . . and had perhaps even lured him into sending his son to his death. As the *Deeds* record,

When my father [Suppiluliuma] heard of the murder of Zannanza, he began to lament for Zannanza, and to the gods he spoke thus: "O Gods! I did no evil, yet the people of Egypt did this to me! They also attacked the frontier of my country!"[62]

It still remains an unsolved mystery as to who ambushed and killed Zannanza. It also remains an open question as to who in Egypt would have sent the letter to Suppiluliuma, for there are two potential queens, both of whom were widowed. One was Nefertiti, wife of Akhenaten; the other was Ankhsenamen, wife of King Tut.[63] However, given the information in the letters—that is, that the queen had no sons—and given the chain of events that followed the murder of Zannanza, with the throne of Egypt going to a man named Ay, who married Ankhsenamen despite being old enough to be her grandfather, the identification of the mysterious royal letter writer as Ankhsenamen makes the most sense. It is unclear whether Ay had anything to do with the actual assassination of the Hittite prince, but since he had the most to gain, suspicion clearly falls upon him.

When Suppiluliuma vowed to enact vengeance for the death of his son, he made plans to attack Egyptian territory. Ay warned him not to do so, in correspondence that still exists in fragmentary condition, but Suppiluliuma declared war anyway and sent the Hittite army into southern Syria, where it attacked numerous cities and brought back thousands of prisoners, including many Egyptian soldiers.[64] Lest anyone wonder whether someone would go to war over a single person, one need only look at the story of the Trojan War, where the Mycenaeans fought the Trojans for ten years, reportedly because of the kidnapping of the beautiful Helen, to which we shall soon turn. One can also point to the assassination of Archduke Ferdinand in Sarajevo on June 28, 1914, which many see as the flash point igniting World War I.

Ironically, as pointed out above and in the *Plague Prayers* of Mursili, the Egyptian prisoners of war who were brought back by the Hittite army are thought to have brought with them a dreadful illness, which spread rapidly throughout the Hittite homelands. Soon thereafter, in approximately 1322 BC, Suppiluliuma died from this plague—perhaps as much a victim of Egyptian-Hittite contretemps as was his son Zannanza.

Hittites and Mycenaeans

One additional note can be made about the Hittites at this time. During Suppiluliuma's reign, there began for the Hittites a period during which they were one of the great powers of the ancient world, on a par with the Egyptians and exceeding the influence of the Mitannians, Assyrians, Kassites/Babylonians, and Cypriots. They maintained their position through a combination of diplomacy, threats, war, and trade. In fact, archaeologists excavating Hittite sites have found trade goods from most of those other countries (we might call them nation-states in modern parlance). Moreover, Hittite goods have been found in virtually all of those countries.

The exception is the area of the Aegean. Hittite objects are close to nonexistent in Bronze Age contexts on mainland Greece, Crete, the Cycladic islands, and even Rhodes, despite the latter's close proximity to Turkey. There are only a dozen such objects that have been discovered, in contrast to hundreds of Egyptian, Canaanite, and Cypriot imports that have been found in the same contexts in the Aegean. Conversely, almost no Mycenaean or Minoan objects were imported into the Hittite homelands in central Anatolia, despite the fact that imported goods from Cyprus, Assyria, Babylon, and Egypt made it through the mountain passes and up onto the central Anatolian plateau. This glaring anomaly in the trade patterns of the ancient Mediterranean world is not restricted just to the time of Suppiluliuma and the fourteenth century BC, but is demonstrable across most of three centuries, from the fifteenth through the thirteenth centuries BC.[65]

It may simply be that neither side produced objects that the other wanted, or that the objects exchanged were perishable (e.g., olive oil, wine, wood, textiles, metals) and have long since disintegrated or been made into other objects, but the dearth of trade may also have been deliberate. We will see, in the next section, a Hittite diplomatic treaty in which a deliberate economic embargo against the Mycenaeans is spelled out—"no ship of the Ahhiyawa may go to him"—and it seems quite likely that we are looking here at one of the earliest examples in history of such an embargo.

As has been pointed out elsewhere,[66] such a scenario, and a motivation for instituting an embargo, is supported by evidence that the Mycenaeans actively encouraged anti-Hittite activities in western Anatolia.[67] As noted at the beginning of this section, if Amenhotep III had sent an embassy to the Aegean, as recorded on his so-called Aegean List at his mortuary temple at Kom el-Hetan, in order to help contain the rising power of the Hittites, such Egyptian anti-Hittite overtures, particularly those that benefited Mycenae, may have found an eager ally in the Aegean.

Alternatively, the hostility and lack of trade between Mycenaeans and Hittites might well have been the *result* of an anti-Hittite treaty signed between Egypt and the Aegean during the time of Amenhotep III. In short, it seems that the politics, trade, and diplomacy of thirty-five hundred years ago, especially during the fourteenth century BC, were not all that dissimilar to those practiced as part and parcel of the globalized economy of our world today, complete with economic embargoes, diplomatic embassies, and both gifts and power plays at the highest diplomatic levels.

ACT III

· · · · ·

FIGHTING FOR GODS AND COUNTRY:

THE THIRTEENTH CENTURY BC

We don't know what happened during the final moments of the ship that sank off the southwestern coast of Turkey at Uluburun (roughly translated as "Grand Promontory") sometime around 1300 BC. Did it capsize in a great storm? Did it founder after striking a submerged object? Did its crew intentionally scuttle it to avoid being taken captive by pirates? Archaeologists do not know, nor are they certain of the vessel's origination, its final destination, or its ports of call, but they did recover its cargo, which suggests that the Bronze Age ship was most likely sailing from the Eastern Mediterranean to the Aegean.[1]

A young Turkish sponge diver discovered the shipwreck in 1982. He reported seeing "metal biscuits with ears" lying on the seabed during one of the first dives that he ever made. His captain realized that the description fit a Bronze Age copper oxhide ingot (so called because it looks like an outstretched hide cut from a slaughtered ox or cow). Archaeologists from the Institute of Nautical Archaeology (INA), at Texas A&M University, had shown him pictures of such objects and told him to keep an eye out for them.

The archaeologists searching for such objects were led by George Bass, who had pioneered the field of underwater archaeology in the 1960s while still a graduate student at the University of Pennsylvania. At that time, modern self-contained underwater breathing apparatus ("scuba") gear was a relatively recent development, and Bass's excavation of a shipwreck at Cape Gelidonya off the coast of Turkey marked the first maritime excavation of a Bronze Age wreck ever officially conducted by professional archaeologists in that region.

Bass's findings at Cape Gelidonya, in which he concluded that the wreck was of a Canaanite ship en route to the Aegean that had sunk in approximately 1200 BC, met with considerable skepticism and debate when his official publication of the excavation appeared in 1967.[2] Most archaeologists had a hard time believing that there was any trade and contact between the Aegean and the Near East that far back in antiquity, more than three thousand years ago, let alone that the Canaanites had the ability to sail the Mediterranean. Bass had therefore sworn to find and excavate another Bronze Age ship at some point during his career, in order to prove that his conclusions about the Cape Gelidonya wreck were plausible. Now his chance had come, in the 1980s, with the wreck at Uluburun, which dated to approximately 1300 BC, about a hundred years older than the Gelidonya ship.

The Uluburun Ship

Current thinking suggests that the Uluburun ship may have begun its journey in either Egypt or Canaan (perhaps at Abu Hawam in what is now modern-day Israel), and made stops at Ugarit in northern Syria and possibly at a port on Cyprus. It then headed west into the Aegean, following the southern coastline of Anatolia (modern Turkey). Along the way, the crew of the vessel had taken on board raw glass, storage jars full of barley, resin, spices, and perhaps wine, and—most precious of all—nearly a ton of raw tin and ten tons of raw copper, which were to be mixed together to form that most wondrous of metals, bronze.

From the ship's cargo, we are reasonably certain that it was traveling westward from the Levant, apparently bound for a port city in the Aegean—perhaps one of the two or three on the Greek mainland that served the capital center of Mycenae, or maybe one of the other major cities, such as Pylos on the mainland or Kommos or even Knossos on Crete. The mere fact that there was another ship sailing from east to west during the Late Bronze Age was enough to confirm Bass's theories and completely alter modern scholars' thoughts about the extent of trade and contacts that took place more than three thousand years ago. Three Bronze Age ships have now been found, but the wreck at Uluburun is the largest, wealthiest, and most completely excavated.

Fig. 8. Reconstruction of the Uluburun ship (Rosalie Seidler/National Geographic Stock; courtesy of the National Geographic Society).

The owner and sponsors of the ship are still unknown. One can speculate about different possibilities to explain the origins of the vessel and the location of its final resting place. It may have been a commercial venture, sent by Near Eastern or Egyptian merchants, perhaps with the blessing of an Egyptian pharaoh or Canaanite king. Or it may have been sent directly by a pharaoh or king, as a greeting-gift from one sovereign to another, as was frequently done during the Amarna Age a few decades earlier. Perhaps the ship was sent by the Mycenaeans on a "shopping expedition" to the Eastern Mediterranean and sank on the return voyage. The merchants on board might have acquired the raw materials and other goods not available in Greece itself, such as the tin and copper, as well as the ton of terebinth resin (from pistachio trees) that could be used in the perfume manufactured at Pylos on mainland Greece and then shipped back to Egypt and the Eastern Mediterranean. There is obviously no shortage of possible scenarios. If the Mycenaeans were the intended recipients, then they might have been waiting impatiently for the cargo on the ship, for it contained enough raw metal to outfit an army of three hundred men with bronze swords, shields, helmets, and armor, in addition to precious ivory and other exotic items. Clearly, when the boat sank that day in approximately 1300 BC, someone or some kingdom lost a fortune.

••꒜ ꒜••

The Uluburun ship sank in fairly deep water—its stern is currently 140 feet below the surface, with the rest of the ship at an angle sloping even farther down, to 170 feet below the surface. Diving to the depth of 140–70 feet is dangerous, for it is beyond the limit of safe scuba diving. The INA divers were allowed only two dives per day, twenty minutes each time. In addition, at those depths, increased levels of inhaled gases can cause a narcotic effect. Working that deep, Bass said, felt as though they had had two martinis before starting—so every dive and every movement to be made underwater had to be planned out in advance.

Over the course of nearly a dozen seasons, from 1984 to 1994, the team dove on the wreck more than twenty-two thousand times without a single major injury, testament to their precautions and the fact that their dives were overseen by an ex–Navy SEAL.[3] The end result was a plan of the ancient wreck and its cargo that is as accurate, down to the millimeter, as any made at a land excavation, despite the great depths at which they were working. The dives also resulted in the retrieval of thousands of objects, which are still being studied.

The boat itself was originally about fifty feet long. It was well constructed, with planks and keel made from Lebanese cedar and using a mortise-and-tenon design for the hull.[4] Previously, the earliest-known wreck in the Mediterranean to use this mortise-and-tenon technique was the Kyrenia wreck found off the coast of Cyprus, dating more than a thousand years later, to about 300 BC.

The copper ingots, of which there were more than 350, were especially difficult to excavate and bring to the surface. During the three thousand years that they had lain underwater, stacked herringbone fashion in four separate rows, many of them had significantly disintegrated and were now in an extremely fragile state. Eventually, a new type of glue had to be used by the archaeological conservators working on Bass's team: an adhesive that could be injected into the remains of an ingot, and which would congeal and harden underwater over the course of a year. The glue would eventually bond together the disparate parts of a decomposed ingot well enough so that it could be hauled to the surface.

But there was far more on board the ship than just the copper ingots. It turned out that the cargo carried in the Uluburun ship consisted of an incredible assortment of goods, truly an international manifest. In all, products from at least seven different countries, states, and empires were on board the ship. In addition to its primary cargo of ten tons of Cypriot copper, one ton of tin, and a ton of terebinth resin, there were also two dozen ebony logs from Nubia; almost two hundred ingots of raw glass from Mesopotamia, most colored dark blue, but others of light blue, purple, and even a shade of honey/amber; about 140 Canaanite storage jars in two or three basic sizes, which contained the terebinth resin, remains of grapes, pomegranates, and figs, as well as spices like coriander and sumac; brand-new pottery from Cyprus and Canaan, including oil lamps, bowls, jugs, and jars; scarabs from Egypt and cylinder seals from elsewhere in the Near East; swords and daggers from Italy and Greece (some of which might have belonged to crew members or passengers), including one with an inlaid hilt of ebony and ivory; and even a stone scepter-mace from the Balkans. There was also gold jewelry, including pendants, and a gold chalice; duck-shaped ivory cosmetic containers; copper, bronze, and tin bowls and other vessels; twenty-four stone anchors; fourteen pieces of hippopotamus ivory and one elephant tusk; and a six-inch-tall statue of a Canaanite deity made of bronze overlaid with gold in places—which, if it was supposed to serve as the protective deity for the ship, didn't do its job very well.[5]

The tin probably came from the Badakhshan region of Afghanistan, one of the few places where it was available during the second millennium BC. The lapis lazuli on board came from the same area, traveling thousands of miles overland before being brought onto the ship. Many of the pieces, such as the lapis lazuli cylinder seals, were tiny and easy to miss during the excavations, especially when the huge vacuum tubes were used to remove the sand that covered the remains. The fact that they were recovered at all is a testament to the skill of the underwater archaeologists excavating the wreck, led first by Bass and then by his chosen successor, Cemal Pulak.

One of the smallest objects found on board the ship was also one of the most important—an Egyptian scarab made of solid gold. Rare as such an object might be, it was made even more unusual by the hieroglyphs inscribed upon it, for they spelled out the name of Nefertiti, wife of the heretic pharaoh Akhenaten. Her name is written on the scarab as "Nefer-neferu-aten"; it is a spelling that Nefertiti used only during the first five years of her reign, at a time when her husband may have been at the height of his heretical condemnation of every Egyptian deity except Aten, the disk of the sun, whom he—and he alone—was allowed to worship directly.[6] The archaeologists used the scarab to help date the ship, for it could not have been made—and therefore the ship could not have sailed—before Nefertiti came to power about 1350 BC.

The archaeologists were able to date the sinking of the ship in three other ways as well. One method involved radiocarbon dating the short-lived twigs and branches that once were used on the deck of the ship. Another involved dendrochronology (counting of tree rings), making use of the wooden beams that made up the hull. The third was the well-used Mycenaean and Minoan pottery that was found on board, which appeared to the specialists to date toward the end of the fourteenth century BC. The four independent dating mechanisms together point to approximately 1300 BC—the very beginning of the thirteenth century BC, give or take a few years in either direction—as the year when the ship went down.[7]

Fragments from a small wooden tablet, originally with ivory hinges, were found on the ship, preserved within a storage jar into which it might have floated while the ship was sinking. Reminiscent of Homer's "tablet with baneful signs" (*Il.* 6.178), it is older by more than five hundred years than similar writing boards that had been found at Nimrud in Iraq. The tablet might once have contained a record of the ship's itinerary, or perhaps the cargo manifest. However, the wax on which the writing was inscribed within the two sides of the tablet vanished long ago, leaving no sign of what had been recorded.[8] It is therefore still impossible to tell whether the cargo on board was meant as a royal gift, perhaps from the king of Egypt to the king at Mycenae, or whether it belonged to a private merchant, selling goods at the principal ports around the Mediterranean. As hypothesized previously, it also could be purchases made on a long-distance shopping trip, for the raw materials on board matched what was needed by the workmen and craft shops of Mycenaean palaces such as Pylos in order to make high-demand concoctions, including perfumes and oils, as well as jewelry such as glass necklaces.

We may never know who sent the Uluburun ship on its voyage or where it was going and why, but it is clear that the ship contained a microcosm of the international trade and contacts that were ongoing in the Eastern Mediterranean, and across the Aegean, during the early thirteenth century BC. Not only were there goods from at least seven different areas, but—judging from the personal possessions the archaeologists found in the shipwreck—there were also at least two Mycenaeans on board, even though this seems to have been a Canaanite ship. Clearly this ship does not belong to a world of isolated civilizations, kingdoms, and fiefdoms, but rather to an interconnected world of trade, migration, diplomacy, and, alas, war. This really was the first truly global age.

Sinaranu of Ugarit

About forty years after the Uluburun ship went down, a text was composed that recorded some of the contents of a similar ship, sent by a merchant named Sinaranu from Ugarit in northern Syria to the island of Crete. It was actually an official proclamation written on a clay tablet in Akkadian, using the cuneiform writing system, which stated that when the ship belonging to Sinaranu returned from Crete, he would not have to pay taxes to the king. The relevant part of the Sinaranu Text, as it is known, reads as follows: "From the present day Ammistamru, son of Niqmepa, King of Ugarit, exempts Sinaranu, son of Siginu . . . His [grain], his beer, his (olive)-oil to the palace he shall not deliver. His ship is exempt when it arrives from Crete."[9]

We know, from other sources, that Sinaranu was a wealthy Ugaritic merchant (the specific term for such a merchant in Akkadian was *tamkār*), who lived and seems to have flourished during the time when Ammistamru II was king of Ugarit. Sinaranu had apparently sent his ship from Ugarit to Crete, and back again, in about 1260 BC, according to our most recent understanding for the dates when Ammistamru II was king (ca. 1260–1235 BC). We do not know the actual content of the cargo brought back from Crete, apart from the seeming likelihood that grain, beer, and olive oil were included. At the very least, this is confirmation that there were direct mercantile connections between northern Syria and Crete during the mid-thirteenth century BC. We also have the name of someone directly involved in international economic and mercantile transactions more than thirty-two hundred years ago. It seems quite likely that the Uluburun ship and the one owned by Sinaranu were not all that different, either in construction or in the cargo being carried.

We also know that Sinaranu was not alone in sending and receiving ships and cargoes during this time period, nor was he the only merchant to be granted exemption from the palace on his taxes. Ammistamru II issued a similar proclamation for other entrepreneurs whose ships sailed to Egypt, Anatolia, and elsewhere: "From this day forth, Ammistamru, son of Niqmepa, King of Ugarit, . . . [text broken] . . . Bin-yasuba and Bin-? . . . and his sons forever, from trips to Egypt and trips to Hatti and in Z-land (?), to the palace and to the palace overseer they need not make any report."[10]

THE BATTLE OF QADESH AND ITS AFTERMATH

At the time that Sinaranu and other merchants were active, Ugarit was under the control of, and a vassal kingdom to, the Hittites in Anatolia. It had been so ever since the time of Suppiluliuma I in the mid-fourteenth century BC, when a treaty was signed detailing Ugarit's obligations as a Hittite vassal.[11] Hittite control had extended as far south as the area of Qadesh, farther to the south in Syria, but went no farther. The Egyptians prevented Hittite efforts at further expansion. A major battle between the Hittites and the Egyptians was fought at the site of Qadesh in the year 1274 BC, some fifteen or twenty years before Sinaranu sent his ship to Crete. This battle resonates as one of the great battles of antiquity and as one of the first instances from the ancient world in which misinformation designed to confuse the enemy was deliberately employed.

The Battle of Qadesh was fought between Muwattalli II of Hatti, who was attempting to expand the Hittite Empire farther south into Canaan, and Ramses II of Egypt, who was determined to keep the border at Qadesh, where it had been located for several decades by that point. Despite not having the Hittites' side of the story, we know virtually every detail of the battle and its outcome, for the Egyptian version is recorded in two different ways at five different temples in Egypt: the Ramesseum (Ramses II's mortuary temple near the Valley of the Kings) and the temples at Karnak, Luxor, Abydos, and Abu Simbel. The shorter version, found in association with a relief depicting the battle, is known as the

"Report" or "Bulletin." The longer version is called the "Poem" or "Literary Record."[12]

We know that the battle was particularly vicious, and that both sides could have won it at one point or another. We also know that it ended in a stalemate, and that the dispute between the two powers was eventually resolved by the signing of a peace treaty.[13]

The most dramatic part of the engagement came after the Hittites sent out two men—Shoshu Bedouin, as we are told in the Egyptian account—to spy on the Egyptian forces, but deliberately in such a way that the men were almost immediately captured by the Egyptians. Under torture, presumably, the spies yielded their contrived disinformation (perhaps one of the first documented instances in human history) and told the Egyptians that the Hittite forces were not yet in the vicinity of Qadesh but were still farther to the north, in the area of Amurru in northern Syria. Upon hearing the news, and without attempting to independently confirm it, Ramses II rode at full speed with the first of his four divisions, the Amun division, aiming to reach Qadesh ahead of the Hittites.[14]

In fact, the Hittites were already at Qadesh, and had gathered their troops together into a tight clump just to the north and east of the city, hiding in the shadow of the city walls where they could not be seen by the Egyptian forces approaching from the south. As the leading regiment of Egyptian troops set up camp just north of the city, Ramses's men caught two more Hittite spies and this time learned the truth, but it was too late. The Hittite forces sped clockwise around almost the entire circumference of the city walls and charged straight into the second Egyptian division, the one known as Re, completely surprising and essentially annihilating them. The remnants of the shattered Re division fled to the north, chased by the entire Hittite army, and joined Ramses and the men in the Amun division at their camp before making a stand.[15]

The battle went back and forth between the two sides. We are told that at one point the Egyptian army was near defeat and Ramses himself was almost killed, but that he had single-handedly saved himself and his men. The account inscribed upon the Egyptian temple walls states:

> Then His Majesty started forth at a gallop, and entered into the host of the fallen ones of Hatti, being alone by himself and none other with him . . .

And he found 2,500 chariots hemming him in on his outer side, consisting of all the fallen ones of Hatti with the many foreign countries which were with them.

It then switches to the first person, related by the pharaoh himself:

I called to you, My Father Amun, when I was in the midst of multitudes I knew not. . . . I found Amun come when I called him; he gave me his hand and I rejoiced . . . All that I did came to pass. . . . I shot on my right and captured with my left . . . I found the 2,500 chariots, in whose midst I was, sprawling before my horse. Not one of them found his hand to fight . . . I caused them to plunge into the water even as crocodiles plunge, fallen upon their faces one upon the other. I killed among them according as I willed.[16]

Although the account of his single-handed prowess is surely exaggerated, for the pharaoh undoubtedly had some help, the numbers involved may not be far from the truth, for elsewhere in the inscription the size of the Hittite forces is given as 3,500 chariots, 37,000 infantry, and a total of 47,500 troops in all.[17] Despite the potential exaggeration, it is clear from the accompanying images and the outcome of the battle that Ramses II and the first two Egyptian divisions were able to hold on until the final two Egyptian divisions caught up and routed the Hittite forces.[18]

In the end, the battle's outcome was a stalemate, and the border between the two powers remained at Qadesh, not to be moved or challenged again. Fifteen years later, in November/December 1259 BC, at about the same time that Sinaranu was sending his ship to Crete from Ugarit, a peace treaty—one of the best preserved and best known from the ancient world—was signed by Ramses II and the current Hittite king Hattusili III, for Muwattalli II had died just two years after the battle. Known as the "Silver Treaty," this agreement survives in several copies, since two versions were created, one by the Hittites and one by the Egyptians. The Hittite version, originally written in Akkadian and inscribed on a tablet of solid silver, was sent to Egypt, where it was translated into Egyptian and copied onto the walls of the Ramesseum and the temple of Amun at Karnak. Similarly, the Egyptian version was translated into Akkadian and inscribed on a tablet of solid silver, then sent to Hattusa, where archaeologists discovered it just a few decades ago.[19] The Hittite version inscribed on the walls of the temples in Egypt begins:

There came the (three royal envoys of Egypt . . .) together with the first and second royal envoys of Hatti, Tili-Teshub, and Ramose, and the envoy of Carchemish, Yapusili, bearing the silver tablet which the Great King of Hatti, Hattusili, had caused to be brought to Pharaoh, by the hand of his envoy Tili-Teshub and his envoy Ramose, to request peace from the Majesty of the King of Southern and Northern Egypt, Usimare Setepenre, son of Re, Ramses II.[20]

Thirteen years later, and possibly after Hattusili had personally visited Egypt, Ramses II married a daughter of Hattusili in a royal wedding ceremony, thereby cementing the treaty and their relationship:[21]

Then he (Hattusili) caused his eldest daughter to be brought, with magnificent tribute (going) before her, of gold, silver, and copper in abundance, slaves, spans of horses without limit, cattle, goats, and sheep by ten-thousands—limitless were the products which they brought to the King of Southern and Northern Egypt, Usimare Setepenre, Son of Re, Ramses II, given life. Then one came to inform His Majesty, saying: 'See, the Great Ruler of Hatti has sent his eldest daughter, with tribute of every kind . . . the Princess of Hatti, together with all the grandees of the Land of Hatti.'[22]

It was probably just as well that the Hittites and Egyptians declared peace and ceased to fight each other, for they likely needed to turn their attention to two other events that may have taken place at about 1250 BC. Although both events are legendary, and although it has yet to be proven that either actually took place, both still resonate in the modern world today: in Anatolia, the Hittites may have had to contend with the Trojan War, while the Egyptians may have had to deal with the Hebrew Exodus. Before we discuss each of these, however, we must set the scene.

The Trojan War

About the same time as the run-up to the Battle of Qadesh, the Hittites were also busy on a second front, in western Anatolia, where they were trying to contain rebellious subjects whose activities were apparently being underwritten by the Mycenaeans.[23] This may be one of the earliest examples that we have of one government deliberately engaging in activities designed to undermine another (think Iranian support for Hezbollah in Lebanon, thirty-two hundred years after the Battle of Qadesh).

It is during the reign of the Hittite king Muwattalli II, in the early- to mid-thirteenth century BC, that we first learn from texts kept in the state archives at the capital city of Hattusa of a renegade Hittite subject named Piyamaradu who was attempting to destabilize the situation in the region of Miletus in western Anatolia. He had already successfully defeated a vassal king of the Hittites in the same region, a man named Manapa-Tarhunta. It is thought that Piyamaradu was probably acting on behalf of, or in collusion with, the Ahhiyawans (i.e., the Bronze Age Mycenaeans).[24]

Piyamaradu's rebellious activities continued during the reign of the next Hittite king, Hattusili III, in the mid-thirteenth century BC, as we know from correspondence called by scholars the "Tawagalawa Letter." The Hittite king sent the letter to an unnamed king of Ahhiyawa, whom he addresses as "Great King" and "brother," implying a level of equality between the two of them. We have already seen that similar terms were employed when the Egyptian pharaohs Amenhotep III and Akhenaten were writing to the kings of Babylonia, Mitanni, and Assyria a century or so earlier. The interpretation of these texts has provided important insights into the status of the Aegean world and Near Eastern affairs at this time.[25]

The Tawagalawa Letter is concerned with the activities of Piyamaradu, who continued to raid Hittite territory in western Anatolia, and who, we are now told, had just been granted asylum and traveled by ship to Ahhiyawan territory—probably an island off the western coast of Anatolia.[26] We are also introduced, on what was once the third page/tablet of the letter (the first two are missing), to Tawagalawa himself, who is identified as the brother of the Ahhiyawan king, and who was present in western Anatolia at that moment, recruiting individuals hostile to the Hittites. Intriguingly, in an indication that relations between the Hittites and the Mycenaeans had previously been better than they were at this point, we are told that Tawagalawa had earlier ridden ("mounted the chariot") with the personal charioteer of the Hittite king himself.[27]

The letter also refers to a dispute between the Mycenaeans and the Hittites over an area known as Wilusa, located in northwestern Anatolia.

This region came up in our discussion of the Assuwan Rebellion that took place nearly two hundred years earlier, and it seems that the Hittites and the Mycenaeans were once again at odds over the territory, which is identified by most scholars with Troy and/or the Troad region. Given the date of the letter, in the mid-thirteenth century BC, it is certainly reasonable to wonder whether there is a link to the later Greek legends regarding the Trojan War.[28]

··✤ ✤··

The tale of the Trojan War, as traditionally related by the blind Greek poet Homer in the eighth century BC, and supplemented by both the so-called Epic Cycle (fragments of additional epic poems now lost) and later Greek playwrights, is well known. Paris, the son of King Priam of Troy, sailed from northwestern Anatolia to mainland Greece on a diplomatic mission to Menelaus, the king of Sparta. While there, he fell in love with Menelaus's beautiful wife, Helen. When Paris returned home, Helen accompanied him—either voluntarily, according to the Trojans, or taken by force, according to the Greeks. Enraged, Menelaus persuaded his brother Agamemnon, king of Mycenae and the leader of the Greeks, to send an armada of a thousand ships and fifty thousand men against Troy to get Helen back. In the end, after a ten-year-long war, the Greeks were victorious. Troy was sacked, most of its inhabitants were killed, and Helen returned home to Sparta with Menelaus.

There are, of course, a number of unanswered questions. Was there really a Trojan War? Did Troy even exist? How much truth is there behind Homer's story? Did Helen really have an astonishingly beautiful face that could have "launched a thousand ships"? Was the Trojan War really fought because of one man's love for a woman . . . or was that merely the excuse for a war fought for other reasons—perhaps for land or power or glory? The ancient Greeks themselves were not entirely certain when the Trojan War had taken place—there are at least thirteen different guesses as to the date made by the ancient Greek writers.[29]

By the time that Heinrich Schliemann went looking for the site of Troy in the mid-nineteenth century AD, most modern scholars believed that the Trojan War was only a legend, and that the site of Troy had never existed. Schliemann set out to prove them wrong. To everyone's surprise, he succeeded. The story has been told many times and therefore will not be repeated in detail here.[30] Suffice it to say that he found nine cities, one on top of another, at the site of Hisarlik (Turkish *Hisarlık*), which is now accepted by most scholars as the location of ancient Troy, but was unable to determine which of the nine cities had been Priam's Troy. Since Schliemann's initial excavations, there have been several additional expeditions to Troy, among them those by his architect, Wilhelm Dörpfeld; by Carl Blegen and the University of Cincinnati in the 1930s; and finally by Manfred Korfmann and now Ernst Pernicka and Tübingen University from the late 1980s until today.

The destruction of the sixth city—Troy VI—is still a matter of debate. Initially dated to ca. 1250 BC, it was probably actually destroyed a bit earlier, about 1300 BC.[31] This was a wealthy city, with imported objects from Mesopotamia, Egypt, and Cyprus, as well as from Mycenaean Greece. It was also what one might call a "contested periphery"—that is, it was located both on the periphery of the Mycenaean world and on the periphery of the Hittite Empire—and was thus caught between two of the great powers of the ancient Mediterranean Bronze Age world.

Dörpfeld believed that the Mycenaeans had captured this city (Troy VI) and burned it to the ground, and that it was this event that formed the basis of Homer's epic tales. Blegen, digging several decades later, disagreed, and published what he said was indisputable evidence for destruction not by humans, but by an earthquake. His argument included positive evidence, such as walls knocked out of line and collapsed towers, as well as negative evidence, for he found no arrows, no swords, no remnants of warfare.[32] In fact, it is now clear that the type of damage that Blegen found was similar to that seen at many sites in the Aegean and Eastern Mediterranean, including Mycenae and Tiryns on mainland Greece. It is also clear that these earthquakes did not all take place at the exact same time during the Late Bronze Age, as will be seen below.

Blegen also thought that the following city, Troy VIIa, was a more likely candidate for Priam's Troy. This city was probably destroyed ca. 1180 BC, and may have been overwhelmed by the Sea Peoples rather than by the Mycenaeans, although this is by no means certain. We shall leave the story here for the moment and pick it up again in the next chapter, when we discuss the events of the twelfth century BC.

Foreign Contacts and the Greek Mainland
in the Thirteenth Century BC

We should note that it is at this time, back at Mycenae on the Greek mainland, that huge fortification walls, which are still visible, were erected in about 1250 BC. These were constructed about the same time as other projects—perhaps defensive measures—were undertaken, including an underground tunnel leading to a water source that inhabitants could access without leaving the protection of the city.

The famous Lion Gate was constructed at the entrance to the citadel of Mycenae in this period, as part of new fortification walls that encircled the city. Were these simply part of the protective measures for the city, or were they built as a demonstration of power and wealth? The fortification walls and the Lion Gate were constructed with huge stones—stones so large that they are now referred to as "Cyclopean masonry," since the later Greeks thought that only the legendary single-eyed Cyclopes, with their brute strength, could have been strong enough to maneuver the blocks into position.

Intriguingly, similar architecture, including corbel-vaulted galleries and secret tunnels to underground water systems, is found not only at several Mycenaean palatial sites, including Mycenae and Tiryns, but also in some Hittite structures, also dating to about the same period.[33] It is a matter of scholarly debate as to which way the influences flowed, but the architectural similarities suggest that the two areas were in contact and influenced each other.

We know, from finds of Mycenaean pottery in the Eastern Mediterranean dating to the thirteenth century BC and Egyptian, Cypriot, Canaanite and other imports found in the Aegean during the same period, that the Mycenaeans were actively trading with Egypt, Cyprus, and other powers in the ancient Near East during these years. They had taken over the trade routes from the Minoans by this time, and trade actually increased during this period, as mentioned above.

In fact, archaeologists excavating at the site of Tiryns, located in the Peloponnese region of mainland Greece, have recently documented evidence indicating that there may have been a specific group of Cypriots living at Tiryns during the late thirteenth century BC, which agrees well with suggestions made previously by other scholars that there was some sort of special commercial relationship between Tiryns and the island of Cyprus during this period. In particular, there seems to have been some sort of metalworking, and perhaps work in ceramics or faience as well, being conducted by Cypriots at Tiryns. It was at this time that Mycenaean clay transport containers, generally used for shipping wine, olive oil, and other commodities, were marked with Cypro-Minoan signs before they were fired. Even though the language of Cypro-Minoan has yet to be fully translated, it seems clear that these vessels were being manufactured for a specific market in Cyprus.[34]

Surprisingly, the Linear B tablets found at Pylos and various other Mycenaean mainland sites do not specifically mention trade or contact with the outside world. The closest that they come is including what seem to be loanwords from the Near East, where the foreign name apparently came with the item. These include the words for sesame, gold, ivory, and cumin—for instance, "sesame" in Linear B is *sa-sa-ma*, coming from the Ugaritic word *ššmn*, the Akkadian word *šammaššammu*, and the Hurrian word *sumisumi*.[35] On these tablets are also terms like *ku-pi-ri-jo*, which has been interpreted as meaning "Cypriot." This appears at least sixteen times in the tablets at Knossos, where it is used to describe spices, but it is used to directly modify wool, oil, honey, vases, and unguent ingredients as well. It is also used at Pylos as an ethnic adjective to describe individuals associated with sheepherding, bronze working, and mixed commodities including wool, cloth, and alum, which might mean that there were ethnic Cypriots living at Pylos at the end of the thirteenth century BC.[36] Similarly, a second term, *a-ra-si-jo*, may also be a reference to Cyprus, as it was known in the Eastern Mediterranean, that is, Alashiya: Akkadian *a-la-ši-ia*, Egyptian ʿ*irs*ʒ, Hittite *a-la-ši-ia*, and Ugaritic *altyy*.[37]

There is also a series of ethnic names interpreted as West Anatolian, primarily female workers, found in the Linear B texts at Pylos. All refer to areas located on the western coast of Anatolia, including Miletus, Halikarnassus, Knidus, and Lydia (Asia). More than one scholar has suggested that there may also be Trojan women mentioned on these Pylos tablets. It has been hypothesized that all of these women may have been captured during Mycenaean raids on the western coast of Anatolia or the neighboring Dodecanese islands.[38]

There are also a few debated words in the Linear B texts at both Pylos and Knossos, which some have suggested may be Canaanite gentilics (personal names). These include *Pe-ri-ta* = "the man from Beirut"; *Tu-ri-jo* = "the Tyrian (man from Tyre)"; and *po-ni-ki-jo* = "Phoenician (man or spice). In addition, *A-ra-da-jo* = "the man from Arad (Arvad)" is also found only in the tablets at Knossos.[39] There are names that seem Egyptian in origin but may have come via Canaan, namely, *mi-sa-ra-jo* = "Egyptian" and a_3*-ku-pi-ti-jo* = "Memphite" or "Egyptian." The former term, *mi-sa-ra-jo*, apparently comes from the Semitic word for Egypt, *Misraim*, more commonly found in Akkadian and Ugaritic documents in Mesopotamia and Canaan. The latter term, a_3*-ku-pi-ti-jo*, may also be derived from a Near Eastern reference to Egypt, for an Ugaritic name for both Egypt and the city of Memphis was Ḥikupta. Strangely enough, the word is found in a Linear B tablet at Knossos as the name of an individual who was in charge of a flock of eighty sheep at a Cretan site; could he have been known as "the Egyptian"?[40]

All of these loanwords and names in the Linear B tablets show unambiguously that the Aegean world was in contact with Egypt and the Near East during the Late Bronze Age. The fact that we do not have any records documenting specific data and exchanges may or may not be surprising, since we possess only the last year of the archives in each case: the tablets that were caught in the destructions and fired accidentally, for normally they would have been erased (by rubbing water on the surface of the clay) and reused each year or as needed. Moreover, we know that the Mycenaeans used these tablets only to record some of the economic activities of the palaces. It is conceivable that the "Foreign Office Archive" was housed elsewhere at the various Mycenaean sites, like similar archives at Amarna in Egypt and Hattusa in Anatolia.

THE EXODUS AND THE ISRAELITE CONQUEST

For the Trojan War, and the city of Troy, about 1250 BC, we have a plethora of data, even if it is still inconclusive. However, for the other event that is said to have taken place at about this same time, we have much less evidence, and what we have is even more inconclusive. This relates to the Exodus of the Hebrews from Egypt, the tale of which is told in the Hebrew Bible.

According to the biblical account, during the reign of an unnamed Egyptian pharaoh, Moses led the Israelites out of slavery in Egypt. They had been enslaved, so we are told, after having lived as free people in Egypt for several centuries. The book of Exodus says that they had been in Egypt for four hundred years following their initial arrival during the lifetime of Jacob, one of the biblical patriarchs, probably in about the seventeenth century BC. If so, they would have arrived in Egypt during the time of the Hyksos and then remained in Egypt during the heyday of the Late Bronze Age, including the Amarna period. In 1987, the French Egyptologist Alain Zivie discovered the tomb of a man named Aper-El, which is a Semitic name, who served as the vizier (the highest appointed official) to Pharaohs Amenhotep III and Akhenaten during the fourteenth century BC.[41]

In any event, as the biblical account goes, the Hebrews led by Moses left Egypt hastily after ten plagues visited on the Egyptians by the Hebrew God convinced the Egyptian pharaoh that it was not worth keeping this minority population in bondage. The Israelites reportedly then embarked upon a forty-year journey that eventually led to the land of Canaan and freedom. During their wanderings, they are said to have followed a pillar of smoke by day and a pillar of fire by night, eating manna from heaven upon occasion. While en route to Canaan, they received the Ten Commandments at Mount Sinai and built the Ark of the Covenant in which to carry them.

This story of the Exodus has become one of the most famous and enduring tales from the Hebrew Bible, still celebrated today in the Jewish holiday of Passover. Yet it is also one of the most difficult to substantiate by either ancient texts or archaeological evidence.[42]

Clues in the biblical stories suggest that *if* the Exodus did take place, it did so during the mid-thirteenth century BC, for we are told that the Hebrews at the time were busy building the "supply cities" named Pithom and Rameses for the pharaoh (Exod. 1:11–14). Archaeological excavations at the sites of these ancient cities indicate that they were begun by Seti I, ca. 1290 BC, who may have been "the Pharaoh who knew not Joseph," and were completed by Ramses II (ca. 1250 BC), who may be the pharaoh of the Exodus.

Ramses II is well known to modern tourists of Egypt and to aficionados of nineteenth-century literature, for it is his fallen statue at the Ramesseum—his mortuary temple in Egypt near the Valley of the Kings—that prompted Percy Bysshe Shelley to write the famous poem "Ozymandias":

I met a traveller from an antique land
Who said: "Two vast and trunkless legs of stone
Stand in the desert. Near them on the sand,
Half sunk, a shattered visage lies, whose frown
And wrinkled lip and sneer of cold command
Tell that its sculptor well those passions read
Which yet survive, stamped on these lifeless things,
The hand that mocked them and the heart that fed.
And on the pedestal these words appear:
'My name is Ozymandias, King of Kings:
Look on my works, ye mighty, and despair!'
Nothing beside remains. Round the decay
Of that colossal wreck, boundless and bare,
The lone and level sands stretch far away.

The poem was published in 1818, just five years before Jean-François Champollion's successful decipherment of Egyptian hieroglyphics. Shelley had to depend upon the ancient Greek historian Diodorus Siculus's incorrect translation of Ramses II's throne name as *Ozymandias*, rather than the correct *User-maat-re Setep-en-re*.[43]

Unfortunately, identifying Ramses II as the pharaoh of the Exodus—which is the identification most frequently found in both scholarly and popular books—does not work if one also wishes to follow the chronology presented by the Bible. The biblical account places the Exodus at approximately 1450 BC, based upon the statement in 1 Kings (6:1) that the event took place some 480 years before Solomon built the Temple in Jerusalem (which is dated to about 970 BC). However, this date of 1450 BC falls near the end of the reign of the pharaoh Thutmose III, at a time when Egypt was an extremely powerful force in the Near East. As we have seen, Thutmose III was in firm control of the land of Canaan, having fought a major battle at the site of Megiddo in 1479 BC. It is extremely unlikely that he would have allowed the Israelites to flee from Egypt to that region, or that his successors would have allowed them to wander around for forty years before settling down, particularly since

Egypt retained firm control of the region even after the reign of Thutmose III. Moreover, there is no evidence for Hebrews/Israelites in the land of Canaan during either the fifteenth or the fourteenth century BC, which there should be if the Exodus had taken place ca. 1450 BC.

Thus, most secular archaeologists favor an alternative date of 1250 BC for the Exodus, which ignores the biblical chronology but makes more sense from an archaeological and historical point of view. It makes more sense because the date falls during the reign of Ramses II, the pharaoh who completed the biblical cities of Pithom and Rameses. It also corresponds to the approximate date for the destructions of a number of cities in Canaan by an unknown hand and allows as much as forty years for the Israelites to wander around in the desert before entering and conquering Canaan, as the biblical account describes, and yet still have them arrive in time to be mentioned by Pharaoh Merneptah in his "Israel Stele"—an inscription that dates to 1207 BC and is the earliest mention outside the Bible of an entity known as Israel.[44]

This inscription, which I have mentioned in passing above, dates to the fifth year of Pharaoh Merneptah's reign. Sir William Matthew Flinders Petrie discovered it in February 1896 within Merneptah's mortuary temple, located near the Valley of the Kings across the Nile River from the modern town of Luxor. On the stele, Merneptah's inscription claims that he conquered a people known as "Israel," located in the region of Canaan. It reads specifically:

> The kings are prostrate, saying: "Mercy!"
> Not one raises his head among the Nine Bows.
> Desolation is for Tehenu; Hatti is pacified;
> Plundered is the Canaan with every evil;
> Carried off is Ashkelon; seized upon is Gezer;
> Yanoam is made as that which does not exist;
> Israel is laid waste, his seed is not;
> Hurru is become a widow for Egypt!
> All lands together, they are pacified;
> Everyone who was restless, he has been bound.[45]

Although numerous sites have been excavated that could potentially be related to the Exodus, including the ongoing and recent digs at Hazor in Israel and Tell el-Borg in the North Sinai,[46] there is currently virtually nothing that sheds a specific light on the historicity of the Exodus—all is inference so far.

On the other hand, what might one expect to find as artifacts of Israelites camped in the desert for forty years more than three thousand years ago? If they were wandering, as opposed to living in permanent structures, they would probably have used tents with postholes, just as the Bedouin of today do. Consequently, an archaeologist searching for visible remnants of the Exodus is probably not going to find the remains of permanent structures, and any tent peg holes would long since have been obliterated.

Similarly, numerous efforts to identify the biblical ten plagues that tormented the Egyptians, including frogs, locusts, boils, flies, hail, and the killing of the Egyptian firstborn children, have been either unsuccessful or unconvincing, although this has certainly not been for lack of trying.[47] There is also no evidence to substantiate the biblical account of the parting of the Red (Reed) Sea. Overall, despite innumerable attempts (many of which have been featured on cable television channels) to propose hypotheses that will account for the phenomena described in the Bible, including efforts to link them to the eruption of the Santorini volcano in the Aegean, definite proof—whether archaeological, geological, or other—has remained elusive.

One could ask what evidence an archaeologist might hope to find for the parting of the sea: the waterlogged remains of the pharaoh's drowned charioteers, along with their horses, chariots, and weapons? Thus far, nothing has come to light, despite occasional claims to the contrary.[48] We cannot entertain even the claim that the parting of the sea was caused by a tsunami (tidal wave) created by the Santorini eruption in the Aegean, since the date of the eruption has now been pushed back to at least 1550 and more likely 1628 BC, based on radiocarbon and ice core dates, while the Exodus is more likely to date to 1250 BC, or 1450 BC at the earliest.[49] Thus, at least a century (from 1550 BC to 1450 BC) and probably more like four centuries (from 1628 BC to 1250 BC) separate the two, which means that efforts to explain the parting of the Red Sea and the biblical plagues as phenomena related to the eruption are just plain wrong.

The book of Joshua in the Hebrew Bible describes in detail the conquest of Canaanite cities by the invading Israelites. Based on this account, one might have expected to find evidence of wholesale destruction at the Canaanite sites that have been excavated, such as Megiddo, Hazor, Bethel, Ai, and so on. We need to keep in mind, though, the somewhat conflicting account in the book of Judges, which gives a slightly different (lengthier and less bloody) picture of the conquest, in which the Israelites and the Canaanites lived together in the various cities. The problem, as has been stressed elsewhere,[50] is that there is very little archaeological evidence to corroborate the Bible's tales of destruction at the Canaanite cities at this time. The sites of Megiddo and Lachish are now thought to have both been destroyed more than a century later, ca. 1130 BC, as we shall see below, and other sites—such as Jericho—show no evidence of destruction anytime in the thirteenth or even the twelfth century BC.

Only Hazor still remains as a possibility, for the Late Bronze Age palace (or temple) on the acropolis was clearly burned and at least part of the city was destroyed, as evidenced by fallen wooden roof beams and jars full of scorched wheat. These edifices—built during the heyday of Hazor in the fourteenth century BC, when it was mentioned in the Egyptian Amarna Letters—suffered tremendously during the destruction, as did the city gate, which was destroyed "in a 'fierce and devastating conflagration,' represented by heaps of fallen mudbricks and ashes reaching a height of 1.5 m[eters]."[51] The most recent excavations on the upper tel of the city uncovered more of the same: "thick layers of ashes, burnt wooden beams, cracked basalt slabs, vitrified mudbricks, fallen walls, and mutilated basalt statues."[52] In particular, the remains of public and religious structures from Stratum 1A in the ceremonial precinct and elsewhere at Hazor were "totally covered and sealed by the thick destruction debris."[53]

The date of this destruction is still debated, however, with the original excavator, Yigael Yadin, and Amnon Ben-Tor, one of the current coexcavators of the site, both favoring ca. 1230 BC. However, it is possible that the destruction took place later, even into the early twelfth century BC. We will have to wait for the results of the radiocarbon testing of the storage jars full of wheat found at the site during the summer of 2012 for a definitive scientific answer.

The identification of the perpetrators is also uncertain. The recent excavators have made a good case for arguing that it was neither the Egyptians nor the Canaanites, for statues belonging to both cultures were defaced during the destruction, which soldiers of those armies would not have done. The Sea Peoples have also been excluded as culprits, on the basis of a lack of identifying pottery and distance from the sea, although these seem less cogent arguments. Ben-Tor generally agrees with the previous excavator Yigael Yadin that the Israelites are the most likely, and logical, agents of destruction, while the other codirector, Sharon Zuckerman, sees a period of decline immediately preceding the destruction and suggests that the devastation was perhaps caused by an internal rebellion of the city-dwellers themselves, after which the city lay abandoned until sometime during the eleventh century BC.[54]

In summary, although it is clear that Hazor was destroyed in the thirteenth or twelfth century BC, and was abandoned for a century or more after that, it is not clear exactly when or by whom it was destroyed. Similarly, the question of whether the Hebrew Exodus from Egypt was an actual event or merely part of myth and legend—which is of interest to many people around the world—also remains unanswered at the moment. Rehashing the available evidence will not yield a final answer. It may be that the question will be resolved by a future discovery either from painstaking archaeological research or by a fortuitous find. It may even be that one of the alternative explanations of the Exodus story is correct. These alternatives include the possibility that the Israelites took advantage of the havoc caused by the Sea Peoples in Canaan to move in and take control of the region; that the Israelites were actually part of the larger group of Canaanites already living in the land; or that the Israelites had migrated peacefully into the region over the course of centuries. If one of these alternatives is the correct explanation of how the Hebrews ended up in the land of Canaan, then the Exodus story was probably made up centuries later, as several scholars have suggested. In the meantime, it will be best to remain aware of the potential for fraud, for many disreputable claims have already been made about events, people, places, and things connected with the Exodus. Undoubtedly more misinformation, whether intentional or not, will be forthcoming in the future.[55]

At the moment, all that we can say for certain is that the archaeological evidence, in the form of pottery, architecture, and other aspects of material culture, indicates that the Israelites as an identifiable group were present in Canaan certainly by the end of the thirteenth century BC, and that it is their culture, along with that of the Philistines and the Phoenicians, that rises up out of the ashes of the destruction of the Canaanite civilization sometime during the twelfth century BC. This, in part, is why the question of the Exodus is relevant here, for the Israelites are among the groups of peoples who will make up a new world order, emerging out of the chaos that was the end of the Late Bronze Age.

HITTITES, ASSYRIANS, AMURRU, AND AHHIYAWA

The last kings of the Hittites—especially Tudhaliya IV (1237–1209 BC) and Suppiluliuma II (1207–? BC)—were very active during the last quarter of the thirteenth century, from ca. 1237 BC, even as their world and civilization were showing signs of coming to an end. Tudhaliya ordered that an entire pantheon of gods and goddesses be carved into the rock of a limestone outcrop at Yazilikaya ("Inscribed Rock"), along with a representation of himself, just a kilometer or so from the Hittite capital city of Hattusa.

At this time, the Hittites were at war with the Assyrians in Mesopotamia. We have already met the Assyrians in an earlier chapter, in a discussion of Assur-uballit I, who ruled over Assyria at the time of the Amarna pharaohs, and who had sacked Babylon after a marriage alliance between the two powers went awry.[56] The Assyrians, after a brief period of relative dormancy following the reign of Assur-uballit, had become resurgent under their king, Adad-nirari I (1307–1275 BC). Under his leadership and that of his successors, the Assyrians emerged as a major power in the Near East at the beginning of the thirteenth century.

Among his other accomplishments, Adad-nirari I fought against the Mitannians, capturing Washukanni and other cities. He placed a client king on their throne and extended the Assyrian Empire sufficiently far to the west that it now bordered the Hittite homeland and almost reached to the Mediterranean Sea. This may not have been as difficult as it sounds, however, since the Hittites under Suppiluliuma I had already inflicted a crushing defeat upon the Mitannians several decades earlier.[57]

Following the reign of Shalmaneser I (1275–1245 BC), who continued many of the policies of Adad-nirari and may finally have brought the Mitannian kingdom to an end,[58] one of the greatest of Assyria's "warrior kings," Tukulti-Ninurta I, who ruled ca. 1244–1208 BC, stepped onto the world stage. He followed in the footsteps of Adad-nirari but was perhaps also emulating his predecessor of the previous century, Assur-uballit, when he decided to attack Babylon. However, Tukulti-Ninurta I surpassed Assur-uballit's achievements: not only did he defeat the Kassite Babylonian king Kashtiliashu IV in battle and bring him to Assur in chains; he also took over their kingdom by ca. 1225 BC, ruling as king himself before installing a puppet king to govern on his behalf. But this was not a particularly successful move, since the puppet king, Enlil-nadin-shumi, was almost immediately attacked and overthrown by an Elamite army marching from their eastern homelands on the Iranian plateau, in what is now southwestern Iran. It would not be the only time that this happened, for we shall encounter the Elamites again soon.[59]

In addition to his other achievements, Tukulti-Ninurta I, the Assyrian warrior king, also defeated the Hittites under Tudhaliya IV, thus dramatically changing the balance of power in the ancient Near East. It has even been suggested that he became so powerful that he sent a mina (a Near Eastern unit of weight, probably the equivalent of a little more than a modern American pound) of lapis lazuli as a gift to the Mycenaean king in Boeotian Thebes on mainland Greece, all the way across the Aegean.[60]

Consequently, by the time of the first Sea Peoples attack on the Eastern Mediterranean in 1207 BC, just one year after Tukulti-Ninurta was assassinated by one of his own sons, Assyria had been one of the major players on the international scene in the ancient Near East for nearly two hundred years. It was a kingdom linked by marriage, politics, war, and trade over the centuries with the Egyptians, Babylonians, Hittites, and Mitanni. It was, without question, one of the Great Powers during the Late Bronze Age.

During the reign of the Assyrian king Tukulti-Ninurta, the Hittites were faced with an obvious and serious threat to their empire and were intent on stopping anyone attempting to move inland from the coast to Assyrian lands in the east. One strategy involved a treaty signed in approximately 1225 BC between Tudhaliya IV, king of the Hittites, and Shaushgamuwa, his brother-in-law by marriage. Shaushgamuwa was the king of Amurru, who controlled the coastal regions of northern Syria that provided potential access to the Assyrian lands. In the treaty, the homage with which we are now familiar is invoked: the enemy of my friend is also my enemy; the friend of my friend is also my friend. Thus, Tudhaliya IV (who refers to himself in the third person as "My Majesty") declared to Shaushgamuwa:

> If the King of Egypt is the friend of My Majesty, he shall be your friend. But if he is the enemy of My Majesty, he shall be your enemy. And if the King of Babylonia is the friend of My Majesty, he shall be your friend. But if he is the enemy of My Majesty, he shall be your enemy. Since the King of Assyria is the enemy of My Majesty, he shall likewise be your enemy. Your merchant shall not go to Assyria, and you shall not allow his merchant into your land. He shall not pass through your land. But if he should come into your land, seize him and send him off to My Majesty. [Let] this matter [be placed] under [oath] (for you).[61]

In our study of the ancient world, there are two items of special interest in this mutual-appreciation treaty. The first is that Tudhaliya IV says to Shaushgamuwa: "[You shall not allow(?)] any ship [of] Ahhiyawa to go to him (that is, the King of Assyria)."[62] This is thought by many scholars to be a reference to an embargo: the one mentioned at the end of the previous chapter. If so, although the embargo is usually thought to be a fairly modern concept, it seems that one may have been put in place by the Hittites against the Assyrians more than three thousand years ago.[63]

The second is the fact that, a few lines earlier, Tudhaliya IV had written, "And the Kings who are my equals in rank are the King of Egypt, the King of Babylonia, the King of Assyria, ~~and the King of Ahhiyawa~~."[64] The strikethrough of the words "King of Ahhiyawa" is not a misprint in this book; it is a strikethrough found on the clay tablet of Tudhaliya IV. In other words, we have here a rough draft of the treaty, in which items could still be deleted, added, or edited. More importantly, we are in possession of an item that indicates that the king of Ahhiyawa was no longer considered to be equal in rank to the other major powers of the Late Bronze Age world: the kings of Egypt, Babylonia, and Assyria, and of the Hittites.

It is reasonable to ask what had happened in the Aegean, or on the western coast of Anatolia, to cause this state of affairs. It must have been a fairly recent occurrence, for recall that in the reign of Hattusili III, Tudhaliya IV's father, the king of Ahhiyawa had been referred to as a

"Great King" and as a "brother" by the Hittite ruler. Perhaps a clue can be found in one of the Ahhiyawa texts, known as the "Milawata Letter." Dating most likely to the time of Tudhaliya IV, the letter makes it clear that the city of Milawata (Miletus) and its surrounding territory on the western coast of Anatolia, which had once been the main footprint of the Mycenaeans in the area, no longer belonged to the Ahhiyawan king but was now under Hittite control.[65] This may have meant that the king of Ahhiyawa was no longer a Great King in the eyes of the Hittite king. However, we should consider the possibility that the Hittite king's "demotion" of the Mycenaean ruler may have been the result of some event of even greater magnitude, perhaps something that had happened back in the Aegean—that is, on the Greek mainland—as we shall see in the next chapter.

The Hittite Invasion of Cyprus

In the meantime, while all of this was going on, Tudhaliya IV decided to attack the island of Cyprus. The island had been a major source of copper throughout the second millennium BC, and it is possible that the Hittites decided to try to control this precious metal, so essential to the creation of bronze. However, we are not certain about his motivation for attacking Cyprus. It may instead have had something to do with the possible appearance of the Sea Peoples in the area or with the drought that is thought to have occurred in the Eastern Mediterranean at this time, as indicated by new scientific discoveries as well as long-known texts that mention an emergency shipment of grain sent from Ugarit in north Syria to the port city of Ura in Cilicia (located in southeastern Turkey).[66]

An inscription, originally written on a statue of Tudhaliya but then recopied onto a tablet from the time of Tudhaliya's son Suppiluliuma II, reads: "I seized the king of Alashiya with his wives, his children, . . . All the goods, including silver and gold, and all the captured people I removed and brought home to Hattusa. I enslaved the country of Alashiya, and made it tributary on the spot."[67] Suppiluliuma II not only recopied Tudhaliya IV's inscription but also conquered Cyprus himself for good measure. The inscription regarding his own military takeover of Cyprus reads: "I, Suppiluliuma, Great King, quickly [embarked upon] the sea.

The ships of Alashiya met me in battle at sea three times. I eliminated them. I captured the ships and set them afire at sea. When I reached dry land once more, then the enemy from the land of Alashiya came against me [for battle] in droves. I [fought against] them."[68]

Clearly, Suppiluliuma was successful in his naval attacks and perhaps in the invasion of Cyprus, but it is unclear why he had to fight and invade the island again, after Tudhaliya IV had already captured it. His attempt might simply have been to gain (or regain) control of the sources of copper or of the international trade routes in increasingly tumultuous times. But we may never know. It is also unclear where the final land battle was fought; scholars have suggested both Cyprus and the coast of Anatolia as possibilities.

Upon assuming the throne following the death of his father, Suppiluliuma II had taken the name of his famous fourteenth-century BC predecessor Suppiluliuma I (though the new king's name was actually spelled slightly differently: Suppiluliama rather than Suppiluliuma). Perhaps he hoped to emulate some of his predecessor's successes. Instead, he ended up presiding over the collapse of the Hittite Empire. In the course of doing so, he and the Hittite army, in addition to invading Cyprus, campaigned in western Anatolia once more.[69] One scholar notes, in a recent article, that many of the documents dated to the time of Suppiluliuma II "point to a growing instability within the Hittite capital and a growing sense of mistrust," though perhaps "unease" would be a better word to use, given what was soon to come.[70]

The Point Iria and Cape Gelidonya Shipwrecks

Another wreck of an ancient sailing vessel, this time presumed to have been from Cyprus, based on the pottery that it carried as cargo, was excavated in 1993 and 1994 by maritime archaeologists off the Argolid coast of mainland Greece, not far from the site of Mycenae. Known as the Point Iria shipwreck, it is dated to approximately 1200 BC and may be evidence that trade between Cyprus and Mycenaean Greece was still ongoing at that time, despite Hittite incursions in Cyprus.[71]

At approximately this same time, yet another ship sank off the coast of Anatolia, not far from where the Uluburun ship had gone down about a century earlier: the Cape Gelidonya shipwreck, named after the location of its watery grave off the southwestern coast of what is now modern Turkey. As noted earlier, this is the shipwreck with which George Bass began his career, and the field of underwater archaeology, in the 1960s. Bass had concluded that the wreck was of a Canaanite ship en route to the Aegean that had sunk in approximately 1200 BC.[72]

Bass has gone back to the site a few times over the years, in order to explore the remains using new equipment that has become available as the result of dramatic improvements in the technology of underwater exploration during the past half century. He has found a few more objects that continue to support his original idea that the ship was probably traveling from the Near East, but, intriguingly, the new finds indicate that it is actually probably Cypriot in origin rather than Canaanite, according to new analyses done of the ship's anchor and some of the ceramics on board.[73]

Regardless of its exact origin in the Eastern Mediterranean, the Cape Gelidonya ship and its cargo are of considerable importance, though admittedly they are not nearly as impressive as the Uluburun shipwreck. The smaller vessel has usually been described as having "tramped" from port to port, exchanging items on a minor scale, rather than sailing on a direct commercial or diplomatic mission.[74] Still, it is one more piece of evidence that international trade was ongoing at the end of the thirteenth century BC, even when things were beginning to fall apart in the Eastern Mediterranean and the Aegean regions.

CHAPTER FOUR

ACT IV
· · · ·

THE END OF AN ERA:
THE TWELFTH CENTURY BC

This is the moment for which we have been waiting: the climax of the play and the dramatic beginning of the end to three hundred and more years of the globalized economy that had been the hallmark of the Late Bronze Age in the Aegean and Eastern Mediterranean. The twelfth century BC, as we will see in this final act, is marked more by tales of woe and destruction than by stories of trade and international relations, although we can begin on the high note of the latter.

THE DISCOVERY OF UGARIT AND MINET EL-BEIDA

Chance is said to favor the prepared spirit, but in some cases even the unprepared spirit is so favored. For it was an accidental discovery by a peasant, presumably untutored in the ways of archaeology, that led to the discovery of the city and kingdom of Ugarit, located on the coast of north Syria. In 1929, the reported finding of a tomb at Minet el-Beida Bay brought French archaeologists to the area. Excavations quickly revealed the ruins of a port city, now referred to as Minet el-Beida. Eight hundred meters farther inland, within a modern mound called Ras Shamra, the capital city of Ugarit was brought to light soon afterward.[1]

Both Ugarit and Minet el-Beida have been under almost continuous French excavation ever since, first by Claude Schaeffer from 1929 onward and, most recently, from 1978 to 1998, by Marguerite Yon. Since 1999, a joint Franco-Syrian team has conducted the excavations.[2] These, all together, have revealed the remnants of a functioning, busy, and prosperous commercial city and port, which were suddenly destroyed and abandoned soon after the beginning of the twelfth century BC. Within the ruins, products from all over the Eastern Mediterranean and Aegean have been found; a warehouse in Minet el-Beida, for example, still held eighty Canaanite storage jars. Unfortunately, these were found in the 1930s, so rigorous scientific analyses of the contents were not conducted.[3]

Within the private houses and the royal palace at Ugarit, a number of important archives have been recovered since the 1950s, documenting the economic activities of several merchants, as well as of Ugarit's royal family. The letters and other items in these archives were written on clay tablets, as was usual in the Bronze Age, but in this case tablets were found inscribed with different languages: sometimes Akkadian, sometimes Hittite, sometimes Egyptian, and sometimes other less widely used languages, such as Hurrian.

Additionally, there was one other language that scholars had never previously seen. It was deciphered fairly rapidly and is now called Ugaritic. It used one of the earliest alphabetic scripts yet known—except that there were actually two alphabetic scripts in the texts, one with twenty-two signs like the Phoenician alphabet and the other with an additional eight signs.[4]

These Ugaritic texts, of which there is now such a large corpus that they have spawned a cottage industry of modern scholarship known as Ugaritic studies, include not only the archives and correspondence of the merchants and the king, but also examples of literature, mythology, history, religion, and other elements belonging to a thriving civilization aware of its own legacy. The result is that we can reconstruct the city of Ugarit from its ruins and can reconstitute as well, from its texts, the daily life and belief systems of its inhabitants. For example, it is clear that they worshipped a pantheon of deities, among whom El and Baal figured prominently. And we know the names of their kings, from Ammistamru I and Niqmaddu II, whose letters to Amenhotep III and Akhenaten are in the Amarna archive in Egypt, to the very last king, Ammurapi, who ruled in the first decade of the twelfth century BC. We also know that the kings of Ugarit married princesses from the neighboring polity of Amurru, and probably also from the larger kingdom of the Hittites, in dynastic marriages complete with dowries that were quite literally fit for a king, though at least one of these marriages ended in a bitter divorce that dragged on in the courts for years.[5]

ECONOMIC AND COMMERCIAL CONNECTIONS OF UGARIT AND ITS MERCHANTS

The citizens and kings of Ugarit carried on lively trade relations throughout the lifetime of the city. It was clearly an international entrepôt, with ships of many nations arriving in the harbor of Minet el-Beida. It may have owed allegiance to Egypt during the first half of the fourteenth century BC, but was definitely a vassal of the Hittites from the second half of that century onward, after Suppiluliuma conquered the area, ca. 1350–1340 BC. Texts at the site, found in the various archives, most of which date to the last half century of the city's existence, document connections between Ugarit and numerous other polities both large and small, including Egypt, Cyprus, Assyria, the Hittites, Carchemish, Tyre, Beirut, Amurru, and Mari. Most recently, the Aegean has been added to this list as well.[6]

The tablets also specifically mention the exportation from Ugarit of perishable goods, including dyed wool, linen garments, oil, lead, copper, and bronze objects, especially to the Assyrians, located far to the east in Mesopotamia, as well as extensive trade connections with Beirut, Tyre, and Sidon on the Phoenician coast.[7] Objects imported from the Aegean, Egypt, Cyprus, and Mesopotamia have been found at Ugarit itself, including Mycenaean vessels, a bronze sword inscribed with the name of the Egyptian pharaoh Merneptah, hundreds of fragments of alabaster jars, and other luxury items.[8] These, and other more mundane goods, such as wine, olive oil, and wheat, reached Ugarit through the efforts of merchants like Sinaranu, whom we met earlier in these pages, whose ship went to Crete and back during the mid-fourteenth century BC. We know that the Ugaritians were sufficiently well-off financially to send the Hittites tribute each year, consisting of five hundred shekels of gold, dyed wool, and garments, in addition to gold and silver cups for the Hittite king, queen, and high officials.[9]

We now know of other Ugaritic merchants who were active later—at the time of the destruction of Ugarit at the beginning of the twelfth century—thanks to additional tablets, many of which have been found in recent decades within their houses, and some of which have changed our understanding of the city's probable end.[10] One such house is known as the "House of Yabninu," located near the southern part of the royal palace. The house itself has still not been completely excavated, but is already known to have covered at least one thousand square meters, so Yabninu must have been a reasonably successful merchant. The sixty or more tablets that were discovered within the ruins of this house are thought to have originally been kept on the second floor, and include documents written in Akkadian, Ugaritic, and the as-yet-undeciphered language known as Cypro-Minoan, chiefly used on the island of Cyprus but also found inscribed on vessels at Tiryns on the Greek mainland. The texts written on the tablets, as well as the imported objects found within the house, document that Yabninu's mercantile activities included connections with Cyprus, the Levantine coast farther to the south, Egypt, and the Aegean.[11]

Another set of tablets was found within the so-called House of Rapanu, which was excavated in 1956 and 1958. The tablets, more than two hundred of them, were quickly studied and then published a decade later, in 1968. They indicate that Rapanu was a scribe and high-ranking adviser to the king of Ugarit, most likely Ammistamru II (ca. 1260–1235 BC). Rapanu was apparently involved in some sensitive negotiations at the highest levels, as the contents of the archive indicate. The texts include a number of letters exchanged between the king of Ugarit and the king of Cyprus (Alashiya), written at the time that the Sea Peoples threatened both. There are also letters exchanged with the king of nearby Carchemish and with the more-distant Egyptian pharaoh; the latter set are concerned with some sort of incident involving Canaanites on the Levantine coast.[12]

One of the letters deals with trade in oil between Ugarit and Cyprus. It is from Niqmaddu III, the penultimate king of Ugarit, and was sent to the king of Alashiya, whom he calls his "father," referring to himself as "your son."[13] Unless the Ugaritic king had married a Cypriot princess, which is not out of the question, it seems that the use of the word "father" follows the general terminology of the time in attempting to establish a familial relationship, while at the same time acknowledging either the superiority or the relative age of the king of Cyprus over the king of

Ugarit. Another of the letters in this house has already been mentioned: the one describing the coming of enemy ships to Ugarit, which Schaeffer thought had been found in a kiln, being baked before its dispatch to the king of Cyprus. We will discuss this text further below.

Some of the most recently discovered tablets are those in the so-called House of Urtenu. This residence was initially uncovered by accident in the southern part of the site during the construction of a modern military bunker in 1973. The archaeologists were allowed to dig through the spoil heap created by the digging of the bunker, which incidentally destroyed the center of the house, and found a number of tablets, all of which have now been published. The newer tablets have come from the careful excavations of 1986–1992, which have also been published, and of 1994–2002, which are currently being studied. Overall, there are more than 500 tablets in this archive—134 were found in 1994 alone—with some texts written in Ugaritic but the majority in Akkadian. The correspondence includes letters from the kings of Egypt, Cyprus, Hatti, Assyria, Carchemish, Sidon, Beirut, and possibly Tyre.[14] One of the oldest was apparently sent by a king of Assyria, probably Tukulti-Ninurta I, to a king of Ugarit, perhaps Ammistamru II or Ibirana, and concerns the battle in which Tukulti-Ninurta and the Assyrians defeated Tudhaliya IV and the Hittites.[15]

As one of the excavators has pointed out, the tablets indicate that Urtenu was active at the beginning of the twelfth century BC, and that he had a high social status. He was apparently an agent in a large commercial firm run by the queen's son-in-law, which had commercial dealings with the city of Emar in inland Syria, as well as with nearby Carchemish. He was also involved in negotiations and trade deals with the island of Cyprus, among other long-distance trade ventures.[16] In fact, the five letters found in the house that were sent from Cyprus are extremely important, for they include—for the first time ever—the name of a king of Bronze Age Cyprus: a man known as Kushmeshusha. There are two letters from this king, as well as two letters from senior governors of the island and, intriguingly, a letter from an Ugaritic scribe who was actually living in Cyprus at the time. These five letters now join the other four from Alashiya that had previously been found in Rapanu's house.[17]

There are two additional letters in the house that contain references to two "Hiyawa-men," who were reportedly waiting in the Lukka lands

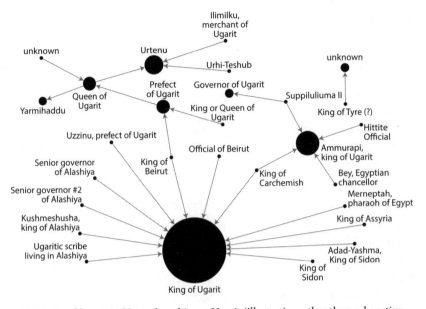

Fig. 9. Royal letters in Urtenu's archive at Ugarit (illustrative rather than exhaustive; nodes = individuals sending or receiving letter(s); edges/lines = pairs between whom letter(s) sent; size of circles = number of letters; created by D. H. Cline).

(later known as Lycia), in southwestern Anatolia, for a ship to arrive from Ugarit. The letters were sent to Ammurapi, the last king of Ugarit, by a Hittite king, probably to be identified as Suppiluliuma II, and one of his top officials. These are the first known references to Aegean people in the Ugarit archives, for "Hiyawa" is undoubtedly related to the Hittite word "Ahhiyawa," which, as we have seen, is taken by most scholars to mean the Mycenaeans and the Bronze Age Aegean.[18]

There is also a letter from Pharaoh Merneptah of Egypt, responding to a request from the king of Ugarit—either Niqmaddu III or Ammurapi—for a sculptor to be sent, so that a statue of the pharaoh could be created and set up in the city, specifically in front of a temple to Baal. At the same time as the pharaoh denies this request in the letter, he gives a long list of luxury goods that were being sent from Egypt to Ugarit. The goods were being loaded onto a ship destined for Ugarit, he said, and included more than a hundred textiles and pieces of clothing, plus assorted other goods such as ebony wood and plaques of red, white, and blue stones.[19] Again, we should note that almost all of these goods are perishable and will not have survived in the archaeological record. It is a good thing that they are mentioned in this text, therefore; otherwise we might never have known that they once existed and were exchanged between Egypt and Ugarit.

Another letter in this archive is from a messenger/representative named Zu-Aštarti, discussing the ship on which he had sailed from Ugarit. He states that he was detained en route. Some scholars have wondered whether he had perhaps even been kidnapped, but he writes only: "On the sixth day I was at sea. As a wind took me, I reached the territory of Sidon. From Sidon to the territory of Ušnatu it bore me, and in Ušnatu I am held up. May my brother know this. . . . Say to the king: 'If they have received the horses which the king gave to the messenger of the land of Alashiya, then a colleague of the messenger will come to you. May they give those horses into his hand.'"[20] It is not completely clear why he was "held up" in Ušnatu or even why the letter is in Urtenu's archives, though it is possible that horse trading was a state-protected industry in Ugarit at that time. A contemporary letter from the Hittite king Tudhaliya IV to Ammistamru II, found in Rapanu's house, states that the Ugarit king must not allow horses to be exported to Egypt by Hittite or Egyptian messengers/merchants.[21]

Destructions in North Syria

The textual evidence from the various archives and houses at Ugarit indicate that international trade and contact was going strong in the city right up until the last possible moment. In fact, one of the scholars publishing the letters from the House of Urtenu noted almost twenty years ago that there was very little indication of trouble, apart from the mention of enemy ships in one letter, and that the trade routes seemed to be open right up until the end.[22] The same was true in Emar, on the Euphrates River far to the east in inland Syria, where it has been noted that "the scribes were conducting normal business until the end."[23]

However, Ugarit was destroyed, apparently quite violently, during the reign of King Ammurapi, most likely between 1190 and 1185 BC. It was not reoccupied until the Persian period, approximately 650 years later.[24] The excavators report "evidence of destruction and fire throughout the city," including "collapsed walls, burnt pisé plaster, and heaps of ashes," with a destruction level that reached two meters high in places. Marguerite Yon, the most recent director of the excavations, says that the ceilings and terraces in the residential quarters were found collapsed, and that elsewhere the walls were "reduced to a shapeless heap of rubble." She believes that the destruction was caused by enemy attack rather than an earthquake, as had previously been suggested by Schaeffer, and that there was violent fighting in the city, including street fighting. This, she says, is indicated by "the presence of numerous arrowheads dispersed throughout the destroyed or abandoned ruins," as well as the fact that the inhabitants—eight thousand, more or less—fled in haste and did not return, not even to collect the hoards of valuables that some had buried before leaving.[25]

The exact date when all of this transpired has been the focus of recent debate. The most conclusive evidence is a letter found in 1986 within the House of Urtenu. The letter was sent to Ammurapi, the king of Ugarit, by an Egyptian chancellor named Bey who, we know from Egyptian sources, was executed in the fifth year of Pharaoh Siptah. Siptah was the penultimate pharaoh of the Nineteenth Dynasty in Egypt, who ruled ca. 1195–1189 BC, that is, just a few years before Ramses III of the Twentieth Dynasty. The letter can therefore be dated with some certainty, specifically before Bey was executed in 1191 BC, which means that the destruction of the city cannot have taken place before this date. Thus, the destruction of the city is usually dated to 1190–1185 BC, though technically it could have been even later.[26] A recent article has pointed out that this date can now be corroborated, on the basis of an astronomical observation found on another tablet at Ugarit. This records an eclipse of the sun that can be dated to January 21, 1192 BC, which also means that the city cannot have been destroyed before this date.[27]

Contrary to previous popular accounts concerning the end of Ugarit,[28] we probably cannot use the famous letter from the Southern Archive, found in Court V of the palace at Ugarit, either to date the destruction or to identify the destroyers. This was the letter that Schaeffer thought had been found in a kiln, before its dispatch to the king of Cyprus. It begins: "My father, now the ships of the enemy have come. They have been setting fire to my cities and have done harm to the land." According to the original report, it was found in a kiln, along with more than seventy

Fig. 10. Sites destroyed ca. 1200 BC.

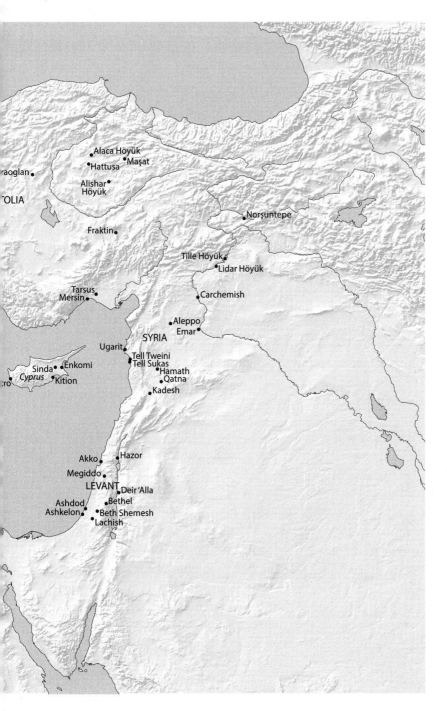

other tablets, where it had been placed for baking. The excavators and other scholars initially hypothesized that the enemy ships had returned and sacked the city before the urgent request for assistance could be dispatched, and this is the story that has been repeated over and over in scholarly and popular accounts from the past several decades. However, a recent reexamination of the find-spot by additional researchers now indicates that it was not found in a kiln after all, but rather was probably stored within a basket that had fallen from the second floor after the building was abandoned.[29]

As a result, although the letter can be used to discuss the presence of enemy ships and probably invaders, it is not clear whether it dates to the final days of Ugarit or to some slightly earlier period. And even if it is a reference to ships of the Sea Peoples, it is possible that it dates to the first wave of invaders, those who attacked Egypt in 1207 BC, rather than to the second wave who fought against Ramses III in 1177 BC.

The site of Emar in inland Syria, with which Ugarit was in contact, was also destroyed at approximately the same time, in 1185 BC, as we know from the date given on a legal document found there. However, it is not clear who caused the destruction at Emar. Tablets found there refer to unnamed "hordes" but do not point specifically to the Sea Peoples, as various scholars have noted.[30]

The site of Ras Bassit, located on the northern border of Ugarit, was also destroyed at approximately this same time. The excavators believe it was an outpost of Ugarit and state that by approximately 1200 BC it was "partly evacuated, partly abandoned, then set on fire, just like the other sites of the region." They attribute this destruction to the Sea Peoples, but the attribution is not definitive.[31]

A similar situation has been described at Ras Ibn Hani, on the coast just to the south of Ugarit, which is thought to have been a secondary residence of the Ugaritic kings during the thirteenth century. The excavators and others envision this site as having been evacuated shortly before the destruction of Ugarit and then destroyed by the Sea Peoples. At least part of the site was immediately reoccupied, as was Ras Bassit, and it is on the basis of the pottery found in these reoccupation levels that the destroyers, and reoccupiers, of both sites are identified by the excavators as the Sea Peoples, a matter that we shall discuss further below.[32]

Perhaps the best, and certainly the most recent, evidence for widespread destruction at this time has been found at Tell Tweini, the site of the Late Bronze Age harbor town of Gibala within the kingdom of Ugarit, located about thirty kilometers south of the modern city of Lattakia. Here, the site was abandoned after a "severe destruction" at the end of the Late Bronze Age. According to the excavators, "The destruction layer contains remains of conflicts (bronze arrowheads scattered around the town, fallen walls, burnt houses), ash from the conflagration of houses, and chronologically well-constrained ceramic assemblages fragmented by the collapse of the town."[33]

By dating this destruction layer using "stratified radiocarbon-based archaeology" and "anchor points in ancient epigraphic-literary sources, Hittite-Levantine-Egyptian kings and astronomical observations," the excavators say that they have finally been able "to precisely date the Sea People invasion in [the] northern Levant," and to "offer the first firm chronology for this key period in human society."[34] The radiocarbon dates from the widespread ash layer (Level 7A) came back from the lab as dating specifically to ca. 1192–1190 BC.[35] However, while they may well have dated the destruction of this Late Bronze Age site, the excavators have offered only circumstantial evidence that the destruction was wreaked by the Sea Peoples, as we will discuss below.

It is also relevant to point out that this date (1192–1190 BC) is fully thirteen to fifteen years before Ramses III meets the Sea Peoples in battle in 1177 BC. Even the destructions elsewhere that are dated to 1185 BC are still eight years before the culminating conflict. Perhaps we should be wondering just how long it would have taken such a proposed migratory group to make its way across the Mediterranean, or even just down the coast of the Levant to Egypt. This, though, would obviously depend upon their organizational ability, means of transportation, and ultimate goals, among other factors, and cannot readily be answered.

Finally, we should also consider a site farther to the south, Tell Kazel, which was located in the region of Amurru, and which may have been the site of ancient Ṣumur, the capital city of that kingdom. The site was destroyed at the end of the Late Bronze Age and the excavators have plausibly hypothesized that the Sea Peoples destroyed it, especially insofar as Ramses III specifically mentions it (that is, Amurru) in his

Sea Peoples inscriptions. Yet, in the occupation level just prior to the destruction, the excavators have identified what appears to be locally produced Mycenaean pottery and other indications of new inhabitants from the Aegean and Western Mediterranean.[36] Thus, Reinhard Jung of the University of Vienna, who has studied this pottery, has hypothesized that "prior to the large Sea Peoples' destruction, smaller groups of people arrived by ship at Tell Kazel and settled together within the local population." He sees this as a pattern of small-scale immigration from the Aegean, but with indications that some of the people involved had earlier roots in southern continental Italy.[37] If correct, this is an indication of the complexity of the period and of the people potentially involved, even to the point that destructions caused by the second wave of Sea Peoples, ca. 1177 BC, may have impacted earlier immigrants from the same origins who had already arrived and settled in the Eastern Mediterranean, perhaps during or after the original Sea Peoples incursions in the fifth year of Merneptah, back in 1207 BC.

Destructions in Southern Syria/Canaan

During this same period, in the twelfth century BC, a number of cities and towns were destroyed in southern Syria and Canaan. Just as in north Syria, it is not clear who destroyed them or when exactly they were destroyed, although in the destruction level at the small site of Deir 'Alla in Jordan, a vase with the cartouche of the Egyptian queen Twosret was found. She was the widow of Pharaoh Seti II and is known to have ruled from 1187 to 1185 BC. Thus, the destruction can probably be dated to shortly after this time. The same holds true for the site of Akko, in what is now modern Israel, where a similar scarab of Twosret was found in the destruction debris.[38] Other evidence of destruction can be seen at Beth Shan, where Yigael Yadin's excavations uncovered a violent end to the Egyptian presence at the site.[39]

Perhaps the best known among the sites in this area with evidence of destruction are Megiddo and Lachish. However, the nature and timing of the collapse in this region are still much debated. Both cities seem to have been destroyed several decades later than would otherwise be expected from the timing at the sites previously discussed, for both

Megiddo and Lachish appear to have been destroyed around 1130 BC rather than 1177 BC.[40]

Megiddo

At Megiddo in the Jezreel Valley of modern-day Israel, the site of biblical Armageddon, some twenty cities have been found layered one on top of another. Of these, the seventh city, with two phases labeled VIIB and VIIA, was violently destroyed either in the thirteenth and the twelfth centuries BC, respectively, or perhaps in a single destruction in the twelfth century.

Traditionally, ever since the University of Chicago excavators published the findings from their excavations at the site during the years 1925–39, it has been accepted that Stratum VIIB ended sometime between 1250 and 1200 BC, while the succeeding city of Stratum VIIA ended sometime around 1130 BC. In these strata were found the remains of a Canaanite palace, or perhaps the remains of two palaces, one built upon the ruins of the other.

According to the Chicago excavators, the Stratum VIIB palace "suffered violent destruction so extensive that the Stratum VIIA builders deemed it more expedient to level off the resulting debris and build over it than to remove it all as was the procedure in previous rebuilding undertakings." The rooms "were filled with fallen stone to a height of about a meter and a half . . . charred horizontal lines found here and there on the walls of the rooms to the north of the court . . . supply a general floor level throughout the palace."[41] The Stratum VIIA palace, built directly on top, was then thought to have lasted until about 1130 BC.

Recently, however, David Ussishkin, a Tel Aviv University archaeologist and the recently retired codirector of the Megiddo Expedition, has convincingly suggested that the Chicago excavators had misinterpreted the levels. Rather than two palaces, one atop the other, he believes we should understand this structure as a single two-story palace, renovated slightly during the transition from VIIB to VIIA, about 1200 BC. There was only a single destruction, he says—a great fire that destroyed the palace at the end of Stratum VIIA. According to Ussishkin, what the Chicago archaeologists thought was the "VIIB palace" was simply the basement or lower story of the palace, while the "VIIA palace" was the upper story. The main city temple (the so-called Tower Temple) was also destroyed at this time, but the most recent excavations at the site indicate that much of the rest of the city survived; it appears that only the elite areas were torched at this time.[42]

This Stratum VIIA destruction is usually dated to ca. 1130 BC, based upon two objects inscribed with Egyptian cartouches found associated with the debris. The first is an ivory pen case inscribed with the name of Ramses III, which was found among other ivory treasures within a room in the palace, in a context sealed by debris from the destruction of the palace.[43] This would imply that the destruction had taken place sometime during or after the time of Ramses III, about 1177 BC or thereafter.

The ivory pieces found in this room within the palace are among the best-known objects recovered from the site of Megiddo. They include fragmentary boxes and bowls, plaques, spoons, disks, game boards and game pieces, jar lids, and combs, among numerous other items. They are on display at the Oriental Institute at the University of Chicago and the Rockefeller Museum in Jerusalem. It is unclear why these ivory pieces were originally collected together, and why they were in this particular part of the palace. Nevertheless, they have received a great deal of attention over the years, for the ivories themselves and the scenes inscribed upon them exhibit a truly globalized style, now commonly called the International Style, which is also seen elsewhere at sites like Ugarit and Mycenae. The distinctive style combines elements found in Mycenaean, Canaanite, and Egyptian cultures, thereby creating hybrid objects unique to, and typifying, this cosmopolitan age.[44]

The second object of relevance from Megiddo is a bronze statue base inscribed with the name of Pharaoh Ramses VI, who ruled a few decades later, ca. 1141–1133 BC. This was not found in a secure archaeological context, but rather was found beneath a Stratum VIIB wall in the residential area at the site. As Ussishkin notes, this is not a reliable context, since Stratum VIIB was much earlier in time than Ramses VI. This means that the statue base must have been deliberately buried in a hole dug by a later inhabitant, either during the VIIA period or even during the following Iron Age VIB-A city. The base is usually attributed to Stratum VIIA by archaeologists, but this is merely a guess.[45]

These two objects, of Ramses III and VI, are always discussed together in relevant publications, and thus the destruction of Megiddo

Fig. 11. Ramses III ivory pen case from Megiddo (after Loud 1939, pl. 62;
courtesy of the Oriental Institute of the University of Chicago).

VIIA is dated after the reign of Ramses VI, or about 1130 BC. However, since the bronze statue base of Ramses VI is not found in a good context, it should not be used to date the ending of Megiddo VIIA. On the other hand, the ivory pen case of Ramses III was indeed sealed within the destruction layer of VIIA and therefore can confidently be used to provide a limiting date before which the city could not have been destroyed, that is, before the reign of this pharaoh. This would indeed fit well with evidence of destruction at several other sites throughout the Near East discussed in these pages.

However, archaeology is a continuously evolving field with new data and new analyses requiring the rethinking of old concepts. In this regard, ongoing studies involving radiocarbon dating of remains found within the destruction of VIIA now are indicating that a date of 1130 BC, or possibly even later, is likely to be correct after all. If this proves to be accurate, it would mean that Megiddo was destroyed more than forty years after the Sea People came through the region in 1177 BC.[46] In any event, as Ussishkin has noted, "Lack of written sources leaves [open] the questions of who was responsible for the destruction of Stratum VIIA . . . the city may have been successfully attacked by invading Sea People groups, by Levantine Canaanite elements, by the Israelites, or by a force combined from different groups."[47] In other words, at Megiddo, we have the same situation as seen at the relevant level at Hazor, described above, where the elite parts of the city were destroyed, but those responsible for the destruction cannot be identified.

Lachish

Lachish, another site in modern Israel, also suffered two destructions during this approximate time period, if David Ussishkin, who excavated at the site from 1973 to 1994, is correct.[48] Here, at this multilayered site located south of Jerusalem, the seventh and sixth cities (Strata VII and VI) are identified as the last Canaanite cities, based on the material remains found during the excavations. This was a period of great prosperity for Lachish, during the period of Egyptian control of the region. It was one of the largest cities in all of Canaan at that time, with some six thousand people living in its territory, and large temples and public buildings within the city itself.[49]

The Stratum VII city is thought to have been destroyed by fire in about 1200 BC, but the excavators have not speculated as to the nature of the destruction or who might have been responsible. In part, this is because it is unclear how much of the city was actually destroyed. At the moment, evidence for a fiery destruction has been found in only the remains of one temple (the so-called Fosse III Temple) and the domestic quarter in Area S.[50] It is conceivable that the destruction could have been caused by the first wave of Sea Peoples, who came through the region in approximately 1207 BC, but there is no proof for such an attribution.

The Stratum VI city has been the major focus of scholarly attention to date. It appears that the survivors of the Stratum VII conflagration simply rebuilt all or part of the city and continued the same material culture that had existed previously. The Stratum VI city is thought to have been an even richer and more prosperous city than the one that had just been destroyed, with a large public building (the Pillared Building) constructed in Area S where domestic structures had previously stood. A new temple was also built, in Area P, but little remains of it because of the destruction that it subsequently suffered. Imported objects from Egypt, Cyprus, and the Aegean, primarily pottery vessels, were found throughout the city in this level, attesting to its international connections.[51]

It is thought that there was an influx of poor refugees into the Stratum VI city just before large portions of it were violently destroyed.[52] One structure in particular, the Pillared Building in Area S, "was destroyed suddenly and violently; ash layers and fallen mudbricks covered the whole structure, and several skeletons of adults, children and babies were found trapped under the collapsed wall."[53] Other buildings at Lachish were also destroyed at this time, after which there ensued a period of abandonment lasting up to three hundred years.[54] According to Ussishkin: "The Level VI city was razed in a violent, fiery destruction, traces of which were detected at every point at which remains of Level VI were uncovered. . . . The destruction was complete, the population liquidated or driven out."[55]

Earlier archaeologists thought that the city had been destroyed in the late thirteenth century BC, ca. 1230 BC (with the Stratum VII city devastated even earlier),[56] but the date of the destruction of Stratum VI has now been changed significantly by Ussishkin, primarily based on the discovery of a bronze plaque, possibly part of a door bolt, with the cartouche of Ramses III. This plaque was part of a cache of broken or defective bronze objects lying buried and sealed beneath the destruction debris of the Stratum VI city.[57]

Just as with the Ramses III pen case at Megiddo, the find context of this object at Lachish indicates that the destruction of the city must have taken place during or after the time of Ramses III. Ussishkin therefore originally dated the destruction to ca. 1150 BC, based on the fact that the bronze plaque could not have been made before the accession of Ramses III to the throne in 1184 BC, and his belief that one must allow time for it "to have been used, then broken and finally discarded and set aside in this cache of defective or broken bronze objects."[58]

He subsequently revised the date to 1130 BC, based upon the discovery that a scarab of Ramses IV had been found at the site, probably in this level, by the previous British excavators, and upon comparison with Megiddo VII: he argued that if Megiddo had lasted that long, then so probably had Lachish.[59] Another scholar has recently noted that there is another possible scarab of Ramses IV in Tomb 570 at Lachish, but he has also emphasized that the reading of the name on both scarabs is not actually certain, and that the stratigraphy for the find-spot of the first one is not completely clear.[60]

Thus, once again, just as with the other sites at which we have looked, it is not at all clear who, or what, caused the destruction, or even when it happened at Lachish; all we can actually say with confidence is that it took place during or after the reign of Ramses III. As Ussishkin states, "The evidence points to the devastation of Level VI by a strong and resolute enemy, but the archaeological data provide no direct clue as to the nature and identity of that enemy or to the immediate circumstances surrounding the city's downfall."[61] He notes that three candidates have been proposed by previous scholars: the Egyptian army, the Israelite tribes, and the invading Sea Peoples, but he also notes that "no remains of a battle were uncovered, apart from a single bronze arrowhead . . . uncovered in the Pillared Building in Area S."[62]

It is unlikely that the Egyptians caused the destruction, for Lachish was prospering during this period of their overlordship and was actively trading with them, as shown by the several items with royal cartouches inscribed upon them that were found in the ruins. It is still possible that the destruction was caused by the Israelites under Joshua, as William F. Albright of Johns Hopkins University thought, although that was when the destruction was believed to date to ca. 1230 BC.[63]

However, Ussishkin identifies the Sea Peoples as the most likely agents of destruction for the city of Stratum VI. In this he is following Olga Tufnell, a previous excavator of Lachish.[64] Yet he presents no evidence that it was actually the Sea Peoples who were responsible; we simply see the end result of the destruction, with no indication as to who brought it about. Moreover, a date of 1130 BC would seem to be far too late for the Sea Peoples, by approximately four decades, just as with the destruction at Megiddo. We should note that Ussishkin may be incorrect in linking the destruction of Lachish to that of Megiddo and placing it that late; there is no good reason to link the two, and so it may be that his original date of ca. 1150 BC (or possibly even earlier, if the Ramses III bronze bolt was not in use for very long) should be embraced instead.

It is also possible that a massive earthquake caused the destruction of the Stratum VI city. The bodies of the four people killed in the Pillared Building were found "apparently trapped and crushed under falling debris while trying to escape it." A child of two–three years had "either been thrown down on its face or had died while crawling along the ground," while an infant "had been thrown or had fallen to the ground."[65] These observations, combined with the fact that no weapons were found in the debris, point to Mother Nature rather than humans as the responsible agent, as may also have been the case at other sites toward the end of the Late Bronze Age.[66] Arguing against this hypothesis is the fact that no other evidence for an earthquake, such as cracked or tilted walls, was found by the excavators. Moreover, the new Canaanite temple built in Area P seems to have been pillaged and looted before its destruction by fire, which would seem to indicate human involvement.[67]

In summary, as with Hazor and Megiddo, it is unclear who destroyed Lachish VI or the earlier city of Lachish VII. Both, or neither, could have been devastated by the Sea Peoples, or by someone—or something—else entirely. As James Weinstein of Cornell University has said, "while the Sea Peoples may have been culpable for the end of Egyptian garrisons in southern and western Palestine, we must allow for the possibility that non–Sea Peoples' groups were responsible for the ruin of sites in other areas of the country."[68]

The Philistine Pentapolis

Of particular interest are the sites in southern Canaan, including those identified in the Bible and elsewhere as belonging to the so-called Philistine pentapolis, the five major Philistine sites: Ashkelon, Ashdod, Ekron, Gath, and Gaza.

At the end of the Late Bronze Age, the earlier Canaanite cities at Ekron and Ashdod were violently destroyed and replaced with new settlements in which there was an almost complete change in material culture, including pottery, hearths, bathtubs, kitchenware, and architecture. This seems to indicate either a change in population or a significant influx of new people—presumably the Philistines—following the collapse of Canaan and the withdrawal of Egyptian forces from the area.[69]

Trude Dothan, professor emerita at the Hebrew University of Jerusalem and former codirector of the Ekron excavations, located at modern Tel Miqne, describes the end of the Late Bronze Age city at Ekron as follows: "In Field I, the upper city or acropolis, we could follow the total destruction of the last Late Bronze Age Canaanite city by fire. Here the destruction is evident: the remains of a large mud-brick storage building, traces of figs and lentils in storage jars, and a large well-preserved silo are buried under the collapsed mud-bricks. . . . The new Philistine city lies flush on the destruction of the Late Bronze Age settlement in the upper city and on the open fields of the Middle Bronze Age lower city."[70]

A similar situation seems to have arisen at Ashkelon, where recent excavations have documented the transformation of the settlement from an Egyptian garrison to a Philistine seaport sometime during the first half of the twelfth century BC—probably just after the reign of Ramses III, to judge from the several scarabs with his cartouche that have been found. In Ashkelon, however, the transition appears to have been peaceful, at least insofar as one can tell from the limited area that has been exposed to date. The excavators have described the "sudden appearance of new cultural patterns expressed in architecture, ceramics, diet, and crafts, particularly weaving." They connect these changes to the Sea Peoples, specifically the Philistines, and describe them as the result of migrations from the Mycenaean world.[71]

However, our understanding of this situation in Canaan at the end of the Late Bronze Age may still be evolving. Although the classic 1995 article on the coming of the Philistines to Canaan by Larry Stager of Harvard University describes the Philistines as "destroy[ing] indigenous cities and supplant[ing] them with their own in the four corners of the territory they conquered,"[72] Assaf Yasur-Landau of the University of Haifa has recently taken issue with this traditional picture, as we shall see below.

DESTRUCTIONS IN MESOPOTAMIA

Even as far to the east as Mesopotamia, evidence of destruction can be seen at multiple sites including Babylon, but these were clearly caused by forces other than the Sea Peoples. We know specifically that the Elamite army, once again marching from southwestern Iran, this time under the command of their king Shutruk-Nahhunte, caused at least some of this devastation.

Shutruk-Nahhunte had come to the Elamite throne in 1190 BC and ruled until 1155 BC. Although Elam (like the other kingdoms in the region) seems to have been a fairly minor player on the world stage during most of the Late Bronze Age, it was connected to some of the great kingdoms through marriage. Shutruk-Nahhunte was married to the daughter of a Kassite Babylonian king, just as many of his predecessors had been. One had married the daughter of Kurigalzu I back in the fourteenth century BC; another had married Kurigalzu's sister; and another had married the daughter of Burna-Buriash later that same century. Shutruk-Nahhunte's own mother was a Kassite princess, as he tells us in a letter that he wrote to the Kassite court, and which the German excavators found at Babylon.[73]

In that letter, he complains that he had been passed over for the Babylonian throne, despite being fully qualified for the position, including by birth. His indignation is palpable as he writes: "Why I, who am a king, son of a king, seed of a king, scion of a king, who am king for the lands, the land of Babylonia and for the land of E[lam], descendant of the eldest daughter of mighty King Kurigalzu, [why] do I not sit on the throne of the land of Babylonia?" He then threatened revenge, saying that he would "destroy your cities, dem[olish] your fortresses, stop up your [irrigation] ditches, cut down your orchards," and proclaiming, "You may climb up to heaven, [but I'll pull you down] by your hem, you may go down to hell, [but I'll pull you up] by your hair!"[74]

He made good on his threats in 1158 BC, invading Babylonia, capturing the city and overthrowing the Kassite king, and then placing his own son on the throne. He also, most famously, brought back to the Elamite city of Susa massive amounts of booty from Babylon, including a diorite stele, nearly eight feet tall, inscribed with the law code of Hammurabi, as well as a victory monument of the even-earlier Akkadian king Naram-Sin, and numerous other items. These were subsequently discovered in 1901 during the French excavations at Susa and sent to Paris, where they are now displayed in the Louvre.[75]

Shutruk-Nahhunte's campaign was apparently motivated by his desire for the kingdom and territory of Babylon and Babylonia, and he may well have taken advantage of the turmoil in the Eastern Mediterranean at the time. Quite possibly he knew that there was almost nobody to whom the Kassite king could turn for assistance. The subsequent campaigns in Mesopotamia undertaken by Shutruk-Nahhunte's son and grandson were very likely also influenced by the fact that the Great Powers of the previous centuries were either no longer in existence or much weakened. However, it is clear that none of the destruction associated with these military activities can be attributed to the Sea Peoples.

DESTRUCTIONS IN ANATOLIA

In Anatolia at this time, a number of cities were also destroyed. Once again, though, the reason in each case is hard to discern; and once again the Sea Peoples have traditionally been credited for the devastation on the basis of little or no evidence. In some cases, additional excavations by subsequent excavators are now overturning long-held attributions and assumptions. For instance, at the site of Tell Atchana, ancient Alalakh, located near the modern Turkish-Syrian border, Sir Leonard Woolley thought the city of Level I had been destroyed by the Sea Peoples in 1190 BC. However, the most recent excavations, by Aslihan Yener of the University of Chicago, have redated this level to the fourteenth century BC and indicate that the majority of the city was abandoned by 1300 BC, long before the possible encursions of the Sea Peoples.[76]

Of those Anatolian sites that were brought to ruin just after 1200 BC, among the better known are Hattusa, the capital city of the Hittites on the interior plateau, and Troy on the western coast. In neither case, however, is it certain beyond a doubt that the destructions were wrought by the Sea Peoples.

Hattusa

It is clear that the Hittite capital city of Hattusa was destroyed and abandoned soon after the beginning of the twelfth century BC. The excavators found "ash, charred wood, mudbricks, and slag formed when mudbricks melted from the intense heat of the conflagration."[77] However, it is not at all clear who destroyed the city. Although scholars and popularizing authors frequently blame the Sea Peoples, largely on the basis of Ramses III's statement "No land could stand before their arms, from Khatte . . . ," we actually have no idea whether "Khatte" in this case was meant as a reference to the Hittites in general or specifically to Hattusa.[78]

It is also not clear precisely when Hattusa fell, especially since it now seems to have been attacked sometime during Tudhaliya IV's reign, perhaps by forces loyal to his cousin Kurunta, who may have attempted to usurp the throne.[79] As the eminent University of Chicago Hittitologist Harry Hoffner, Jr., has remarked, the usual *terminus ante quem* for the final destruction (i.e., the date before which this must have happened) is based on the statement made by Ramses III in 1177 BC, which would probably place the destruction sometime earlier, perhaps ca. 1190–1180 BC. However, we have no real idea how accurate Ramses's statement was.[80]

By the 1980s, Hittitologists and other scholars were seriously suggesting that an older and better-known enemy, namely, the Kashka, who were located to the northeast of the Hittite homelands, had instead been responsible for destroying the city. This group is thought to have also sacked the city earlier, at a time just before the Battle of Qadesh in the early thirteenth century BC, when the Hittites temporarily abandoned Hattusa and moved their entire capital south for a number of years, to a region known as Tarhuntassa.[81] This makes much more sense, for as James Muhly of the University of Pennsylvania once wrote, "it has always been difficult to explain how Sea Raiders [i.e., Sea Peoples] destroyed the massive fortifications . . . of Hattusa, located hundreds of miles from the sea in what today seems a rather isolated part of the upland plateau of central Anatolia."[82]

The archaeological evidence indicates that parts of Hattusa were destroyed by an intense fire, which consumed portions of both the Upper and the Lower City, as well as the royal acropolis and the fortifications. However, it has now become clear that only the public buildings were destroyed, including the palace and some of the temples, and a few of the city gates. These buildings had been emptied out, rather than looted, before being put to the torch, while the domestic quarters in both the Upper and the Lower City show no signs of destruction at all.[83] A recent director of the excavations, Jürgen Seeher, suggested that the city was attacked only after it had been abandoned for some time, that the royal family had taken all of their possessions and moved elsewhere long before the final destruction. If so, the Kashka—longtime enemies of the Hittites—are more likely than the Sea Peoples to have been responsible for the actual destruction, though it may well have taken place only after the Hittite Empire had been severely weakened through other agencies, such as drought, famine, and interruption of the international trade routes.[84]

The same possible explanations may be given for the devastation visible at three other well-known central Anatolian sites reasonably near Hattusa: Alaca Höyük, Alishar, and Masat Höyük. All were destroyed by fire at approximately this same time, though it is unclear whether the Kashka, the Sea Peoples, or someone else entirely was responsible. Mersin and Tarsus, in southeastern Anatolia, were also destroyed, although both later recovered and were reoccupied.[85] The site of Karaoglan, which lies not very far to the west of Hattusa in central Anatolia, was also destroyed at this time, with bodies found in the destruction layer, but again it is not clear who was responsible.[86]

There is relatively little destruction farther to the west in Anatolia. In fact, the Australian scholar Trevor Bryce has noted that "the sites destroyed by fire [in Anatolia] seem to have been limited to the regions east of the Marassantiya river . . . there is no evidence of such a catastrophe further west. Indications from archaeological excavations are that only a small number of sites of the Hittite world were actually destroyed; the majority were simply abandoned."[87]

Troy

The one site in the west that was destroyed by fire early in the twelfth century BC was Troy, specifically Troy VIIA, located on the western coast of Anatolia.[88] Although Carl Blegen, the excavator from the University of Cincinnati, dated its destruction to ca. 1250 BC, the devastation has now been redated to 1190–1180 BC by Penelope Mountjoy, a noted expert on Mycenaean pottery.[89] The inhabitants of this city simply took the remnants of Troy VIh, which was probably destroyed by an earthquake perhaps as early as 1300 BC, as discussed in detail earlier, and rebuilt the city. Thus, the large houses originally built during Troy VI now had partitioning walls installed and several families living where there had been only one before. Blegen saw the dwellings as evidence of a city under siege, but Mountjoy suggests instead that the inhabitants were trying to recover from the earthquake, with temporary shanties erected among the ruins.[90] However, the city did eventually come under siege, as shown by evidence found by both Blegen and the next excavator of Troy, Manfred Korfmann from the University of Tübingen, who dug at the site from 1988 to 2005.

Both excavators found bodies in the streets of Troy VIIA and arrowheads embedded in the walls, and both were convinced that it had been destroyed in warfare.[91] Korfmann, who also located the long-lost lower city at Troy, which all the previous excavators had missed, said at one point: "The evidence is burning and catastrophe with fire. Then there are skeletons; we found, for example, a girl, I think sixteen, seventeen years old, half buried, the feet were burned by fire. . . . It was a city which was besieged. It was a city which was defended, which protected itself. They lost the war and obviously they were defeated."[92]

However, the date of this destruction might make it difficult to argue that the Mycenaeans were responsible, as in Homer's story of the Trojan War in the *Iliad*, unless the Mycenaean palaces back on the Greek mainland were being attacked and destroyed precisely because all their warriors were away fighting at Troy. In fact, Mountjoy suggests that the Sea Peoples, rather than the Mycenaeans, destroyed Troy VIIA. This would fit well with the mention of the former by Ramses III just three years later, but she presents no substantial evidence to support her hypothesis, which remains speculative.[93]

DESTRUCTIONS ON THE GREEK MAINLAND

If the Mycenaeans were not involved in the destruction of Troy VIIA, it may have been because they were also under attack at approximately the same time. It is universally accepted by scholars that Mycenae, Tiryns, Midea, Pylos, Thebes, and many other Mycenaean sites on the Greek mainland suffered destructions at this same approximate time, at the end of the thirteenth century BC, and early in the twelfth.[94] In fact, a recent survey published in 2010 by British archaeologist Guy Middleton presents a stark picture of the devastation on the Greek mainland during the period from 1225 to 1190 BC: "In the Argolid and Corinthia there were destructions at Mycenae, Tiryns, Katsingri, Korakou and Iria . . . in Lakonia at the Menelaion; in Messenia, at Pylos; in Achaea, at Teikhos Dymaion; in Boeotia and Phokis, at Thebes, Orchomenos, Gla . . . and Krisa, while the following sites appear to have been abandoned without destructions: Argolid and Corinthia: Berbati, Prosymna, Zygouries, Gonia, Tsoungiza; Lakonia: Ayios Stephanos; Messenia: Nichoria; Attica: Brauron; Boeotia and Phokis: Eutresis."[95] As Middleton further notes, there were additional destructions during the period from 1190 to 1130 BC at Mycenae, Tiryns, Lefkandi, and Kynos.

As Carl Blegen and Mabel Lang, of Bryn Mawr College, wrote back in 1960, this seems to have been "a stormy period of Mycenaean history. Widespread destruction by fire was visited on Mycenae, both inside and outside the acropolis. Tiryns, too, was subjected to a catastrophe of the same kind. The palace at Thebes was probably likewise looted and burned down in the same general period. Many other settlements were overthrown, abandoned altogether, and never reinhabited: among the better known examples may be mentioned Berbati . . . Prosymna . . . Zygouries . . . and other smaller places."[96] It is clear that something tumultuous occurred, although some scholars see this as merely the final stages of a dissolution or collapse that had begun as early as 1250 BC. Jeremy Rutter of Dartmouth College, for example, believes that "the destruction of the palaces was anything but an unforeseen catastrophe which precipitated a century of crisis in the Aegean, but was instead the culmination of an extended period of unrest which afflicted the Mycenaean world from the mid-thirteenth century onwards."[97]

Pylos

At Pylos, the destruction of the palace, originally thought by the excavator to date to ca. 1200 BC, is now usually dated to about 1180 BC, for the same reasons that the destruction of Troy VIIA has been down-dated, that is, on the basis of the redating of the pottery found in the remains.[98] Its destruction is generally assumed to have been caused by violence, in part because there is much burning associated with the final levels at the site, after which it was apparently abandoned. In 1939, during the first season of excavations at the palace, Blegen noted, "It must have been a conflagration of great intensity, for the interior walls have in many places been fused into shapeless masses, stones converted into lime, and, resting on the blackened carbonized rubbish and ashes covering the floors, is a thick layer of fine dry red-burnt earth, presumably the disintegrated debris of crude bricks that once formed the material of the superstructure."[99]

The later excavations further confirmed his initial impressions; as Jack Davis of the University of Cincinnati and the former director of the American School of Classical Studies in Athens, later noted, "the Main Building burned with such intensity that the Linear B tablets in its Archive Room were fired, and jars in some of the storerooms even melted."[100] Blegen himself wrote in 1955 that "everywhere . . . vivid evidence of devastation by fire was brought to light. The abundant, not to say extravagant, use of massive wooden timbers in the construction of the stone walls provided almost unlimited fuel for the flames, and the entire structure was reduced to a heap of crumbling ruins in a conflagration hot enough to calcine stone and even to melt ornaments of gold."[101]

Earlier scholars occasionally pointed to mentions in the Linear B tablets found at the site which suggest that there were "watchers of the sea" in place during the final year(s) of the site's occupation, and have hypothesized that they were waiting and watching for the Sea Peoples. However, it is not clear what these tablets are documenting, and, even if the inhabitants of Pylos were watching the sea, we do not know why or for what they were watching.[102]

In short, the palace at Pylos was destroyed in a cataclysmic fire ca. 1180 BC, but it is not clear who (or what) caused the fire. As with the other sites that were devastated at this time, we are uncertain as to whether it was human perpetrators or an act of nature.

Mycenae

Mycenae suffered a major destruction during the middle of the thirteenth century BC, ca. 1250, which was probably caused by an earthquake. There was also a second destruction, ca. 1190 BC or shortly thereafter, whose cause is unknown but which spelled the end of the city as a major power.

This latter destruction was marked by fire. One of the principal directors of the Mycenae excavations, the late Spyros Iakovidis of the University of Pennsylvania, noted that "locally limited and not necessarily simultaneous fires broke out in the Cult Centre, Tsountas' House, part of the Southwest Building, Panagia House II . . . and perhaps the palace."[103] In the Cult Center, for instance, "the intensity of the fire has served to preserve these walls in their original state, though off axis."[104]

In a nearby deposit, found on the causeway within the citadel, the excavators found a mass of rubble, which included "calcined stone, burnt mud-brick, patches of ash, and carbonized beams," and which "blocked the doorways of the rooms to the southeast, and lay nearly 2 m. deep against the terrace wall to the north-east." The terrace wall itself "was contorted by the intense heat generated by the destruction fire, and in many places had achieved the consistency of concrete." The excavators concluded that the rubble came from the mud-brick walls associated with buildings on the terrace above, which collapsed "in a blazing mass."[105] However, there is no indication of the cause of any of this, whether it was invaders, internal rebellion, or an accident.

One senior researcher and excavator of Mycenae, Elizabeth French of Cambridge University, has remarked: "Immediately after the '1200 Destruction,' however it may have been caused, the citadel of Mycenae was a mess. As far as we can tell almost all structures were unusable. Both fire and collapse were widespread and we have evidence of a layer of mud wash covering large areas of the west slope which we surmise was the result of heavy rain on the debris."[106] However, both French and Iakovidis note that this did not mark the end of Mycenae, for it was reoccupied, albeit on a smaller scale, immediately afterward. As Iakovidis said, this "was a period of retrenchment and of accelerating regression but not one of danger and distress."[107]

Interestingly, Iakovidis further remarked that "the archaeological context . . . offers no evidence for migrations or invasions on any scale or for local disturbances during the 12th and the 11th century B.C. Mycenae did not meet with a violent end. The area was never . . . deserted but by then, due to external and faraway causes, the citadel had lost its political and economic significance. The complex centralized system which it housed and represented had broken down, the authority which had created it could maintain no longer and a general decline set in, during which the site fell slowly and gradually into ruins."[108] In other words, it is unclear, according to Iakovidis, what caused the fires that destroyed large portions of Mycenae just after 1200 BC, but he eschews the notion of invasions or other dramatic events, preferring to attribute the gradual decline of the site during the following decades to the collapse of the palatial system and of long-distance trade. Recent research by other archaeologists may prove his thesis to be correct.[109]

Tiryns

Just a few kilometers from Mycenae, the excavations at Tiryns in the Argolid region of mainland Greece have been ongoing since the days of Heinrich Schliemann in the late 1800s. Evidence for destructions at the site has been recorded by most of the excavators, but most recently by Joseph Maran, of the University of Heidelberg.

In 2002 and 2003, Maran continued the excavation of two structures, known as Buildings XI and XV within the Lower Citadel at the site, portions of which had been excavated by his predecessor Klaus Kilian. They are believed to have been in use for only a very short time before being destroyed. In destruction debris dated to ca. 1200 BC or just after, he found a number of very interesting artifacts, including a small ivory rod with a cuneiform inscription, which was either imported or made/used by a foreigner living at Tiryns during this tumultuous period.[110]

Maran reports that this destruction was the result of a "catastrophe that struck Tiryns . . . [and which] destroyed the palace and the settlement in the Lower Citadel." He further notes, as Kilian had already suggested, that based on "undulating walls" visible in some buildings, the probable cause of the destruction was a strong earthquake, and that "recent excavations in neighboring Midea have [now] supported this interpretation."[111]

Kilian had long argued that an earthquake destroyed Tiryns and also affected several other sites in the Argolid, such as Mycenae; other archaeologists are now in agreement with this hypothesis.[112] Kilian wrote, "The evidence consists of building remains with tilted and curved walls and foundations, as well as skeletons of people killed and buried by the collapsed walls of houses."[113]

We have already noted that Mycenae suffered a major destruction, ca. 1250 BC, which was probably caused by an earthquake. As described in more detail below, there is substantial evidence for one or more earthquakes severely impacting numerous sites in Greece at about this time, and not just Mycenae and Tiryns in the Argolid.

However, archaeological evidence from the ongoing excavations has conclusively shown that Tiryns was not completely destroyed. The city continued in use for another round of occupation lasting several more decades, with significant rebuilding in some portions, especially in the lower city.[114]

DESTRUCTIONS IN CYPRUS

In the Eastern Mediterranean, the Sea Peoples have been blamed for the Bronze Age disruptions on Cyprus, ca. 1200 BC, as well. It used to be thought that the case was pretty clear-cut. Thirty years ago, Vassos Karageorghis, then the director of antiquities on the island, wrote: "The peaceful conditions . . . were to change towards the end of Late Cypriot II [i.e., ca. 1225 BC]. Although we may not accept as entirely accurate the boastful assertion of the Hittites that they exercised control over Cyprus . . . we cannot ignore the fact that during the reign of Shuppiluliuma II conditions in the East Mediterranean could not have been calm."[115]

Karageorghis went on to suggest that "large numbers of refugees" left mainland Greece when the "Mycenaean empire" (as he called it) collapsed, and that they became plunderers and adventurers, who eventually reached Cyprus in the company of others, ca. 1225 BC. He attributed to them the destructions on Cyprus at this time, including the major sites of Kition and Enkomi on the eastern coast, as well as activity at other sites such as Maa-*Palaeokastro*, Kalavasos-*Ayios Dhimitrios*, Sinda, and Maroni.[116]

The small site of Maa-*Palaeokastro* is especially interesting, as it was built specifically during this period of troubles, that is, toward the end of the thirteenth century BC. Karageorghis, who excavated the site, described it as "a fortified [military] outpost on a headland of the western coast." As he pointed out, it was naturally fortified by the steep sides of the headland and surrounded on three sides by the sea, so that it needed to be fortified only at the point where it joined the mainland. He believed that this outpost was established by the invaders from the Aegean, who then raided Enkomi and Kition from this enclave, only to be destroyed in turn by a second influx of settlers from the Aegean, probably ca. 1190 BC, who then established permanent residency on the island.[117]

Karageorghis believed that other similar foreign enclaves or outposts had been established at Cypriot sites like Sinda and Pyla-*Kokkinokremos*. For example, he noted that the fortified settlement of Sinda, which is located just inland and to the west of Enkomi, was violently destroyed ca. 1225 BC. New floors were then laid and new buildings constructed directly on top of this burned destruction layer, possibly by the invaders from the Aegean.[118]

These destructions, and constructions, however, are probably too early to fit the dates of incursions of the Sea Peoples—at least those described by Merneptah in 1207 BC or Ramses III in 1177 BC. Consequently, Karageorghis suggested that an earlier wave of bellicose peoples from the Aegean had arrived on Cyprus even before the Sea Peoples, by ca. 1225 BC at the latest. The subsequent arrival of the Sea Peoples could be seen in the excavations at Enkomi, on the coast of Cyprus, which "revealed a second catastrophe . . . associated by some scholars with the raids of the Sea Peoples." This second level of destruction, he said, dated to ca. 1190 BC.[119]

There is, however, no real evidence to identify who was to blame for any of the destructions of 1225–1190 BC at any of these sites on Cyprus. It is quite possible that Tudhaliya and the Hittites—who, after all, did claim to have attacked and conquered Cyprus at this approximate time—caused at least some of the destructions ca. 1225 BC. Furthermore, we have already seen that another Hittite attack on the island also reportedly took place during the reign of Suppiluliuma II (who came to the Hittite throne ca. 1207 BC), as he claims in his records. Thus, it may be that it is the Hittites, rather than the Sea Peoples, who were responsible for most of the destructions on Cyprus during this turbulent period. There is even one text, sent by the governor of Cyprus (Alashiya), which seems to indicate that ships from Ugarit may have caused some of the damage, as well as a possibility that at least some of the devastation could have been caused by an earthquake or earthquakes. At Enkomi, the excavators discovered the bodies of children who had been killed by falling mud-bricks from the superstructure of the building, which would seem to indicate the hand of Mother Nature rather than that of humans.[120]

The scenario envisioned by Karageorghis has now been amended to form a more complex view of the proceedings on Cyprus during this period at the end of the Late Bronze Age. Even Karageorghis had been quickly persuaded that, at each of the sites in question, there was only one set of destructions, and not two; and that they ranged from as early as 1190 BC to as late as 1174 BC, rather than from 1225 BC onward.[121] A more recent history of the period, written by British scholar Louise Steel, states that the "traditional view of the . . . period is of a Mycenaean colonization of Cyprus (and the southern Levant) following the collapse of Mycenaean palaces. However . . . there was no simple imposition of Mycenaean culture on the island. Instead, the . . . material demonstrates a syncretism of influences that reflect the cosmopolitan nature of the [Late Cypriot] cultural identity. Mycenaean (or Aegean) culture is not simply transposed from the Aegean to Cyprus but merges with the indigenous Cypriot culture."[122]

Steel also calls Karageorghis's conclusions, and the conventional view of the Aegean colonization of Cyprus, into question. For instance, rather than seeing sites such as Maa-*Palaeokastro* and Pyla-*Kokkinokremos* as foreign or Aegean "defensive outposts," she states that the evidence seems to better support identification of these as local Cypriot strongholds, with the latter established, for example, "to ensure movement of goods, in particular metals, between the harbour towns . . . and the Cypriot hinterland."[123] She states further that "the conventional interpretation of Maa-Palaeokastro as an early Aegean stronghold has yet to be rigorously tested," and suggests that both Maa-*Palaeokastro* and Pyla-*Kokkinokremos* might actually be examples of indigenous Cypriot strongholds, analogous to the defensive settlements built at approximately this time on the island of Crete.[124]

Other scholars, including Bernard Knapp of the University of Edinburgh, have now suggested that the so-called Mycenaean colonization so prevalent in earlier scholarly literature was neither Mycenaean nor a colonization. Instead, it was more probably a period of hybridization, during which aspects of Cypriot, Aegean, and Levantine material culture were appropriated and reused to form a new elite social identity.[125] In other words, we are looking once again at a globalized culture, reflecting a multitude of influences at the end of the Bronze Age, just before the collapse.

On the other hand, we still have Paul Åström's comments about his excavation at the site of Hala Sultan Tekke, on the coast of Cyprus near the modern city of Larnaka, which he described as "a town partly destroyed by fire and deserted in haste." Here, sometime around or after 1200 BC, "loose objects were left abandoned in the courtyards and valuables were hidden in the ground. Bronze arrowheads—one of them found stuck in the side of a wall of a building—and numerous lead sling bullets scattered all over the place are eloquent proof of war."[126] This is one of the few clear instances of enemy attackers, and yet they did not leave a calling card, either here or anywhere else for that matter. There is also now recent scientific evidence from the lagoon at Hala Sultan Tekke that the region was quite possibly suffering from the effects of a severe drought at this same time, as we shall discuss below.[127]

Thus, we are now faced with a situation in which our current knowledge is being reassessed and conventional historical paradigms are being overthrown, or at least called into question. While it is clear that there were destructions on Cyprus either just before or after 1200 BC, it is by no means clear who was responsible for this damage; possible culprits range from the Hittites to invaders from the Aegean to Sea Peoples and even earthquakes. It is also conceivable that what we see in the archaeological record is merely the material culture of those who took advantage of these destructions and settled into the now fully or partially abandoned cities and settlements, rather than the material culture of those who were actually responsible for the destructions.

Regardless, Cyprus seems to have survived these depredations essentially intact. There is now every indication that the island was flourishing during the remainder of the twelfth and into the eleventh century BC; evidence includes Egyptian texts such as "The Report of Wenamun," concerning an Egyptian priest and emissary who was shipwrecked on the island ca. 1075 BC.[128] However, Cyprus's resilience came about only as a result of the rather dramatic restructuring of its political and economic organization, which allowed the island and its polities to last until the end finally came, ca. 1050 BC.[129]

FIGHTING IN EGYPT AND THE HAREM CONSPIRACY

Returning to Egypt for a moment, we find a picture similar to that characterizing sites elsewhere in the Eastern Mediterranean and in the Aegean, and yet different. The Egyptians had ended the thirteenth century BC on a relatively high note, having defeated the first wave of Sea Peoples during the reign of Merneptah, in 1207 BC. The twelfth century began calmly, under the rule of Seti II and then Queen Twosret, but by the time Ramses III came to the throne in 1184 BC, events were growing tumultuous. In the fifth year of his rule, and again in his eleventh year, he fought major wars against the neighboring Libyans.[130] In between, in his eighth year, he fought the battles against the Sea Peoples that we have been discussing here. And then, in 1155, after ruling for thirty-two years, he was apparently assassinated.

We are told the story of the assassination in a number of documents, the longest of which is the Turin Judicial Papyrus. It is thought that some of these documents might be connected with one another and may originally have been part of a single fifteen-foot-long papyrus scroll. All are concerned with the trial of his accused assailants, known to Egyptologists as the Harem Conspiracy.

The conspiracy seems to be unrelated to anything else going on in the Eastern Mediterranean at the time and was simply a plot hatched by a minor queen in the royal harem to have her son succeed Ramses III. There were as many as forty accused conspirators, both members of the harem and court officials, who were tried in four groups. A number of them were found guilty and received the death penalty; several were forced to commit suicide right in the court. The minor queen and her son were among those sentenced to death.[131]

Although it is known that Ramses III died before the verdicts were reached in this case, it is not clear in these documents whether the plot had actually succeeded. But apparently it had, although this fact has only recently come to light.

Ramses III's mummy has long been known. He had originally been buried in the Valley of the Kings in his own tomb (known as KV 11) but had later been moved by priests for safekeeping, along with a number of other royal mummies. These were all found in 1881, in the Deir el-Bahari cache near Hatshepsut's mortuary temple.[132]

In 2012, Egyptologists and forensic scientists conducted an autopsy of Ramses III's body and reported in the *British Medical Journal* that his throat had been cut. The sharp knife that caused the wound had been thrust into his neck immediately under the larynx, all the way down to the cervical vertebra, cutting his trachea and severing all of the soft tissue in the area. Death was instantaneous. Subsequently, during the embalming process, a protective Horus-eye amulet had been placed in the wound, either for protection or for healing, though it was far too late to help the king in this life. In addition, a thick collar of linen was placed around his neck, in order to hide the stab wound (70 mm wide). It was only during the X-ray analysis that the scientists were able to see through the thick cloth and identify the injury that killed the king.[133]

A second body, of a male aged between eighteen and twenty and known only as "Man E," was found with Ramses III. Wrapped in a ritually impure goatskin and not properly mummified, the body may be that of the guilty prince, according to DNA tests which indicate that he was probably Ramses III's son. The forensic evidence, including facial contortions and injuries on his throat, suggests that he was probably strangled.[134]

With the death of Ramses III, the true glory of the Egyptian New Kingdom came to an end. There would be eight more pharaohs during the Twentieth Dynasty before it ended in 1070 BC, but none of them accomplished anything of merit. Of course, it would have been fairly remarkable had they done so, given the state of affairs elsewhere in the Eastern Mediterranean, although the last king, Ramses XI, did send his emissary Wenamun to Byblos in order to purchase cedars of Lebanon, only to have him shipwrecked on Cyprus on the homeward voyage in about 1075 BC.

SUMMATION

Although it is clear that there were massive destructions in the Aegean and Eastern Mediterranean regions at the end of the thirteenth and the beginning of the twelfth century BC, it is far from clear who—or what—was responsible. Among the open questions is even the identity of the manufacturers of the pottery known as "Mycenaean IIIC1b," which appears at many of these Eastern Mediterranean sites following the destructions of ca. 1200 BC, including Ras Ibn Hani and Ras Bassit near Ugarit.[135] This pottery, which was earlier seen as the product of displaced Mycenaeans who had fled to the east, following the destructions of their hometowns and cities on the Greek mainland, seems instead to have been produced in Cyprus and the Eastern Mediterranean, most likely after importation of the real Aegean ware had ceased.

As Annie Caubet, of the Louvre Museum, has said regarding the reoccupation of Ras Ibn Hani, near Ugarit: "Certainly, resettlement on the site in a stable and continuous way is undeniable. What remains to be proved is that the inhabitants were now a part of the Sea Peoples and not the local population which had returned after the troubles were over."[136] Other innovations observable in Cyprus and the Levant at this time, such as the use of ashlar masonry in architectural building techniques, and new funerary rituals and vase types,[137] may indicate contact with the Aegean or even the presence of displaced Aegean individuals, but Aegean styles do not necessarily indicate Aegean people, so these could also be simply a manifestation of the globalization that was in place even during the tumultuous years that characterized the end of the Late Bronze Age.

As for the end itself, it may have taken much more than the simple depredations of the roving marauders recorded by the Egyptians—the "Sea Peoples," as we call them now. So often fingered by earlier scholars as the sole culprits responsible for the end of civilization in this widespread area, they may have been as much the victims as the oppressors, as we shall see in the next chapter.

CHAPTER FIVE

A "PERFECT STORM" OF CALAMITIES?

. . . . .

We are now finally in a position to attempt to solve our mystery, by pulling together all of the different strands of evidence and the clues that are available, so that we may determine why the stable international system of the Late Bronze Age suddenly collapsed after surviving for centuries. However, we must come to this with an open mind and employ "the scientific use of the imagination," as the immortal Sherlock Holmes once said, for "we must balance probabilities and choose the most likely."[1]

To begin with, it will be apparent by now that the Sea Peoples and the so-called Collapse or Catastrophe at the end of the Late Bronze Age are both topics that have been much discussed by scholars over the course of the past century, and that they are linked more often than not in such discussions. This was especially true during the 1980s and 1990s, when Nancy Sandars published the revised edition of her book, simply called *The Sea Peoples*, in 1985 and Robert Drews published his book *The End of the Bronze Age* in 1993. There were also at least two academic conferences or seminars specifically devoted to these topics, held in 1992 and 1997, and many other books, theses, and conferences were tangentially related.[2] However, as noted at the beginning of this volume, a wealth of new data has become available in the past few decades, which need to be considered in our evolving understanding of both the Sea Peoples and the complex forces that brought to a close the era of magnificent civilizations that we have been discussing.[3]

We need to acknowledge first and foremost, as frequently noted in the preceding pages, that it is not always clear who, or what, caused the destruction of the Late Bronze Age cities, kingdoms, and empires of the Aegean and Eastern Mediterranean. The destruction of the Palace of Nestor at Pylos, ca. 1180 BC, is an excellent example, as one scholar has recently acknowledged: "Some have suggested that the agents of this calamity were invaders from outside the kingdom; others that the people of Pylos themselves revolted against their king. The precise causes remain undetermined."[4]

Second, we need to admit that there is currently no scholarly consensus as to the cause or causes of the collapse of these multiple interconnected societies just over three thousand years ago; culprits recently blamed by scholars include "attacks by foreign enemies, social uprising, natural catastrophes, systems collapse, and changes in warfare."[5] It is therefore worth our time to reconsider, as scholars have done for approximately the past eighty years, what the possible causes might be. In so doing, however, we should objectively consider the available evidence that supports or fails to support each of the hypothetical possibilities.

EARTHQUAKES

For instance, the idea that earthquakes caused, or might have contributed to, the destruction of some of the Late Bronze Age cities has been around since the days of Claude Schaeffer, the original excavator of Ugarit. He thought that an earthquake caused the final destruction of the city, for he found visible indications that an earthquake had rocked the city in the distant past. Photographs from Schaeffer's excavations, for example, show long stone walls knocked off kilter, which is one of the hallmarks of earthquake damage.[6]

However, current thinking on the subject puts the date of this earthquake at Ugarit at 1250 BC or a bit thereafter. Moreover, because there are signs of restoration activities in the decades between the earthquake and the final demise of the city, it is now thought that the quake only damaged the city and did not completely destroy it.[7]

It is, admittedly, frequently difficult to distinguish between a city destroyed by an earthquake and a city destroyed by humans and warfare. However, there are several markers that characterize a destructive earthquake and which can be noted by archaeologists during excavations. These include collapsed, patched, or reinforced walls; crushed skeletons, or bodies found lying under fallen debris; toppled columns lying parallel to one another; slipped keystones in archways and doorways; and walls leaning at impossible angles or offset from their original position.[8] In contrast, a city destroyed during warfare will usually have weapons of various sorts within the destruction debris. At the site of Aphek, in Israel, for example, which was destroyed toward the end of the thirteenth century BC, the excavators found arrowheads stuck in the walls of the buildings, just as there are in Troy VIIA.[9]

Thanks to recent research by archaeoseismologists, it is now clear that Greece, as well as much of the rest of the Aegean and Eastern Mediterranean, was struck by a series of earthquakes, beginning about 1225 BC and lasting for as long as fifty years, until about 1175 BC. The earthquake at Ugarit identified and described by Schaeffer was not an isolated event; it was just one of many such quakes that occurred during this time period. Such a series of earthquakes in antiquity is now known as an "earthquake storm," in which a seismic fault keeps "unzipping" by unleashing a series of earthquakes over years or decades until all the pressure along the fault line has been released.[10]

In the Aegean, earthquakes probably struck during this time period at Mycenae, Tiryns, Midea, Thebes, Pylos, Kynos, Lefkandi, the Menelaion, Kastanas in Thessaly, Korakou, Profitis Elias, and Gla. In the Eastern Mediterranean, earthquake damage dating to this period is also visible at numerous sites, including Troy, Karaoglun, and Hattusa in Anatolia; Ugarit, Megiddo, Ashdod, and Akko in the Levant; and Enkomi on Cyprus.[11]

And, just as people are killed during the collapse of buildings and are buried in the rubble when an earthquake hits a populated area today, so too at least nineteen bodies of people killed in these ancient earthquakes have been found during excavations at the devastated Late Bronze Age cities. At Mycenae, for example, the skeletons of three adults and a child were found in the basement of a house two hundred meters north of the citadel, where they had been crushed beneath fallen stones during an earthquake. Similarly, in a house built on the west slope of the ridge north of the Treasury of Atreus, the skeleton of a middle-aged woman whose skull had been crushed by a falling stone was found in the doorway between the main room and the front room. At Tiryns, the skeletons of a woman and a child were found buried by the collapsed walls of Building X inside the Acropolis; two other human skeletons were found near the fortification walls, where they had been killed and then covered by debris falling from the walls. Similarly, at nearby Midea, other skeletons were found, including one of a young girl in a room near the East Gate, whose skull and backbone were smashed under fallen stones.[12]

However, we must concede that although these earthquakes undoubtedly caused severe damage, it is unlikely that they alone were sufficient to cause a complete collapse of society, especially since some of the sites were clearly reoccupied and at least partially rebuilt afterward. Such was the case at Mycenae and Tiryns, for example, although they never again functioned at the level that they had achieved prior to the destruction.[13] Thus, we must look elsewhere for a different, or perhaps complementary, explanation for the end of the Late Bronze Age in the Aegean and Eastern Mediterranean.

CLIMATE CHANGE, DROUGHT, AND FAMINE

One suggestion favored by scholars, especially those seeking to explain not only the end of the Late Bronze Age but also why the Sea Peoples may have begun their migrations, is climate change, particularly in the form of drought, resulting in famine. Although theories formulated by archaeologists frequently reflect the era, decade, or even the year in which they are publishing, such hypotheses regarding the effects of possible climate change at the end of the second millennium BC predate by several decades our current preoccupation with climate change.

For example, drought was long the favored explanation of earlier scholars for the movement of the Sea Peoples out of the regions of the Western Mediterranean and into the lands to the east. They postulated that a drought in northern Europe had pressured the population to migrate down into the Mediterranean region, where they displaced the inhabitants of Sicily, Sardinia, and Italy, and perhaps those in the Aegean as well. If this occurred, it might have initiated a chain reaction that culminated in the movement of peoples far away in the Eastern Mediterranean. For examples of droughts initiating large-scale human migrations, one need only look back to the United States of the 1930s and the drought that caused the infamous "Dust Bowl," which led to a huge migration of families from Oklahoma and Texas to California.

This type of migration is frequently referred to as "push-pull," with negative conditions in the home area pushing the inhabitants out and positive conditions in the area of destination beckoning or pulling the new migrants in that direction. To these, as the British archaeologist

Guy Middleton has pointed out, may be added the categories of "stay" and "ability": the factors contributing to the desire to stay at home after all, and the factors regarding the ability to actually migrate, including knowledge of sailing, passable routes, and so on.[14]

Perhaps the most famous of the arguments in favor of a drought as an influential factor in the demise of the Late Bronze Age in the Aegean was put forth fully fifty years ago, in the mid-1960s, by Rhys Carpenter, a professor of archaeology at Bryn Mawr College. He published a very short but extremely influential book in which he argued that the Mycenaean civilization had been brought down by a prolonged drought that had severely affected the Mediterranean and Aegean regions. He based his arguments on what appeared to be a rather dramatic drop in population on mainland Greece following the end of the Bronze Age.[15]

However, subsequent archaeological surveys and excavations have shown that the population decrease was not nearly as dramatic as Carpenter had thought. Instead, there was a shift in population to other areas of Greece during the Iron Age, which may have had little to do with a possible drought. And so Carpenter's ingenious theory has now fallen by the wayside, although perhaps it should be resurrected in light of new data (see below).[16]

Leaving drought aside for the moment, and turning to famine, we may note that scholars have long pointed to the written texts that speak plainly of famines and the need for grain in the Hittite Empire and elsewhere in the Eastern Mediterranean at the end of the Bronze Age.[17] They have also correctly noted that the occurrence of famine in this region was not unique to the final years of the Late Bronze Age.

For example, decades earlier, during the mid-thirteenth century BC, a Hittite queen wrote to the Egyptian pharaoh Ramses II, stating, "I have no grain in my lands." Soon thereafter, probably in a related move, the Hittites sent a trade embassy to Egypt in order to procure barley and wheat for shipment back to Anatolia.[18] An inscription of the Egyptian pharaoh Merneptah, in which he states that he had "caused grain to be taken in ships, to keep alive this land of Hatti," further confirms famine in the land of the Hittites toward the end of the thirteenth century BC.[19] Additional correspondence sent from the Hittite capital city attests to the ongoing crisis during the following decades, including one letter in which the writer rhetorically asks, "Do you not know that there was a famine in the midst of my lands?"[20]

Some of the letters found at Ugarit are concerned with the immediate shipment of large quantities of grain to the Hittites. One missive sent from the Hittite king to the king of Ugarit is concerned specifically with a shipment of two thousand units of barley (or simply grain). The Hittite king ends his letter dramatically, stating, "It is a matter of life or death!"[21] Another letter is similarly concerned with the shipment of grain, but it also requests that many boats be sent as well. This led the original excavators to hypothesize that it was a reaction to the incursions of the Sea Peoples, which it may or may not be.[22] Even the last king of Ugarit, Ammurapi, received several letters from the Hittite king Suppiluliuma II in the early twelfth century BC, including one chastising him for being late in sending a much-needed shipment of food to the Hittite homeland sometime in the years just before the final destructions.[23]

Itamar Singer of Tel Aviv University was convinced that the extent of famine during the last years of the thirteenth and the early decades of the twelfth century BC was unprecedented, and that it affected far more areas than simply Anatolia. In his estimation, the evidence, both textual and archaeological, indicates that "climatological cataclysms affected the entire eastern Mediterranean region towards the end of the second millennium BCE."[24] He may well have been correct, for one of the letters found in the House of Urtenu at Ugarit in northern Syria refers to a famine ravaging the city of Emar in inland Syria at the time that it was destroyed in 1185 BC. The relevant lines in this letter, apparently sent by someone from Urtenu's commercial firm stationed in that city, read: "There is famine in your [i.e., our] house; we will all die of hunger. If you do not quickly arrive here, we ourselves will die of hunger. You will not see a living soul from your land."[25]

Even Ugarit itself seems not to have been immune, for a letter from Merneptah found in the House of Urtenu specifically mentions "consignments of grain sent from Egypt to relieve the famine in Ugarit,"[26] and one king of Ugarit wrote to an unidentified, but probably royal and senior, correspondent, saying, "(Here) with me, plenty (has become) famine."[27] There is also a text from the king of Tyre, located in the coastal area of what is now Lebanon, to the king of Ugarit. It informs the Ugaritic king that his ship, which was returning from Egypt loaded with grain, had been caught in a storm: "Your ship that you sent to Egypt, died [was wrecked] in a mighty storm close to Tyre. It was recovered and the salvage master [or captain] took all the grain from their jars. But I have taken all their grain, all their people, and all their belongings from the salvage master [or captain], and I have returned (it all) to them. And (now) your ship is being taken care of in Akko, stripped." In other words, the ship had either sought refuge or been successfully salvaged. Either way, the crew and the grain it carried were safe and awaiting the command of the Ugaritic king.[28] The ship itself, it seems, was berthed in the port city of Akko, where today one can sit in a pleasant seaside restaurant and imagine the bustle of activities that took place there more than three thousand years ago.

But what factor, or combinations of factors, may have caused the famine(s) in the Eastern Mediterranean during these decades remains uncertain. Elements that might be considered include war and plagues of insects, but climate change accompanied by drought is more likely to have turned a once-verdant land into an arid semidesert. However, until recently, the Ugaritic and other Eastern Mediterranean textual documents containing reports of famine provided the only potential evidence for climate change or drought, and even that was indirect. As a result, the issue has been debated on and off by scholars for decades.[29]

The topic has recently been given new impetus, though, as a result of findings published by an international team of scholars, including David Kaniewski and Elise Van Campo of the Université de Toulouse in France and Harvey Weiss of Yale University, who suggest that they may have direct scientific evidence for climate change and drought in the Mediterranean region at the end of the thirteenth and into the beginning of the twelfth century BC. Their research, which first suggested that the end of the Early Bronze Age in Mesopotamia, toward the end of the third millennium BC, might have been caused by climate change, has now expanded to propose that the same thing may have occurred at the end of the Late Bronze Age as well.[30]

Using data from the site of Tell Tweini (ancient Gibala) in north Syria, the team noted that there may have been "climate instability and a severe drought episode" in the region at the end of the second millennium BC.[31] In particular, they studied pollen retrieved from alluvial deposits near the site, which suggest that "drier climatic conditions occurred in the Mediterranean belt of Syria from the late 13th/early 12th centuries BC to the 9th century BC."[32]

Kaniewski's team has now also published additional evidence of a probable drought on Cyprus at this same time, using pollen analysis from the lagoon system known as the Larnaca Salt Lake Complex, located by the site of Hala Sultan Tekke.[33] Their data suggest that "major environmental changes" took place in this area during the end of the Late Bronze Age and the beginning of the Iron Age, that is, during the period from 1200 to 850 BC. At this time, the area around Hala Sultan Tekke, which had been a major Cypriot port earlier in the Late Bronze Age, "turned into a drier landscape [and] the precipitation and groundwater probably became insufficient to maintain sustainable agriculture in this place."[34]

If Kaniewski and his colleagues are correct, they have retrieved the direct scientific evidence that scholars have been seeking for a drought that may have contributed to the end of the Late Bronze Age. In fact, they conclude that the data from both coastal Syria and coastal Cyprus strongly suggest "that the LBA crisis coincided with the onset of a ca. 300-year drought event 3200 years ago. This climate shift caused crop failures, dearth and famine, which precipitated or hastened socioeconomic crises and forced regional human migrations at the end of the LBA in the Eastern Mediterranean and southwest Asia."[35]

Working independently, Brandon Drake of the University of New Mexico has provided additional scientific data to add to those of Kaniewski and his team. Publishing in the *Journal of Archaeological Science*, he cites three additional lines of evidence that all support the view that the Early Iron Age was more arid than the preceding Bronze Age. First, oxygen-isotope data from mineral deposits (speleothems) within Soreq Cave in northern Israel indicate that there was a low annual precipitation during the transition from the Bronze Age to the Iron Age. Second, stable carbon isotope data in pollen cores from Lake Voulkaria in western Greece show that plants were adapting to arid environments at this time. Third, sediment cores from the Mediterranean reveal that there was a drop in the temperature of the surface of the sea, which in turn would have caused a reduction in precipitation on land (by reducing the temperature differential between land and sea).[36] He notes that while it "is difficult to directly identify a point in time when the climate grew more arid," the change most likely occurred before 1250–1197 BC,[37] which is precisely the time period under discussion here.

He notes also not only that there was a sharp increase in Northern Hemisphere temperatures immediately before the collapse of the Mycenaean palatial centers, possibly causing droughts, but that there was a sharp decrease in temperature during the abandonment of these centers, meaning that it first got hotter and then suddenly colder, resulting in "cooler, more arid conditions during the Greek Dark Ages." As Drake says, these climatic changes, including a decline in the surface temperature of the Mediterranean Sea before 1190 BC that resulted in less rainfall (or snow), could have dramatically affected the palatial centers, especially those that were dependent upon high levels of agricultural productivity, such as in Mycenaean Greece.[38]

Israel Finkelstein and Dafna Langgut of Tel Aviv University, in conjunction with Thomas Litt at the University of Bonn in Germany, have now added additional data to the picture. They note that fossil pollen particles from a twenty-meter-long core drilled through sediments at the bottom of the Sea of Galilee also indicate a period of severe drought beginning ca. 1250 BC in the southern Levant. A second core drilled on the western shore of the Dead Sea provided similar results, but the two cores also indicate that the drought in this region may have ended already by ca. 1100 BC, thereby allowing life to resume in the region, albeit perhaps with new peoples settling down.[39]

Nevertheless, exciting as these findings are, at this point we must also acknowledge that droughts have been frequent in this region throughout history, and that they have not always caused civilizations to collapse. Again it would seem that, on their own, climate change, drought, and famines, even if they "influenced social tensions, and eventually led to competition for limited resources," are not enough to have caused the end of the Late Bronze Age without other mitigating factors having been involved, as Drake is careful to point out.[40]

INTERNAL REBELLION

Some scholars have suggested that internal rebellions may have contributed to the turmoil at the end of the Late Bronze Age. Such revolts could have been triggered by famine, whether caused by drought or otherwise, or earthquakes or other natural disasters, or even a cutting of the international trade routes, any and all of which could have dramatically impacted the economy in the affected areas and led dissatisfied peasants or lower classes to rebel against the ruling class, in a revolution akin to that in 1917 czarist Russia.[41]

Such a scenario might be invoked to explain the destruction seen, for instance, at Hazor in Canaan, where there is no evidence for an earthquake, nor is there specific evidence for warfare or invaders. Although Yadin and Ben-Tor, two of the primary excavators of the site, have both suggested a destruction by warfare, probably at the hands of the Israelites, the other codirector of the current excavations, Sharon Zuckerman of Hebrew University in Jerusalem, has recently suggested that the destruction of Hazor Stratum IA, dating somewhere between 1230 and the early decades of the twelfth century BC, was caused by an internal rebellion of the city's inhabitants, rather than an invasion by external peoples. As she states simply, "there is no archaeological evidence of warfare, such as human victims or weapons, anywhere in the site . . . the view of the final destruction of the LBA city of Hazor as a sudden unexpected attack on a strong flourishing kingdom does not concur with the archaeological evidence."[42] She suggests instead that "mounting internal conflicts and gradual decline, culminating in the final assault on the major political and religious foci of the city's elite, provides the most plausible alternative framework for the explanation of the destruction and abandonment of Hazor."[43]

Although there is no doubting the destructions observable at the various Mycenaean palatial centers and Canaanite cities, there is, quite frankly, no way to tell whether revolting peasants were responsible. It thus remains a plausible, but unproven, hypothesis. And again, many civilizations have successfully survived internal rebellions, often even flourishing under a new regime. Thus, on its own, the hypothesis of internal rebellions is not enough to account for the collapse of the Late Bronze Age civilizations in the Aegean and Eastern Mediterranean.

(Possible) Invaders and the Collapse of International Trade

Among events that could have led to an internal rebellion, we have just glimpsed the specter of outside invaders cutting the international trade routes and upsetting fragile economies that might have been overly dependent upon foreign raw materials. Carol Bell's comparison of the strategic importance of tin in the Bronze Age to that of crude oil in today's world might be particularly apt in this hypothetical situation.[44]

However, even if an internal rebellion were not the outcome, the cutting of the trade routes could have had a severe, and immediate, impact upon Mycenaean kingdoms such as Pylos, Tiryns, and Mycenae, which needed to import both the copper and the tin needed to produce bronze, and which seem to have imported substantial quantities of additional raw materials as well, including gold, ivory, glass, ebony wood, and the terebinth resin used in making perfume. While natural disasters such as earthquakes could cause a temporary disruption in trade, potentially leading to higher prices and perhaps to what we today would call inflation, more permanent disruptions would more likely have been the result of outside invaders targeting the affected areas. However, who would these invaders have been? Or is this where we invoke the Sea Peoples?

Rather than the Sea Peoples, the ancient Greeks—ranging from historians like Herodotus and Thucydides in fifth-century BC Athens to the much-later traveler Pausanias—believed that a group known as the Dorians had invaded from the north at the end of the Bronze Age, thereby initiating the Iron Age.[45] This concept was once much discussed by archaeologists and ancient historians of the Bronze Age Aegean; among their considerations was a new type of pottery called "Handmade Burnished Ware" or "Barbarian Ware." However, in recent decades it has become clear that there was no such invasion from the north at this time and no reason to accept the idea of a "Dorian Invasion" bringing the Mycenaean civilization to an end. Despite the traditions of the later classical Greeks, it is clear that the Dorians had nothing to do with the collapse at the end of the Late Bronze Age and entered Greece only long after those events had transpired.[46]

Moreover, recent studies now indicate that even during the decline of the Mycenaean world and the early years of the succeeding Iron Age, mainland Greece may still have retained its trade connections to the Eastern Mediterranean. These connections, however, were probably no longer under the control of the elite classes who had dwelt in the Bronze Age palaces.[47]

In northern Syria, on the other hand, we have numerous documents attesting to the fact that maritime invaders attacked Ugarit during this time period. Although we have little firm evidence for the origins of these marauders, we cannot dismiss the possibility that they included the Sea Peoples. In addition, scholars have recently pointed out that many of the city-states in the Eastern Mediterranean, and Ugarit in particular, may have been hard-hit by the collapse of the international trade routes, which would have been vulnerable to depredations by maritime marauders.

Itamar Singer, for instance, has suggested that Ugarit's downfall may have been due to "the sudden collapse of the traditional structures of international trade, which were the lifeblood of Ugarit's booming economy in the Bronze Age." Christopher Monroe of Cornell University has put this into a larger context, pointing out that the wealthiest city-states in the Eastern Mediterranean were the hardest-hit by the events taking place during the twelfth century BC, since they were not only the most attractive targets for the invaders but also the most dependent on the international trade network. He suggests that dependence, or perhaps overdependence, on capitalist enterprise, and specifically long-distance trade, may have contributed to the economic instability seen at the end of the Late Bronze Age.[48]

However, we should not overlook the fact that Ugarit would have been a tempting target for both external invaders and homegrown pirates, as well as other possible groups. In this regard, we should consider again the letter from the Southern Archive, found in Court V of the palace in Ugarit (but not within a kiln), which mentions seven enemy ships that had been causing havoc in the Ugaritic lands. Whether or not these particular ships had anything to do with the final destruction of Ugarit, such enemy ships would have disrupted the international trade upon which Ugarit was vitally dependent.

When such dramatic situations occur today, it seems that everyone has a piece of advice to give. Things were no different back then, during the Late Bronze Age. One letter found at Ugarit, possibly sent by the Hittite viceroy of Carchemish, gives the Ugarit king advice on how to deal with such enemy ships. He begins, "You have written to me: 'Ships of the enemy have been seen at sea!'" and then advises: "Well, you must remain firm. Indeed, for your part, where are your troops, your chariots stationed? Are they not stationed near you? . . . Surround your cities with walls. Bring (your) infantry and chariotry into (them). Be on the lookout for the enemy and make yourself very strong!"[49]

Another letter, found in the House of Rapanu and sent by a man named Eshuwara who was the senior governor of Cyprus, is undoubtedly related. In this letter, the governor says that he is not responsible for any damage done to Ugarit or its territory by the ships, especially since it is—he claims—Ugarit's own ships and men who are committing the atrocities, and that Ugarit should be prepared to defend itself: "As for the matter concerning those enemies: (it was) the people from your country (and) your own ships (who) did this! And (it was) the people from your country (who) committed these transgressions(s) . . . I am writing to inform you and protect you. Be aware!" He then adds that there are twenty enemy ships, but that they have gone off in an unknown direction.[50]

Finally, a letter in the Urtenu archive from an official in Carchemish, located in inland northern Syria, states that the king of Carchemish was on his way from Hittite territory to Ugarit with reinforcements, and that the various people named in the letter, including Urtenu and the city elders, should try to hold out until they arrived.[51] It is unlikely that they arrived in time. If they did, they were of little use, for an additional, private letter usually thought to be one of the last communications from Ugarit describes an alarming situation: "When your messenger arrived, the army was humiliated and the city was sacked. Our food in the threshing floors was burnt and the vineyards were also destroyed. Our city is sacked. May you know it! May you know it!"[52]

As noted above, the excavators of Ugarit report that the city was burned, with a destruction level reaching two meters high in some places, and that numerous arrowheads were found scattered throughout the ruins.[53] There were also a number of hoards found buried in the city; some contained precious gold and bronze items, including figurines, weapons, and tools, some of them inscribed. All appear to have been items hidden just before the destruction took place; their owners never returned to retrieve them.[54] However, even a severe and complete destruction of the city does not explain why the survivors did not rebuild, unless there were no survivors.

Rather than complete annihilation, it may be the cutting of the trade routes, and the collapse of the international trading system as a whole, that are the most logical and complete explanations as to why Ugarit was never reoccupied after its destruction. In the words of one scholar, "The fact that Ugarit never rose from its ashes, as did other LBA cities of the Levant which suffered a similar fate, must have more substantial grounds than the destruction inflicted upon the city."[55]

However, there is a counterargument to this suggestion. Ugarit's international connections apparently continued right up until the sudden end of the city, for there is a letter from the king of Beirut sent to an Ugaritic official (the prefect) that arrived after the king of Ugarit had already fled the city.[56] In other words, Ugarit was destroyed by invaders and was never rebuilt, despite the fact that the international trade connections were at least partially if not still completely intact at the time of destruction.

In fact, what jumps out from the materials in the Rapanu and Urtenu archives is the tremendous amount of international interconnection that apparently still existed in the Eastern Mediterranean even at the end of the Late Bronze Age. Moreover, it is clear from the few texts published from the Urtenu archive that these international connections continued right up until almost the last moment before Ugarit's destruction. This seems to be a clear indication that the end was probably sudden, rather than a gradual decline after trade routes had been cut or because of drought and famine, and that Ugarit specifically was destroyed by invaders, regardless of whether these forces had also cut the international trade routes.

Decentralization and the Rise of the Private Merchant

There is one other point to be considered, which has been suggested relatively recently and may well be a reflection of current thinking about the role of decentralization in today's world.

In an article published in 1998, Susan Sherratt, now at the University of Sheffield, concluded that the Sea Peoples represent the final step in the replacement of the old centralized politico-economic systems present in the Bronze Age with the new decentralized economic systems of the Iron Age—that is, the change from kingdoms and empires that controlled the international trade to smaller city-states and individual entrepreneurs who were in business for themselves. She suggested that the Sea Peoples can "usefully be seen as a structural phenomenon, a product of the natural evolution and expansion of international trade in the 3rd and early 2nd millennium, which carried within it the seeds of the subversion of the palace-based command economies which had initiated such trade in the first place."[57]

Thus, while she concedes that the international trade routes might have collapsed, and that at least some of the Sea Peoples may have been migratory invaders, she ultimately concludes that it does not really matter where the Sea Peoples came from, or even who they were or what they did. Far more important is the sociopolitical and economic change that they represent, from a predominantly palatial-controlled economy to one in which private merchants and smaller entities had considerably more economic freedom.[58]

Although Sherratt's argument is elegantly stated, other scholars had earlier made similar suggestions. For example, Klaus Kilian, excavator of Tiryns, once wrote: "After the fall of the Mycenaean palaces, when 'private' economy had been established in Greece, contacts continued with foreign countries. The well-organized palatial system was succeeded by smaller local reigns, certainly less powerful in their economic expansion."[59]

Michal Artzy, of the University of Haifa, even gave a name to some of the private merchants envisioned by Sherratt, dubbing them "Nomads of the Sea." She suggested that they had been active as intermediaries who carried out much of the maritime trade during the fourteenth and thirteenth centuries BC.[60]

However, more recent studies have taken issue with the type of transitional worldview proposed by Sherratt. Carol Bell, for instance, respectfully disagrees, saying: "It is simplistic . . . to view the change between the LBA and the Iron Age as the replacement of palace administered exchange with entrepreneurial trade. A wholesale replacement of one paradigm for another is not a good explanation for this change and restructuring."[61]

While there is no question that privatization may have begun as a by-product of palatial trade, it is not at all clear that this privatization then ultimately undermined the very economy from which it had come.[62] At Ugarit, for example, scholars have pointed out that even though the city was clearly burned and abandoned, there is no evidence either in the texts found at the site or in the remains themselves that the destruction and collapse had been caused by decentralized entrepreneurs undermining the state and its control of international trade.[63]

In fact, combining textual observations with the fact that Ugarit was clearly destroyed by fire, and that there are weapons in the debris, we may safely reiterate that although there may have been the seeds of decentralization at Ugarit, warfare and fighting almost certainly caused the final destruction, with external invaders as the likely culprits. This is a far different scenario from that envisioned by Sherratt and her like-minded colleagues. Whether these invaders were the Sea Peoples is uncertain, however, although it is intriguing that one of the texts at Ugarit specifically mentions the Shikila/Shekelesh, known from the Sea Peoples inscriptions of Merneptah and Ramses III.

In any event, even if decentralization and private individual merchants were an issue, it seems unlikely that they caused the collapse of the Late Bronze Age, at least on their own. Instead of accepting the idea that private merchants and their enterprises undermined the Bronze Age economy, perhaps we should consider the alternative suggestion that they simply emerged out of the chaos of the collapse, as was suggested by James Muhly of the University of Pennsylvania twenty years ago. He saw the twelfth century BC not as a world dominated by "sea raiders, pirates, and freebooting mercenaries," but rather as a world of "enterprising merchants and traders, exploiting new economic opportunities, new markets, and new sources of raw materials."[64] Out of chaos comes opportunity, at least for a lucky few, as always.

Was It the Sea Peoples and Where Did They Go?

We come, finally, to a consideration of the Sea Peoples, who remain as enigmatic and elusive as ever. Whether they are seen as sea raiders or migrating populations, the archaeological and textual evidence both indicate that the Sea Peoples, despite their moniker, most likely traveled both by land and by sea—that is, by any means possible.

Those proceeding by sea would most likely have hugged the coastline, perhaps even putting in to a safe harbor every evening. However, questions remain as to whether the enemy ships mentioned in the Ugaritic texts belonged to the Sea Peoples or to renegade members of their own kingdom, as implied in the letter sent by Eshuwara, the governor of Alashiya.[65] In this regard, we should take into account the letter just mentioned, from the House of Urtenu in Ugarit, that mentions the "Shikila people," who, more likely than not, can be identified with the Shekelesh of the Egyptian records. The letter was sent by the Hittite king, probably Suppiluliuma II, to the governor of Ugarit, and refers to a young king of Ugarit, who "does not know anything." Singer, among other scholars, sees this as a probable reference to Ammurapi, who was the new king of Ugarit at the time. In the letter, the Hittite king says that he wishes to interview a man named Ibnadushu, who had been captured by the Shikila people "who live on ships," in order to find out more information about these Shikila/Shekelesh.[66] However, we do not know whether the interview ever took place or what else might have been learned from Ibnadushu.

It is generally agreed that this document contains the only specific mention by name of the Sea Peoples outside of Egyptian records, although it has also been suggested that there might be others. The "enemy from the land of Alashiya" who attacked the last Hittite king, Suppiluliuma II, on land after he had fought three sea battles against Alashiyan (i.e., Cypriot) forces is possibly a reference to the Sea Peoples. So too is an inscription found at Hattusa in 1988, which may contain an indication that Suppiluliuma II was already fighting the Sea Peoples who had landed on the southern coast of Anatolia and were advancing north.[67] Most documents and inscriptions, other than the Egyptian records, simply contain the more general phrase "enemy ships," though, and do not specifically name the Sea Peoples.

Those of the Sea Peoples who came by land possibly, and perhaps likely, proceeded along a predominantly coastal route, where the destruction of specific cities would have opened up entire new areas to them, in much the same way that Alexander the Great's battles at the Granicus River, Issus, and Gaugamela opened up specific portions of the ancient Near East to his army almost a thousand years later. Assaf Yasur-Landau of the University of Haifa has suggested that some of the Sea Peoples could have begun their journey in Greece and passed through the Dardanelles to western Turkey/Anatolia. Others—perhaps most of them, he says—would simply have begun their journey at this point, perhaps joining those coming from the Aegean, with the route continuing along the southern coast of Turkey to Cilicia at its eastern end, and then down to the southern Levant via a route running along the coast. If they followed this route, they would have encountered the city of Troy, the kingdoms of Arzawa and Tarhuntassa in Anatolia, and the cities of Tarsus and Ugarit in southeastern Anatolia and northern Syria, respectively. Some or all of these sites do show signs of destruction and/or subsequent abandonment that occurred about the time that the Sea Peoples are presumed to have been active, but it is unclear whether they were actually responsible.[68]

In fact, the archaeological evidence now seems to suggest that most of the sites in Anatolia were simply either completely or mostly abandoned at this time, rather than put to the torch by the Sea Peoples. We can speculate that if the international trade, transportation, and communication routes were disrupted by wars, famines, or other forces, the cities dependent upon these routes might have withered and died, with the result that their populations would have left gradually or fled rapidly, depending upon the speed of commercial and cultural decline. As one scholar has recently said, "while it is reasonable to assume that Cilicia and the Syrian coast were affected by the actions of the Sea Peoples, so far neither historical nor archaeological evidence for any kind of activity of the Sea Peoples in the Hittite homelands is attested . . . the real causes for the collapse of the Hittite state seem to be internal rather than external."[69]

A prime example of assigning blame without proof is the recent claim related to the radiocarbon dating at Tell Tweini, the site of the Late Bronze Age harbor town of Gibala within the kingdom of Ugarit. Here, the laboratory results led the excavators and their colleagues to conclude that they have found evidence of destruction wreaked by the Sea Peoples, and to specifically date it to 1192–1190 BC.[70] They state, without caveat: "The Sea Peoples were seaborne foes from different origins. They launched a combined land-sea invasion that destabilized the already weakened power base of empires and kingdoms of the old world, and attempted to enter or control the Egyptian territory. The Sea Peoples symbolize the last step of a long and complex spiral of decline in the ancient Mediterranean world."[71]

Although there is little doubt that the city was destroyed at about the time identified by the excavators, as confirmed by the radiocarbon dates, the attribution to the Sea Peoples as the agents of the destruction is speculative, although it is certainly quite possible. The excavators have not offered any definitive proof regarding a role for the Sea Peoples; they simply point out that the material culture of the settlement that was established on the tell after the destruction includes "the appearance of Aegean-type architecture, locally-made Mycenaean IIIC Early pottery, hand-made burnished pottery, and Aegean-type loam-weights."[72] As they state, "these materials, also known from Philistine settlements, are cultural markers of foreign settlers, most probably the Sea Peoples."[73] While Tweini could be the best example yet of a site possibly destroyed and then resettled by the Sea Peoples, we cannot say so with absolute certainty. Moreover, as Annie Caubet has noted with regard to Ras Ibn Hani (above), one cannot always be sure that the people who resettled a site after its destruction are necessarily the same ones who destroyed it in the first place.

We can further speculate that in at least some cases groups designated as the Sea Peoples might have entered the vacuum created by the destruction and/or abandonment of the cities, whether caused by themselves or others, and settled down without moving on, eventually leaving their artifacts behind them, as may have been the case at Tweini. In such circumstances, these Sea Peoples are likely to have occupied primarily, although not exclusively, the coastal cities, including sites like Tarsin and Mersin on the coast of southeastern Anatolia. The same may be true for the region now on the border between southwestern Turkey and northern Syria, in the area of Tell Ta'yinat, which recent evidence suggests became known as the "Land of Palistin" during the Iron Age.[74]

In fact, there are traditions, especially literary traditions, which specifically state that the Sea Peoples settled Tel Dor, in the north of what is now modern Israel. For example, the Egyptian story called "The Report of Wenamun," which dates to the first half of the eleventh century BC, refers to Dor as a town of the Tjekker or Sikils (Shekelesh). Another Egyptian text, the "Onomasticon of Amenemope," which dates to ca. 1100 BC, lists the Shardana, the Tjekker, and the Peleset, and also mentions the sites of Ashkelon, Ashdod, and Gaza (three of the five sites considered to be part of the Philistine "pentapolis"). Sites along the Carmel Coast and in the Akko Valley, as well as perhaps Tel Dan, have also been suggested as having been settled by the Sea Peoples, such as the Shardana and the Danuna. At many of these sites, including those with occupation levels designated as "Philistine," such as at Ashdod, Ashkelon, Gaza, Ekron, and elsewhere, degenerate Aegean-style pottery and other cultural identifiers have been found.[75] These may well be the only physical remains that we have of the elusive Sea Peoples, but the archaeological remains at many of these sites, and even farther north, seem to have more direct connections with Cyprus than with the Aegean. Nevertheless, there are clear links to non-Canaanite peoples in the twelfth century BC.[76]

Interestingly, there seem to be no such remains, nor any such destruction, in the area that came to be known as Phoenicia, in what is now modern Lebanon. Despite scholarly discussions, it is still unclear why this should be so, or whether it is simply an illusion caused by the relative lack of excavation here, compared to the other coastal regions of the Near East.[77]

Among the many scenarios suggested to explain the final days of the Late Bronze Age in the Aegean and Eastern Mediterranean, the proposal made by Israel Finkelstein of Tel Aviv University a decade ago still seems most likely. He argues that the migration of the Sea Peoples was not a single event but a long process involving several phases, with the first phase starting in the early years of Ramses III, ca. 1177 BC, and the last phase ending during the time of Ramses VI, ca. 1130 BC. He says specifically that

> despite the description in the Egyptian texts of a single event, the migration of the Sea Peoples was at least a half-century-long process that had several phases. . . . It may have started with groups that spread destruction along the Levantine coast, including northern Philistia, in the beginning of the twelfth century and that were defeated by Ramesses III in his eighth year. Consequently, some of them were settled in Egyptian garrisons in the delta. Later groups of Sea Peoples, in the second half of the twelfth century, succeeded in terminating Egyptian rule in southern Canaan. After destroying the Egyptian strongholds . . . they settled in Philistia and established their major centers at Ashdod, Ashkelon, Tel Miqne, and other places. These people—the Philistines of the later biblical text—are easily identifiable by several Aegean-derived features in their material culture.[78]

Most scholars agree with Finkelstein that the archaeological evidence seems to indicate that we should be looking primarily at the Aegean region, perhaps via the filter of western Anatolia and Cyprus as intermediate stops for some or most along the way,[79] rather than Sicily, Sardinia, and the Western Mediterranean for the origin of many of the Sea Peoples. However, Yasur-Landau suggests that if they were Mycenaeans, they were not those fleeing the ruins of their palaces, at Mycenae and elsewhere, just after those places were destroyed. He points out that there is no evidence of Linear B writing or other aspects of the wealthy palatial period from the thirteenth century BC on the Greek mainland at these Anatolian and Canaanite sites. Rather, the material culture of these settlers indicates that they were from "the rather humbler culture that came [immediately] afterward" during the early twelfth century BC. He also notes that some may even have been farmers rather than raiding warriors, looking to improve their lives by moving to a new area. Regardless, they were "an entire population of families on the move to a new home."[80] In any event, he believes that these migrants were not the cause of the collapse of the Late Bronze Age civilizations in this area but were instead "opportunists" who took advantage of the collapse to find themselves new homes.[81]

Yasur-Landau now takes issue with the traditional picture of a Philistine military takeover of Canaan. He says: "The circumstances of the settlement do not reflect a violent incursion. Recent discoveries at Ashkelon show that the migrants [actually] settled on a deserted site, on top of the unfinished remains of an Egyptian garrison. . . . There are no clear signs for any violent destruction at Ashdod . . . the signs of destruction described by the excavators [there] may be no more than evidence for cooking. . . . At Ekron, the small Canaanite village . . . was indeed destroyed by fire, but . . . [was] replaced by another Canaanite village . . . before the arrival of the migrants."[82]

Rather than a hostile military-style takeover, Yasur-Landau sees instead intercultural marriages and intercultural families, maintaining both Canaanite and Aegean traditions, mostly in the domestic arena. As he puts it, "material remains from early Iron Age Philistia reveal intricate, and predominantly peaceful, interactions between migrants and locals. . . . I would therefore venture to suggest that the general lack of violence connected with the foundation of the Philistine cities . . . and the co-existence of both Aegean and local cultural traditions indicate that these were joint foundations of Aegean migrants and local populations, rather than colonial enterprises."[83]

Other scholars agree, pointing out that, at most, the Philistines destroyed only the elite portions at some of the sites—the palace and its environs, for instance—and that the components that we now identify with the Philistines were "of a mixed nature and include features from the Aegean, Cyprus, Anatolia, Southeast Europe and beyond."[84] It does not appear that completely foreign elements simply replaced the previous Canaanite material culture lock, stock, and barrel (in terms of pottery, building practices, and so on); rather, what we now identify as Philistine culture may be the result of a hybridization and a mingling of different cultures, containing both the older local Canaanite and newer foreign intrusive elements.[85]

In other words, although there is no question that there were new peoples entering and settling down in Canaan at this time, in this reconstruction the bogeyman specter of the invading Sea Peoples/Philistines has been replaced by a somewhat more peaceful picture of a mixed group of migrants in search of a new start in a new land. Rather than militant invaders intent only on destruction, they were more likely to have been refugees who did not necessarily always attack and conquer the local peoples but frequently simply settled down among them. Either way, they are unlikely, all by themselves, to have ended civilization in the Aegean and Eastern Mediterranean.[86]

ARGUMENTS FOR A SYSTEMS COLLAPSE

In 1985, when Nancy Sandars published a revised edition of her classic book on the Sea Peoples, she wrote, "In the lands surrounding the Mediterranean, there have *always* been earthquakes, famines, droughts and floods, and in fact dark ages of a sort are recurrent." Furthermore, she stated, "catastrophes punctuate human history but they are generally survived without too much loss. They are often followed by a much greater effort leading to greater success."[87] So what was different about this period, the end of the Late Bronze Age? Why didn't the civilizations simply recover and carry on?

As Sandars mused, "many explanations have been tried and few have stood. Unparalleled series of earthquakes, widespread crop-failures and famine, massive invasion from the steppe, the Danube, the desert—all may have played some part; but they are not enough."[88] She was correct. We must now turn to the idea of a systems collapse, a systemic failure with both a domino and a multiplier effect, from which even such a globalized international, vibrant, intersocietal network as was present during the Late Bronze Age could not recover.

Colin Renfrew of Cambridge University, one of the most respected scholars ever to study the prehistoric Aegean region, had already suggested the idea of a systems collapse back in 1979. At the time, he framed it in terms of catastrophe theory, wherein "the failure of a minor element started a chain reaction that reverberated on a greater and greater scale, until finally the whole structure was brought to collapse."[89] A potentially useful metaphor that comes to mind is the so-called butterfly effect, whereby the initial flapping of a butterfly's wings may eventually result in a tornado or hurricane some weeks later on the other side of the world.[90] We might, for example, cite the attack by the Assyrian king Tukulti-Ninurta I on the vaunted Hittite forces. His defeat of their army, at the end of the thirteenth century BC during Tudhaliya IV's reign, may in turn have emboldened the neighboring Kashka to subsequently attack and burn the Hittite capital city of Hattusa.

Renfrew noted the general features of systems collapse, itemizing them as follows: (1) the collapse of the central administrative organization; (2) the disappearance of the traditional elite class; (3) a collapse of the centralized economy; and (4) a settlement shift and population decline. It might take as much as a century for all aspects of the collapse to be completed, he said, and noted that there is no single, obvious cause for the collapse. Furthermore, in the aftermath of such a collapse, there would be a transition to a lower level of sociopolitical integration and the development of "romantic" Dark Age myths about the previous period. Not only does this fit the Aegean and the Eastern Mediterranean region ca. 1200 BC, but, as he pointed out, it also describes the collapse of the Maya, Old Kingdom Egypt, and the Indus Valley civilization at various points in time.[91] As mentioned, such topics and discussions of "collapses" throughout history, and of the possibly cyclical rise and fall of empires, have subsequently been taken up by other scholars, most popularly and recently by Jared Diamond.[92]

Not surprisingly, not every scholar agrees with the idea of a systems collapse at the end of the Late Bronze Age. Robert Drews of Vanderbilt

University, for instance, dismisses it out of hand because he does not think that it explains why the palaces and cities were destroyed and burned.[93]

However, as we have seen, soon after 1200 BC, the Bronze Age civilizations collapsed in the Aegean, Eastern Mediterranean, and Near East, exhibiting all of the classic features outlined by Renfrew, from disappearance of the traditional elite class and a collapse of central administrations and centralized economies to settlement shifts, population decline, and a transition to a lower level of sociopolitical integration, not to mention the development of stories like those of the Trojan War eventually written down by Homer in the eighth century BC. More than the coming of the Sea Peoples in 1207 and 1177 BC, more than the series of earthquakes that rocked Greece and the Eastern Mediterranean during a fifty-year span from 1225 to 1175 BC, more than the drought and climate change that may have been ravaging these areas during this period, what we see are the results of a "perfect storm" that brought down the flourishing cultures and peoples of the Bronze Age—from the Mycenaeans and Minoans to the Hittites, Assyrians, Kassites, Cypriots, Mitannians, Canaanites, and even Egyptians.[94]

In my opinion, and Sandars's before me, none of these individual factors would have been cataclysmic enough on their own to bring down even one of these civilizations, let alone all of them. However, they could have combined to produce a scenario in which the repercussions of each factor were magnified, in what some scholars have called a "multiplier effect."[95] The failure of one part of the system might also have had a domino effect, leading to failures elsewhere. The ensuing "systems collapse" could have led to the disintegration of one society after another, in part because of the fragmentation of the global economy and the breakdown of the interconnections upon which each civilization was dependent.

In 1987, Mario Liverani, of the University of Rome, laid the blame upon the concentration of power and control in the palaces, so that when they collapsed, the extent of the disaster was magnified. As he wrote, "the particular concentration in the Palace of all the elements of organization, transformation, exchange, etc.—a concentration which seems to reach its maximum in the Late Bronze Age—has the effect of transforming the physical collapse of the Palace into a general disaster for the entire kingdom."[96] In other words, to put it in modern investment terms, the Bronze Age rulers in the Aegean and the Near East should have diversified their portfolios, but they did not.

Two decades later, Christopher Monroe cited Liverani's work and suggested that the economy of the Late Bronze Age became unstable because of its increasing dependency on bronze and other prestige goods. Specifically, he saw "capitalist enterprise"—in which he included long-distance trade, and which dominated the palatial system present in the Late Bronze Age—as having transformed traditional Bronze Age modes of exchange, production, and consumption to such an extent that when external invasions and natural catastrophes combined in a "multiplier effect," the system was unable to survive.[97]

In writing about the situation at the end of the Late Bronze Age in his book *Scales of Fate*, Monroe describes the interactions of the various powers in the Aegean and Eastern Mediterranean as an "intersocietal network," which agrees with the picture presented here. He points out, as I have, that this period is "exceptional in the treaties, laws, diplomacy, and exchange that created the first great international era in world history."[98]

However, most interestingly, Monroe further notes that such networks have ways of postponing the inevitable collapse, which comes to all societies eventually. As he says, "revolts are quelled, raw materials are found, new markets are opened, price controls are put into effect, merchants' properties are confiscated, embargoes [are] placed, and war is waged."[99] He also says, though, that "generally the rulers of the core power or powers treat the symptoms rather than the causes of instability," and concludes that the "violent destruction of the Late Bronze palatial civilization, as attested in the textual and archaeological record, was, like many collapses, the inevitable result of limited foresight."[100]

I am in agreement with Monroe up until this last point, for I do not think that we are justified in blaming the collapse simply on "limited foresight," given the multiple probable factors explored above, which the ancient leaders could not possibly have completely predicted. An unanticipated systems collapse—quite possibly triggered by climate change, as hypothesized recently by Brandon Drake and the team led by David Kaniewski,[101] or precipitated by earthquakes or invasion— seems much more likely, but Monroe's words might serve as something of a warning for us today, for his description of the Late Bronze Age, especially in terms of its economy and interactions, could well apply to our current globalized society, which is also feeling the effects of climate change.

A Review of Possibilities and Complexity Theory

As noted at the beginning of this chapter, the so-called Collapse or Catastrophe at the end of the Late Bronze Age has been much discussed by scholars. Robert Drews tried to attack this problem systematically, devoting each chapter in his 1993 book to a discussion of a different potential cause. However, he may have misjudged and underestimated some of these; for instance, he dismissed out of hand the idea of a systems collapse, in favor of his own theory that changes in warfare were actually responsible—a hypothesis upon which not all scholars agree.[102]

Now, twenty years after the publication of Drews's book, and even after all of the continuous debate and constant stream of academic publications on the topic, there is still no general consensus as to who, or what, caused the destruction or abandonment of each of the major sites within the civilizations that came to an end in the twilight of the Bronze Age. The problem can be concisely summarized as follows:

Major Observations

1. We have a number of separate civilizations that were flourishing during the fifteenth to thirteenth centuries BC in the Aegean and Eastern Mediterranean, from the Mycenaeans and the Minoans to the Hittites, Egyptians, Babylonians, Assyrians, Canaanites, and Cypriots. These were independent but consistently interacted with each other, especially through international trade routes.

2. It is clear that many cities were destroyed and that the Late Bronze Age civilizations and life as the inhabitants knew it in the Aegean, Eastern Mediterranean, Egypt, and the Near East came to an end ca. 1177 BC or soon thereafter.

3. No unequivocal proof has been offered as to who or what caused this disaster, which resulted in the collapse of these civilizations and the end of the Late Bronze Age.

Discussion of Possibilities

There are a number of possible causes that may have led, or contributed, to the collapse at the end of the Late Bronze Age, but none seems capable of having caused the calamity on its own.

A. Clearly there were earthquakes during this period, but usually societies can recover from these.

B. There is textual evidence for famine, and now scientific evidence for droughts and climate change, in both the Aegean and the Eastern Mediterranean, but again societies have recovered from these time and time again.

C. There may be circumstantial evidence for internal rebellions in Greece and elsewhere, including the Levant, although this is not certain. Again, societies frequently survive such revolts. Moreover, it would be unusual (notwithstanding recent experience in the Middle East to the contrary) for rebellions to occur over such a wide area and for such a prolonged period of time.

D. There is archaeological evidence for invaders, or at least newcomers probably from the Aegean region, western Anatolia, Cyprus, or all of the above, found in the Levant from Ugarit in the north to Lachish in the south. Some of the cities were destroyed and then abandoned; others were reoccupied; and still others were unaffected.

E. It is clear that the international trade routes were affected, if not completely cut, for a period of time, but the extent to which this would have impacted the various individual civilizations is not altogether clear—even if some were overly dependent upon foreign goods for their survival, as has been suggested in the case of the Mycenaeans.

It is true that sometimes a civilization cannot recover from invaders or an earthquake, or survive a drought or a rebellion, but at the moment, for lack of a better explanation, it looks as though the best solution is to suggest that all of these factors together contributed to the collapse of what had been the dominant Late Bronze Age kingdoms and societies in these regions. Based on the evidence presently available, therefore, we may be seeing the result of a systems collapse that was caused by a series of events linked together via a "multiplier effect," in which one factor affected the others, thereby magnifying the effects of each. Perhaps the inhabitants could have survived one disaster, such as an earthquake or a drought, but they could not survive the combined effects of earthquake, drought, and invaders all occurring in rapid succession. A "domino effect" then ensued, in which the disintegration of one civilization led to the fall of the others. Given the globalized nature of their world, the effect upon the international trade routes and economies of even one society's collapse would have been sufficiently devastating that it could have led to the demise of the others. If such were the case, they were not too big to fail.

However, despite my comments above, systems collapse might be just too simplistic an explanation to accept as the entire reason for the ending of the Late Bronze Age in the Aegean, Eastern Mediterranean, and Near East.[103] It is possible that we need to turn to what is called complexity science, or, perhaps more accurately, complexity theory, in order to get a grasp of what may have led to the collapse of these civilizations.

Complexity science or theory is the study of a complex system or systems, with the goal of explaining "the phenomena which emerge from a collection of interacting objects." It has been used in attempts to explain, and sometimes solve, problems as diverse as traffic jams, stock market crashes, illnesses such as cancer, environmental change, and even wars, as Neil Johnson of Oxford University has recently written.[104] While it has made its way from the realm of mathematics and computational science to international relations, business, and other fields over the past several decades, it has only rarely been applied in the field of archaeology. Intriguingly, and perhaps presciently, Carol Bell explored the topic briefly in her 2006 book on the evolution of, and changes in, long-distance trading relationships in the Levant from the Late Bronze Age to the Iron Age. She noted that it was a promising theoretical approach that might be of use as an explanatory model for the cause of the collapse and for the restructuring that followed.[105]

For a problem to be a potential candidate for a complexity theory approach, Johnson states that it has to involve a system that "contains a collection of many interacting objects or 'agents.'"[106] In our case, those would be the various civilizations active during the Late Bronze Age: the Mycenaeans, Minoans, Hittites, Egyptians, Canaanites, Cypriots, and so on. In one aspect of complexity theory, behavior of those objects is affected by their memories and "feedback" from what has happened in the past. They are able to adapt their strategies, partly on the basis of their knowledge of previous history. Automobile drivers, for example, are generally familiar with the traffic patterns in their home area and are able to predict the fastest route to take to work or back home again. If a traffic jam arises, they are able to take alternative routes to avoid the problem.[107] Similarly, toward the end of the Late Bronze Age, seafaring merchants from Ugarit or elsewhere might have taken steps to avoid enemy ships or areas in which such ships and marauders were frequently based, including the coastal portions of the Lukka lands (i.e., the region later known as Lycia, in southwestern Anatolia).

Johnson also states that the system is typically "alive," meaning that it evolves in a nontrivial and often complicated way, and that it is also "open," meaning that it can be influenced by its environment. As he puts it, this means that the complicated stock markets today, about which analysts often talk as if they were living, breathing organisms, can be influenced or driven by outside news about the earnings of a particular company or an event on the other side of the world. Just so, Sherratt—in her analogy published a decade ago, and quoted above in the preface—described the similarities between the Late Bronze Age world and our own "increasingly homogenous yet uncontrollable global economy and culture, in which . . . political uncertainties on one side of the world can drastically affect the economies of regions thousands of miles away."[108] Such influences or stressors on the "system" in the Aegean and Eastern Mediterranean at the end of the Late Bronze Age might well be the probable, possible, and conceivable earthquakes, famine, drought, climate change, internal rebellion, external invasion, and cutting of the trade routes discussed above.

The most important premise, we might argue, is that Johnson asserts that such a system exhibits phenomena that "are generally surprising, and may be extreme." As he says, this "basically means that anything can happen—and if you wait long enough, it generally will." For example, as he notes, all stock markets will eventually have some sort of crash, and all traffic systems will eventually have some kind of jam. These are generally unexpected when they arise, and could not have been specifically predicted in advance, even though one knew full well that they could and would occur.[109]

In our case, since there has never been a civilization in the history of the world that hasn't collapsed eventually, and since the reasons are frequently the same, as Jared Diamond and a host of others have pointed out, the eventual collapse of the Late Bronze Age civilizations was predictable, but it is unlikely that we would have been able to predict when it would happen, or that they would all collapse at the same time, even with a full working knowledge of each civilization. As Johnson writes, "even a detailed knowledge of the specifications of a car's engine, colour and shape, is useless when trying to predict where and when traffic jams will arise in a new road system. Likewise, understanding individuals' personalities in a crowded bar would give little indication as to what large-scale brawls might develop."[110]

So what use might complexity theory be in the effort to explain the collapse at the end of the Late Bronze Age, if it cannot help us predict when it would happen or why? Carol Bell pointed out that the trading networks of the Aegean and Eastern Mediterranean are examples of complex systems. She therefore cited the work of Ken Dark, of the University of Reading, who noted that "as such systems become more complex, and the degree of interdependence between their constituent parts grows, keeping the overall system stable becomes more difficult."[111] Known as "hyper-coherence," this occurs, as Dark says, "when each part of the system becomes so dependent upon each other that change in any part produces instability in the system as a whole."[112] Thus, if the Late Bronze Age civilizations were truly globalized and dependent upon each other for goods and services, even just to a certain extent, then change to any one of the relevant kingdoms, such as the Mycenaeans or the Hittites, would potentially affect and destabilize them all.

Moreover, it is especially relevant that the kingdoms, empires, and societies of the Late Bronze Age Aegean and Eastern Mediterranean can each be seen as an individual sociopolitical system. As Dark says, such "complex socio-political systems will exhibit an internal dynamic which leads them to increase in complexity. . . . [T]he more complex a system is, the more liable it is to collapse."[113]

Thus, in the Late Bronze Age Aegean and Eastern Mediterranean, we have individual sociopolitical systems, the various civilizations, that were growing more complex and thus apparently more liable to collapse. At the same time, we have complex systems, the trading networks, that were both interdependent and complicated in their relationships, and thus were open to instability the minute there was a change in one of the integral parts. Here is where one malfunctioning cog in an otherwise well-oiled machine might turn the entire apparatus into a pile of junk, just as a single thrown rod can wreck the engine of a car today.

Therefore, rather than envisioning an apocalyptic ending overall—although perhaps certain cities and kingdoms like Ugarit met a dramatic, blazing end—we might better imagine that the end of the Late Bronze Age was more a matter of a chaotic although gradual disintegration of areas and places that had once been major and in contact with each other, but were now diminished and isolated, like Mycenae, because of internal and/or external changes that affected one or more of the integral parts of the complex system. It is clear that such damage would have led to a disruption of the network. We might picture a modern power grid that has been disrupted, perhaps by a storm or an earthquake, wherein the electric company can still produce power but cannot get it out to the individual consumers; we see such events on an annual basis in the United States, caused by anything and everything from tornadoes in Oklahoma to snowstorms in Massachusetts. If the disruption is permanent, as might be the case in a major catastrophe, such as a nuclear explosion today, eventually even the production of the electricity will halt. The analogy may hold for the Late Bronze Age, albeit at a lower technological level.

Moreover, as Bell noted, the consequence of such instability is that when the complex system does collapse, it "decomposes into smaller entities," which is exactly what we see in the Iron Age that follows the end of these Bronze Age civilizations.[114] Thus, it seems that employing complexity theory, which allows us to take both catastrophe theory and systems collapse one step further, may be the best approach to explaining the end of the Late Bronze Age in the Aegean and Eastern Mediterranean in the years following 1200 BC. The real questions are not so much "Who did it?" or "What event caused it?"—for there seem to have been any number of elements and people involved—as "Why did it happen?" and "How did it happen?" Whether it could have been avoided is yet another question entirely.

However, in suggesting that complexity theory should be brought to bear on the analysis of the causes of the Late Bronze Age collapse, we may just be applying a scientific (or possibly pseudoscientific) term to a situation in which there is insufficient knowledge to draw firm conclusions. It sounds nice, but does it really advance our understanding? Is it more than just a fancy way to state a fairly obvious fact, namely, that complicated things can break down in a variety of ways?

There is little doubt that the collapse of the Late Bronze Age civilizations was complex in its origins. We do know that many possible variables may have had a contributing role in the collapse, but we are not even certain that we know all of the variables and we undoubtedly do not know which ones were critical—or whether some were locally important but had little systemic effect. To carry our analogy of a modern traffic jam further: we do know most of the variables in a traffic jam. We know something about the number of cars and the roads they traveled along (whether wide or narrow) and we are certainly able to predict to a large extent the effect of some external variables, for example, a blizzard on a major thruway. But for the Late Bronze Age, we suspect, though we do not know for certain, that there were hundreds more variables than there are in a modern traffic system.

Moreover, the argument that the Bronze Age civilizations were increasing in complexity and were therefore prone to collapse does not really make all that much sense, especially when one considers their "complexity" relative to that of the Western European civilizations of the last three hundred years. Thus, while it is possible that complexity theory might be a useful way to approach the collapse of the Late Bronze Age once we have more information available as to the details of all the relevant civilizations, it may not be of much use at this stage, except as an interesting way to reframe our awareness that a multitude of factors were present at the end of the Late Bronze Age that could have helped destabilize, and ultimately led to the collapse of, the international system that had been in place, functioning quite well at various levels, for several previous centuries.

And yet, scholarly publications still continue to suggest a linear progression for the collapse of the Late Bronze Age, despite the fact that it is not accurate to simply state that a drought caused famine, which eventually caused the Sea Peoples to start moving and creating havoc, which caused the Collapse.[115] The progression wasn't that linear; the reality was much more messy. There probably was not a single driving force or trigger, but rather a number of different stressors, each of which forced the people to react in different ways to accommodate the changing situation(s). Complexity theory, especially in terms of visualizing a nonlinear progression and a series of stressors rather than a single driver, is therefore advantageous both in explaining the collapse at the end of the Late Bronze Age and in providing a way forward for continuing to study this catastrophe.

THE AFTERMATH

• • • • •

We have seen that for more than three hundred years during the Late Bronze Age—from about the time of Hatshepsut's reign beginning about 1500 BC until the time that everything collapsed after 1200 BC—the Mediterranean region played host to a complex international world in which Minoans, Mycenaeans, Hittites, Assyrians, Babylonians, Mitannians, Canaanites, Cypriots, and Egyptians all interacted, creating a cosmopolitan and globalized world system such as has only rarely been seen before the current day. It may have been this very internationalism that contributed to the apocalyptic disaster that ended the Bronze Age. The cultures of the Near East, Egypt, and Greece seem to have been so intertwined and interdependent by 1177 BC that the fall of one ultimately brought down the others, as, one after another, the flourishing civilizations were destroyed by acts of man or nature, or a lethal combination of both.

However, even after all that has been said, we must acknowledge our inability to determine with certainty the precise cause (or multitude of causes) for the collapse of civilizations and the transition from the end of the Late Bronze Age to the Iron Age in the Aegean and Eastern Mediterranean, or even to definitively identify the origins and motivations of the Sea Peoples. Nevertheless, if we pull together the threads of evidence that have been presented throughout our discussions, there are some things that we can say about this pivotal period with relative confidence.

For instance, we have reasonably good evidence that at least some international contacts and perhaps trade continued right up until the sudden end of the era, and possibly even beyond (if recent studies are any indication).[1] This is shown, for instance, by the last letters in the Ugarit archives documenting contacts with Cyprus, Egypt, the Hittites, and the Aegean, as well as by the gifts sent by the Egyptian pharaoh Merneptah to the king of Ugarit just a few decades, at most, before the city was destroyed. At the very least, there is no evidence of a discernible decrease in contact and trade—except perhaps for momentary fluctuations in intensity—across the Aegean and Eastern Mediterranean until the troubles began.

But then, the world as they had known it for more than three centuries collapsed and essentially vanished. As we have seen, the end of the Late Bronze Age in the Aegean and Eastern Mediterranean regions, an area that extended from Italy and Greece to Egypt and Mesopotamia, was a fluid event, taking place over the course of several decades and perhaps even up to a century, not an occurrence tied to a specific year. But the eighth year of the reign of the Egyptian pharaoh Ramses III—1177 BC, to be specific, according to the chronology currently used by most modern Egyptologists—stands out and is the most representative of the entire collapse. For it was in that year, according to the Egyptian records, that the Sea Peoples came sweeping through the region, wreaking havoc for a second time. It was a year when great land and sea battles were fought in the Nile delta; a year when Egypt struggled for its very survival; a year by which time some of the high-flying civilizations of the Bronze Age had already come to a crashing halt.

In fact, one might argue that 1177 BC is to the end of the Late Bronze Age as AD 476 is to the end of Rome and the western Roman Empire. That is to say, both are dates to which modern scholars can conveniently point as the end of a major era. Italy was invaded and Rome was sacked several times during the fifth century AD, including in AD 410 by Alaric and the Visigoths and in AD 455 by Geiseric and the Vandals. There were also many other reasons why Rome fell, in addition to these attacks, and the story is much more complex, as any Roman historian will readily attest. However, it is convenient, and considered acceptable academic shorthand, to link the invasion by Odoacer and the Ostragoths in AD 476 with the end of Rome's glory days.

The end of the Late Bronze Age and the transition to the Iron Age is a similar case, insofar as the collapse and transition was a rolling event, taking place between approximately 1225 and 1175 BC or, in some places, as late as 1130 BC. However, the second invasion by the Sea Peoples, ending in their cataclysmic fight against the Egyptians under Ramses III during the eighth year of his reign, in 1177 BC, is a reasonable benchmark and allows us to put a finite date on a rather elusive pivotal moment and the end of an age. We can say with certainty that the far-reaching civilizations that were still flourishing in the Aegean and the ancient Near East in 1225 BC had begun to vanish by 1177 BC and were almost completely gone by 1130 BC. The mighty Bronze Age kingdoms and empires were gradually replaced by smaller city-states during the following Early Iron Age. Consequently, our picture of the Mediterranean and Near Eastern world of 1200 BC is quite different from that of 1100 BC and completely different from that of 1000 BC.

We have firm evidence that it took decades, and even centuries in some areas, for the people in these regions to rebuild and reclaim their societies, and to forge new lives that would bring them back up out of the darkness into which they had been plunged. Jack Davis of the University of Cincinnati has pointed out, for instance, that "the destruction to the Palace of Nestor ca. 1180 BC was so devastating that neither the palace nor the community subsequently recovered. . . . The area of the Mycenaean kingdom of Pylos remained, as a whole in fact, severely depopulated for nearly a millennium."[2] Joseph Maran, of the University of Heidelberg, has further noted that, although we don't know how contemporaneous the final destructions actually were in Greece, it is clear that after the catastrophes were over, "there were no palaces, the use of writing as well as all administrative structures came to an end, and the concept of a supreme ruler, the *wanax*, disappeared from the range of political institutions of Ancient Greece."[3] In terms of literacy and writing, the same holds true for Ugarit and the other entities that had flourished in the Eastern Mediterranean during the Late Bronze Age, for with their end came also the end of cuneiform writing in the Levant, replaced by other, perhaps more useful or convenient, writing systems.[4]

In addition to the artifacts, it is through writing that we have tangible, concrete evidence for the interconnectedness and globalization of these regions during those years, particularly in terms of explicit relationships between the specific individuals named in the letters. Especially important are the archive of letters at Amarna in Egypt, from the time of the pharaohs Amenhotep III and Akhenaten in the mid-fourteenth century BC, the archives at Ugarit in north Syria during the late thirteenth and early twelfth centuries, and those at Hattusa in Anatolia during the fourteenth–twelfth centuries. The letters in these various archives document the fact that numerous types of networks were in simultaneous existence in the Aegean and Eastern Mediterranean region during the

Late Bronze Age, including diplomatic networks, commercial networks, transportation networks, and communication networks, all of which were needed to keep the globalized economy of that time functioning and flowing smoothly. The cutting, or even partial dismantling, of those related networks would have had a disastrous effect back then, just as it would on our world today.

However, as was the case with the fall of the western Roman Empire, the end of the Bronze Age empires in the Eastern Mediterranean was not the result of a single invasion or cause, but came about because of multiple incursions and manifold reasons. Many of the same invaders responsible for the destructions in 1177 BC had been active during the reign of Pharaoh Merneptah in 1207 BC, thirty years earlier. Earthquakes, drought, and other natural disasters had also ravaged the Aegean and Eastern Mediterranean for decades. Therefore, no single incident can really be imagined to have brought about the end of the Bronze Age; rather, the end must have come as the consequence of a complex series of events that reverberated throughout the interconnected kingdoms and empires of the Aegean and Eastern Mediterranean and eventually led to a collapse of the entire system, as we have seen.

In addition to the loss of populations and the collapse of ordinary buildings and palaces alike, it seems likely that there was a loss, or at least a significant decline, in the relationships among the various kingdoms of the region. Even if not all of the places crashed and collapsed at exactly the same time, by the mid-twelfth century BC they had lost their interconnectedness and the globalization that had existed, especially during the fourteenth and thirteenth centuries BC. As Marc Van De Mieroop of Columbia University has said, the elites lost the international framework and the diplomatic contacts that had supported them, at the same time as foreign goods and ideas stopped arriving.[5] They now had to start afresh.

When the world emerged from the collapse of the Bronze Age, it was indeed a new age, including new opportunities for growth, particularly with the demise of the Hittites and the decline of the Egyptians, who, in addition to ruling their own regions, had also between them controlled most of Syria and Canaan for much of the Late Bronze Age.[6] Although there was a certain amount of continuity in some areas, particularly with the Neo-Assyrians in Mesopotamia, overall it was time for a new set of powers and a fresh start with new civilizations, including the Neo-Hittites in southeastern Anatolia, north Syria, and points farther east; the Phoenicians, Philistines, and Israelites in what had once been Canaan; and the Greeks in geometric, archaic, and then classical Greece. Out of the ashes of the old world came the alphabet and other inventions, not to mention a dramatic increase in the use of iron, which gave its name to the new era—the Iron Age. It is a cycle that the world has seen time and time again, and that many have come to believe is an inexorable process: the rise and fall of empires, followed by the rise of new empires, which eventually fall and are replaced in turn by even newer empires, in a repeated cadence of birth, growth and evolution, decay or destruction, and ultimately renewal in a new form.

One of the most interesting, and fertile, fields of current research on the ancient world lies in the consideration of what happens after civilizations collapse, "beyond collapse," but this is a topic for another book.[7] An example of this research is the work of William Dever, professor emeritus at the University of Arizona and Distinguished Professor of Near Eastern Archaeology at Lycoming College, who said of the ensuing period in the region of Canaan: "Perhaps the most important conclusion to be drawn about the 'Dark Age' . . . is that it was nothing of the sort. Gradually being illuminated by archaeological discovery and research, [this period] emerges rather as the catalyst of a new age—one that would build upon the ruins of Canaanite civilization and would bequeath to the modern Western world a cultural heritage, especially through the Phoenicians and Israelites, of which we are still the benefactors."[8]

Moreover, as Christopher Monroe has stated, "all civilizations eventually experience violent restructuring of material and ideological realities such as destruction or re-creation."[9] We see this in the constant rise and fall of empires over time, including the Akkadians, Assyrians, Babylonians, Hittites, Neo-Assyrians, Neo-Babylonians, Persians, Macedonians, Romans, Mongols, Ottomans, and others, and we should not think that our current world is invulnerable, for we are in fact more susceptible than we might wish to think. While the 2008 collapse of Wall Street in the United States pales in comparison to the collapse of the entire Late Bronze Age Mediterranean world, there were those who warned that something similar could take place if the banking institutions with a global reach were not bailed out immediately. For instance, the *Washington Post* quoted Robert B. Zoellick, then the president of the World Bank, as saying that "the global financial system may have reached a 'tipping point,'" which he defined as "the moment when a crisis cascades into a full-blown meltdown and becomes extremely difficult for governments to contain."[10] In a complex system such as our world today, this is all it might take for the overall system to become destabilized, leading to a collapse.

WHAT IF?

The period of the Late Bronze Age has rightfully been hailed as one of the golden ages in the history of the world, and as a period during which an early global economy successfully flourished. So we might ask, would the history of the world have taken a different turn, or followed a different path, if the civilizations in these regions had not come to an end? What if the series of earthquakes in Greece and the Eastern Mediterranean had not taken place? What if there had been no drought, no famine, no migrants or invaders? Would the Late Bronze Age have eventually come to an end anyway, since all civilizations seem to rise and fall? Would any of the developments that followed have eventually come about no matter what? Would progress have continued? Would additional advances in technology, literature, and politics have been made centuries earlier than they actually were?

Of course, these are rhetorical questions, and ones that cannot be answered, because the Bronze Age civilizations *did* come to an end and development *did* essentially have to begin completely anew in areas from Greece to the Levant and beyond. As a result, new peoples and/or new city-states like the Israelites, Aramaeans, and Phoenicians in the Eastern Mediterranean, and later the Athenians and Spartans in Greece, were able to establish themselves. From them eventually came fresh developments and innovative ideas, such as the alphabet, monotheistic religion, and eventually democracy. Sometimes it takes a large-scale wildfire to help renew the ecosystem of an old-growth forest and allow it to thrive afresh.

··✤ DRAMATIS PERSONAE ✤··
(Listed in Alphabetical Order)

The chronology for Egyptian regnal dates follows the most commonly accepted scheme, for which see, for example, Kitchen 1982 and Clayton 1994. The following list does not include all names mentioned in the text, but rather those of the major rulers and related personnel.

Adad-nirari I: King of Assyria; ruled 1307–1275 BC. Conquered kingdom of Mitanni.

Ahmose: Egyptian queen, Eighteenth Dynasty; ca. 1520 BC. Wife of Thutmose I and mother of Hatshepsut.

Ahmose I: Pharaoh and founder of the Eighteenth Dynasty; ruled 1570–1546 BC. Responsible, along with his brother Kamose, for expelling the foreign Hyksos from Egypt.

Akhenaten: Heretic pharaoh, Eighteenth Dynasty; ruled 1353–1334 BC. Banned all gods and goddess except for Aten; possible monotheist. Husband of Nefertiti; father of Tutankhamen.

Amenhotep III: Pharaoh, Eighteenth Dynasty; ruled 1391–1353 BC. Extensive correspondence with fellow royal rulers found at the site of Amarna; established trade connections as far away as Mesopotamia and the Aegean.

Ammistamru I: King of Ugarit; ruled ca. 1360 BC. Corresponded with the Egyptian pharaohs.

Ammistamru II: King of Ugarit; ruled 1260–1235 BC. In charge during the time that Sinaranu sent his ship from Ugarit to Crete.

Ammurapi: Last king of Ugarit; ruled ca. 1215–1190/85 BC.

Ankhsenamen: Egyptian queen, Eighteenth Dynasty; ca. 1330 BC. Daughter of Akhenaten and wife of Tutankhamen.

Apophis: Hyksos king; ruled in Egypt ca. 1574 BC as part of the Fifteenth Dynasty. Quarreled with Seknenre, the Egyptian pharaoh ruling simultaneously elsewhere in the country.

Assur-uballit I: King of Assyria; ruled 1363–1328 BC. Corresponded with Amarna pharaohs; major player in the world of realpolitik.

Ay: Pharaoh, Eighteenth Dynasty; ruled 1325–1321 BC. Military man who became pharaoh by marrying Ankhsenamen after the death of Tutankhamen.

Burna-Buriash II: Kassite king of Babylon; ruled 1359–1333 BC. Corresponded with Amarna pharaohs.

Hammurabi: King of Babylon; ruled 1792–1750 BC. Renowned for his law code.

Hatshepsut: Egyptian queen/pharaoh, Eighteenth Dynasty; ruled 1504–1480 BC. Came to the throne as regent for her stepson Thutmose III; ruled as pharaoh for approximately twenty years.

Hattusili I: Hittite king; ruled 1650–1620 BC. Probably responsible for moving the Hittite capital to Hattusa.

Hattusili III: Hittite king; ruled 1267–1237 BC. Signed peace treaty with Egyptian pharaoh Ramses II.

Idadda: King of Qatna; presumably defeated by Hanutti, commander in chief of the Hittite army under Suppiluliuma I, ca. 1340 BC.

Kadashman-Enlil I: Kassite king of Babylon; ruled ca. 1374–1360 BC. Corresponded with Amarna pharaohs; daughter married Egyptian pharaoh Amenhotep III.

Kamose: Pharaoh; last king of the Seventeenth Dynasty; ruled 1573–1570 BC. Responsible, along with his brother Ahmose, for expelling the foreign Hyksos from Egypt.

Kashtiliashu IV: Kassite king of Babylon; ruled ca. 1232–1225 BC. Defeated by Tukulti-Ninurta I of Assyria.

Khyan: Hyksos king, Fifteenth Dynasty; ruled ca. 1600 BC. One of the best known of the Hyksos kings; items with his name inscribed on them have been found in Anatolia, Mesopotamia, and the Aegean region.

Kukkuli: King of Assuwa in northwestern Anatolia; ruled ca. 1430 BC. Initiated Assuwan Rebellion against the Hittites.

Kurigalzu I: Kassite king of Babylon; ruled ca. 1400–1375 BC. Corresponded with Amarna pharaohs; daughter married Egyptian pharaoh Amenhotep III.

Kurigalzu II: Kassite king of Babylon; ruled ca. 1332–1308 BC. Puppet king who was placed on the throne by Assur-uballit I of Assyria.

Kushmeshusha: King of Cyprus; ruled early twelfth century BC; a letter from this king was found in the House of Urtenu at Ugarit.

Manetho: Egyptian priest who lived and wrote during the Hellenistic period, in the third century BC.

Merneptah: Pharaoh, Nineteenth Dynasty; ruled 1212–1202 BC. Best known for his stele mentioning Israel and for fighting the first wave of the Sea Peoples.

Mursili I: Hittite king; ruled 1620–1590 BC. Destroyed Babylon in 1595 BC, bringing an end to Hammurabi's dynasty.

Mursili II: Hittite king; ruled 1321–1295 BC. Son of Suppiluliuma I; wrote *Plague Prayers* and other historically important documents.

Muwattalli II: Hittite king; ruled 1295–1272 BC. Fought against Egyptian pharaoh Ramses II at the battle of Qadesh.

Nefertiti: Egyptian queen, Eighteenth Dynasty; ruled ca. 1350 BC. Married to Akhenaten, the heretic pharaoh; may have been a power behind the throne.

Niqmaddu II: King of Ugarit; ruled ca. 1350–1315 BC. Corresponded with the Egyptian pharaohs during the Amarna Period.

Niqmaddu III: Penultimate king of Ugarit; ruled ca. 1225–1215 BC.

Niqmepa: King of Ugarit; ruled ca. 1313–1260 BC. Son of Niqmaddu II and father of Ammistamru II.

Ramses II: Pharaoh, Nineteenth Dynasty; ruled 1279–1212 BC. Opponent of Hittite king Muwattalli II at the battle of Qadesh and later cosignatory of peace treaty with Hattusili III.

Ramses III: Pharaoh, Twentieth Dynasty; ruled 1184–1153 BC. Fought against the second wave of Sea Peoples; assassinated in a harem conspiracy.

Saushtatar: King of Mitanni; ruled ca. 1430 BC. Expanded the Mitannian kingdom by attacking the Assyrians and may have fought against the Hittites.

Seknenre: Pharaoh, Seventeenth Dynasty; ruled ca. 1574 BC. Probably killed in battle, with at least one mortal head wound visible.

Shattiwaza: King of Mitanni; ruled ca. 1340 BC. Son of Tushratta.

Shaushgamuwa: King of Amurru, on northern coast of Syria; ruled ca. 1225 BC. Signed treaty with Hittites in late thirteenth century BC, mentioning Ahhiyawa.

Shutruk-Nahhunte: Elamite king in southwestern Iran; ruled 1190–1155 BC. Related to the Kassite dynasty ruling Babylon, he attacked the city and overthrew its king in 1158 BC.

Shuttarna II: King of Mitanni; ruled ca. 1380 BC. Corresponded with Amarna pharaohs; daughter married Egyptian pharaoh Amenhotep III.

Sinaranu: Merchant in Ugarit; ca. 1260 BC. Sent ship(s) to Minoan Crete; exempt from taxation.

Suppiluliuma I: Hittite king; ruled ca. 1350–1322 BC. Powerful king; expanded Hittite holdings throughout much of Anatolia and down into northern Syria. Corresponded with Egyptian queen who requested one of his sons as her husband.

Suppiluliuma II: Last Hittite king; ruled ca. 1207 BC onward. Fought several naval battles and invaded Cyprus during his reign.

Tarkhundaradu: King of Arzawa, in southwestern Anatolia; ruled ca. 1360 BC. Corresponded with Amarna pharaohs; daughter married Egyptian pharaoh Amenhotep III.

Thutmose I: Pharaoh, Eighteenth Dynasty; ruled 1524–1518 BC. Father of Hatshepsut and Thutmose II.

Thutmose II: Pharaoh, Eighteenth Dynasty; ruled 1518–1504 BC. Half brother and husband of Hatshepshut; father of Thutmose III.

Thutmose III: Pharaoh, Eighteenth Dynasty; ruled 1479–1450 BC. One of the most powerful Egyptian pharaohs; fought the battle of Megiddo during the first year of his reign.

Tiyi: Egyptian queen, eighteenth Dynasty; ruled ca. 1375 BC. Wife of Amenhotep III; mother of Akhenaten.

Tudhaliya I/II: Hittite king; ruled ca. 1430 BC. Put down the Assuwan Rebellion, dedicating Mycenaean sword(s) at Hattusa afterward.

Tudhaliya IV: Hittite king; ruled 1237–1209 BC. Responsible for the sanctuary at Yazlikaya, near Hattusa.

Tukulti-Ninurta I: King of Assyria; ruled 1243–1207 BC.

Tushratta: King of Mitanni; ruled ca. 1360 BC. Son of Shuttarna II; corresponded with Amarna pharaohs; daughter married Egyptian pharaoh Amenhotep III.

Tutankhamen: Pharaoh, Eighteenth Dynasty; ruled 1336–1327 BC. Famous boy king who died young, with fabulous wealth placed in his tomb.

Twosret: Egyptian queen, last ruler of the Nineteenth Dynasty; widow of Pharaoh Seti II; known to have ruled 1187–1185 BC.

Zannanza: Hittite prince, son of Suppiluliuma I; lived ca. 1324 BC; promised in marriage to widowed Egyptian queen but assassinated while en route to Egypt.

Zimri-Lim: King of Mari in what is now modern Syria; ruled 1776–1758 BC. Contemporary of Hammurabi of Babylon and author of some of the "Mari Letters," which give insight into life in Mesopotamia during the eighteenth century BC.

··⟩ NOTES ⟨··

PREFACE

1. In this, I agree with Jennings 2011, who has written recently about globalizations and the ancient world. See also previously Sherratt 2003, in an article published a decade ago before the correlations became even more vivid, and now the MA thesis written under my direction by Katie Paul (2011).

2. Diamond 2005; see previously the volume by Tainter 1988 and the edited volume by Yoffee and Cowgill 1988; also discussions in Killebrew 2005: 33–34; Liverani 2009; Middleton 2010: 18–19, 24, 53; and now Middleton 2012; Butzer 2012; Butzer and Endfield 2012. On the rise and fall of empires, particularly from a world-systems viewpoint, which has engendered much discussion, see Frank 1993; Frank and Gillis 1993; Frank and Thompson 2005. In addition, a conference was recently held in Jerusalem (December 2012) entitled "Analyzing Collapse: Destruction, Abandonment and Memory" (http://www.collapse.huji.ac.il/the-schedule), but the proceedings have not yet been published.

3. Bell 2012: 180.

4. Bell 2012: 180–81.

5. Sherratt 2003: 53–54. See now also Singer 2012.

6. Braudel 2001: 114.

7. See Mallowan 1976; McCall 2001; Trumpler 2001.

PROLOGUE

1. Roberts 2008: 5 notes that Emmanuel de Rougé was the first to coin this term, "peuples de la mer," in a publication dating to 1867; see also Dothan and Dothan 1992: 23–24; Roberts 2009; Killebrew and Lehmann 2013: 1.

2. See, for instance, the recent discussions in Killebrew 2005, Yasur-Landau 2010a, and Singer 2012.

3. Kitchen 1982: 238–39; cf. Monroe 2009: 33–34 and n. 28. Some Egyptologists put the eighth year of Ramses III slightly earlier (1186 BC) or slightly later (1175 BC), since the dates for the ancient Egyptian pharaohs and their years of rule are not completely certain but rather are approximate and are often adjusted according to the whims and desire of individual archaeologists and historians; here the years of Ramses's rule are taken to be 1184–1153 BC.

4. Raban and Stieglitz 1991; Cifola 1994; Wachsmann 1998: 163–97; Barako 2001, 2003a, 2003b; Yasur-Landau 2003a; Yasur-Landau 2010a: 102–21, 171–86, 336–42; Demand 2011: 201–3.

5. Following Edgerton and Wilson 1936: pl. 46; revised trans., Wilson 1969: 262–63; see also Dothan, T. 1982: 5–13, with illustrations.

6. See now the compilation of all the Egyptian and other primary sources mentioning the various Sea Peoples, from the time of Amenhotep III in the Eighteenth Dynasty through the period of Ramses IX in the Twentieth Dynasty and beyond, by Adams and Cohen (2013) in Killebrew and Lehmann (eds.) 2013: 645–64 and tables 1–2.

7. Roberts 2008: 1–8; Sandars 1985: 117–37, 157–77; Vagnetti 2000; Cline and O'Connor 2003; Van De Mieroop 2007: 241–43; Halpern 2006–7; Middleton 2010: 83; Killebrew and Lehmann 2013: 8–11; Emanuel 2013: 14–27. See also additional references below regarding the pottery and other material culture remains.

8. See discussion in Cline and O'Connor 2003; also Sandars 1985: 50, 133 and now Emanuel 2013: 14–27. Killebrew and Lehmann 2013: 7–8 note that the Lukka and Danuna are also mentioned in earlier Egyptian inscriptions, from the time of Amenhotep III and Akhenaten; see tables 1–2 and the appendix by Adams and Cohen 2013, as well as Artzy 2013: 329–32, in the volume edited by Killebrew and Lehmann.

9. See Amos 9:7 and Jer. 47:4, where Crete is referred to by one of its ancient names, Caphtor. See now Hitchcock in press.

10. Roberts 2008: 1–3; Dothan and Dothan 1992: 13–28. See also Finkelstein 2000: 159–61 and Finkelstein 2007: 517 for lucid descriptions of how the early biblical archaeologists such as Albright correlated the Peleset and the Philistines; Dothan, T. 1982, Killebrew 2005: 206–234, and Yasur-Landau 2010a: 2–3, 216–81 on the material remains usually identified as Philistine; and now the most recent, and complex, discussion and definition of the Philistines by Maeir, Hitchcock, and Horwitz 2013; Hitchcock and Maeir 2013; also the related discussions by Hitchcock 2011 and Stockhammer 2013.

11. See, e.g., Cifola 1991; Wachsmann 1998; Drews 2000; Yasur-Landau 2010b, 2012b; Bouzek 2011.

12. Breasted 1930: x–xi. See now the biography of Breasted by Abt (2011). As Abt notes on p. 230, Rockefeller secretly authorized an additional fifty thousand dollars, should Breasted need it, but did not inform him of that.

13. See, e.g., Raban and Stieglitz 1991.

14. Following Edgerton and Wilson 1936: pl. 46; revised trans., Wilson 1969: 262–63.

15. Following Breasted 1906 (reprinted 2001) 4:201; Sandars 1985: 133. See now Zwickel 2012.

16. See most recently Kahn 2012, with many further references.

17. Following Edel 1961; see Bakry 1973.

18. Breasted 1906 (2001) 3:253.

19. Following Breasted 1906 (2001) 3:241, 243, 249.

20. See discussion in Sandars 1985: 105–15; Cline and O'Connor 2003; Halpern 2006–7.

21. http://www.livescience.com/22267-severed-hands-ancient-egypt-palace.html and http://www.livescience.com/22266-grisly-ancient-practice-gold-of-valor.html (last accessed August 15, 2012).

22. Following Edgerton and Wilson 1936: pls. 37–39.

23. Ben Dor Evian 2011: 11–22.

24. RS 20.238 (*Ugaritica* 5.24); translation following Beckman 1996a: 27; original publication in Nougayrol et al. 1968: 87–89. See also Sandars 1985: 142–43; Yon 1992: 116, 119; Lebrun 1995: 86; Huehnergard 1999: 376–77; Singer 1999: 720–21; Bryce 2005:

333 (with incorrect RS tablet number). The precise interpretation of this letter is a matter of scholarly debate, for it is not clear whether it is actually a request for assistance or even what the main point of the letter might have been.

25. Schaeffer 1962: 31–37; also Nougayrol et al. 1968: 87–89; Sandars 1985: 142–43; Drews 1993: 13–14.

26. See, e.g., discussions in Sandars 1985; Drews 1993; Cifola 1994; and the papers in conference volumes edited by Ward and Joukowsky (1992) and by Oren (1997). But see already a protest to the contrary in Raban and Stieglitz 1991 and now the papers in Killebrew and Lehmann 2013.

27. See, e.g., Monroe 2009; Yasur-Landau 2010a; and the papers in the conference volumes edited by Bachhuber and Roberts (2009), Galil et al. (2012), and Killebrew and Lehmann (2013); also the brief summation of the situation in Hitchcock and Maeir 2013 and the synopsis in Strobel 2013.

28. Bryce 2012: 13.

29. Roberts 2008: 1–19. See also discussion in Roberts 2009; Drews 1992: 21–24; Drews 1993: 48–72; Silberman 1998; Killebrew and Lehmann 2013: 1–2.

CHAPTER ONE

1. Cline 1995b, with references; see, most recently, Cline, Yasur-Landau, and Goshen 2011, also with references.

2. See, e.g., Bietak 1996, 2005; now also Bietak, Marinatos, and Palyvou 2007.

3. See, most recently, Kamrin 2013.

4. Oren 1997.

5. Wente 2003a: 69–71.

6. Translation following Pritchard 1969: 554–55; Habachi 1972: 37, 49; Redford, D. B. 1992: 120; Redford, D. B. 1997: 14.

7. E.g., Bietak 1996: 80.

8. Heimpel 2003: 3–4.

9. Dalley 1984: 89–93, esp. 91–92.

10. For such requests, at Mari and elsewhere, see Cline 1995a: 150; previously Zaccagnini 1983: 250–54; Liverani 1990: 227–29. For contacts specifically between the Minoans and Mesopotamia, see Heltzer 1989 and now also Sørensen 2009; previously also Cline 1994: 24–30 on the larger question of contacts between the Aegean and Mesopotamia.

11. See items listed in Cline 1994: 126–28 (D.3–12).

12. Translation following Durard 1983: 454–55; see also Cline 1994: 127 (D.7).

13. See discussions in Cline 1994, 1995a, 1999a, 2007a, and 2010, with further references.

14. See Cline 1994: 126 (D.2), with previous references; also Heltzer 1989.

15. Evans 1921–35.

16. Momigliano 2009.

17. Numerous books have been published on the Minoans and/or various aspects of their society; see, for example, Castleden 1993 and Fitton 2002; also most recently, the specific articles found in Cline (ed.) 2010.

18. On the Khyan lid, see Cline 1994: 210 (no. 680) with additional references.

19. On the Thutmose III vase, see Cline 1994: 217 (no. 742) with additional references.

20. Cline 1999a: 129–30, with earlier references.

21. Pendlebury 1930. On Pendlebury himself, see now Grundon 2007. Pendlebury's original book has now been replaced by a recent study in two volumes; see Phillips 2008.

22. As previously noted in Cline and Cline 1991.

23. Panagiotopoulos 2006: 379, 392–93.

24. Translation following Strange 1980: 45–46. See also Wachsmann 1987: 35–37, 94; Cline 1994: 109–10 (A.12) with additional information and references; Rehak 1998; Panagiotopoulos 2006: 382–83.

25. Troy 2006: 146–50.

26. Panagiotopoulos 2006: 379–80.

27. Panagiotopoulos 2006: 380–87.

28. Translation following Strange 1980: 97–98. See also Wachsmann 1987: 120–21; Cline 1994: 110 (A.13).

29. Strange 1980: 74; Wachsmann 1987: 119–21; Cline 1994: 110 (A.14).

30. Panagiotopoulos 2006: 380–83.

31. I first pointed this out in a conference paper presented at the annual meetings of the Archaeological Institute of America; see Cline 1995a: 146. See also Cline 1994: 110–11 (A.16); Panagiotopoulos 2006: 381–82.

32. Panagiotopoulos 2006: 372–73, 394; but see protestations by Liverani 2001: 176–82. See previously Cline 1995a: 146–47; Cline 1994: 110 (A.15).

33. Clayton 1994: 101–2; Allen 2005: 261; Dorman 2005a: 87–88; Keller 2005: 96–98.

34. Tyldesley 1998: 1; Dorman 2005a: 88. See also http://www.drhawass.com/blog /press-release-identifying-hatshepsuts-mummy (last accessed December 29, 2010).

35. Clayton 1994: 105; Dorman 2005b: 107–9.

36. Tyldesley 1998: 144.

37. Clayton 1994: 106–7; Tyldesley 1998: 145–53; Liverani 2001: 166–69; Keller 2005: 96–98; Roth 2005: 149; Panagiotopoulos 2006: 379–80.

38. Panagiotopoulos 2006: 373.

39. Translation following Strange 1980: 16–20, no. 1; see Cline 1997a: 193.

40. Cline 1997a: 194–96, with previous references.

41. Ryan 2010: 277, see also 5–28, 260–81 for general discussions of Ryan's reexcavation of tomb KV 60. See also news reports, such as http://www.guardians.net/hawass /hatshepsut/search_for_hatshepsut.htm and http://www.drhawass.com/blog/press-release -identifying-hatshepsuts-mummy (both last accessed December 29, 2010).

42. On Thutmose III's campaign and capture of Megiddo, see Cline 2000: chap. 1, with further references; also, for a very brief account, Allen 2005: 261–62.

43. Cline 2000: 28.

44. Darnell and Manassa 2007: 139–42; Podany 2010: 131–34.

45. Podany 2010: 134.

46. The classic and authoritative translation was published in German by Kammenhuber in 1961. For a modern example of a horse-trainer attempting to use Kikkuli's methods, see now Nyland 2009.

47. Redford, D. B. 2006: 333–34; Darnell and Manassa 2007: 141; Amanda Podany, personal communication, May 23, 2013.

48. Bryce 2005: 140.

49. I have suggested this previously in Cline 1997a: 196. Further, for my previous discussions of this material concerning the Assuwa Rebellion and Ahhiyawa, including similar details and wording in the following paragraphs and further below, see Cline 2013: 54–68;

also Cline 1996, with previous references, and Cline 1997a. See also Bryce 2005: 124–27, with previous references, and the relevant sections in Beckman, Bryce, and Cline 2011.

50. Translation and transliteration following Unal, Ertekin, and Ediz 1991: 51; Ertekin and Ediz 1993: 721; Cline 1996: 137–38; Cline 1997a: 189–90.

51. On the Hittites, and the material presented in the following paragraphs, see especially the overviews by Bryce 2002, 2005, 2012; Collins 2007.

52. See now the discussion on Hittites and the Bible in Bryce 2012: 64–75.

53. See now Bryce 2012: 47–49 and passim on the Neo-Hittites and their world.

54. See now Bryce 2012: 13–14; previously Bryce 2005.

55. Hittite Law no. 13; translation following Hoffner 2007: 219.

56. As mentioned above, for my previous discussions of this material, including the details in the following paragraphs and further below, see now Cline 2013: 54–68; also Cline 1996, with previous references, Cline 1997a, and the relevant sections in Beckman, Bryce, and Cline 2011.

57. Full transliteration and translation in Carruba 1977: 158–61; see also Cline 1996: 141 for additional discussion and relevant references.

58. Translation following Houwink ten Cate 1970: 62 (cf. also 72 n. 99, 81); see also Cline 1996: 143 for additional relevant references.

59. See Cline 1996: 145–46; Cline 1997a: 192.

60. See references given in Cline 2010: 177–79.

61. See references given in Cline 1994, 1996, and 1997a for the arguments regarding the proper location of Ahhiyawa; see now also Beckman, Bryce, and Cline 2011, as well as alternative perspectives presented in Kelder 2010 and Kelder 2012.

62. For a brief introduction to Schliemann, with additional bibliography given, see now Rubalcaba and Cline 2011.

63. See Schliemann 1878; Tsountas and Manatt 1897.

64. Blegen and Rawson 1966: 5–6; previously, Blegen and Kourouniotis 1939: 563–64.

65. On the most current thinking regarding the Mycenaeans, see, most recently, the articles found in Cline (ed.) 2010.

66. On the Mycenaean goods found in Egypt and elsewhere in the Near East, see Cline 1994 (republished 2009), with further bibliographical references.

67. Cline 1996: 149; see now Cline 2013: 54–68.

68. See Cline 1997a: 197–98 and Cline 2013: 43–49, with further references.

69. Translation following Fagles 1990: 185.

70. As previously stated in Cline 1997a: 202–3.

71. Kantor 1947: 73.

72. Panagiotopoulos 2006: 406 n. 1 says, "There is no reason to believe that Hatshepsut was a pacifist, since there is reliable evidence for at least four, and perhaps even six, military campaigns during her reign, at least one of which she led in person." See previously Redford, D. B. 1967: 57–62.

CHAPTER TWO

1. Cline 1998: 236–37; Sourouzian 2004. See Cambridge classicist Mary Beard's rumination on these statues, found online at http://timesonline.typepad.com/dons_life /2011/01/the-colossi-of-memnon.html (last accessed January 16, 2011).

2. Work on the Aegean List began in 2000; the whole base was finally reassembled in the spring of 2005, reconstructed from eight hundred separate fragments. See discussion in Sourouzian et al. 2006: 405–6, 433–35, pls. XXIIa, c.

3. Kitchen 1965: 5–6; see also Kitchen 1966.

4. For the primary publication of these lists, see Edel 1966; Edel and Görg 2005. For other scholars' thoughts, commentaries, and hypotheses, see, e.g., Hankey 1981; Cline 1987 and 1998, with citations of earlier publications.

5. Cline and Stannish 2011.

6. Cline 1987, 1990, 1994, and 1998; Phillips and Cline 2005.

7. Cline 1987: 10; see also Cline 1990.

8. Cline 1994: xvii–xviii, 9–11, 35, 106; Cline 1999a.

9. Cline 1998: 248; see also previously Cline 1987 and now also Cline and Stannish 2011: 11.

10. Mynářová 2007: 11–39.

11. See Amarna Letters EA 41–44; Moran 1992: 114–17.

12. See Cohen and Westbrook 2000.

13. See Moran 1992 for an English translation of all the letters.

14. Amarna Letter EA 17; translation following Moran 1992: 41–42.

15. Amarna Letter EA 14; Moran 1992: 27–37.

16. For instance, Amarna Letters EA 22, 24, and 25; Moran 1992: 51–61, 63–84.

17. Liverani 1990; Liverani 2001: 135–37. See now also Mynářová 2007: 125–31, specifically on the Amarna Letters.

18. On such anthropological studies, see the discussion in Cline 1995a: 143, with further references and bibliography noted there in fn. 1.

19. Ugarit Letter RS 17.166, cited in Cline 1995a: 144, following translation by Liverani 1990: 200.

20. Hittite Letter KUB XXIII 102: I 10–19, cited in Cline 1995a: 144, following translation by Liverani 1990: 200.

21. See again Cline 1995a, for previous and more full discussion of this topic.

22. Amarna Letter EA 24; translation following Moran 1992: 63. See now discussion on the relations between Tushratta and Amenhotep III in Kahn 2011.

23. See Amarna Letter EA 20, sent to Amenhotep III, Moran 1992: 47–50, and then Amarna Letters EA 27–29, subsequently sent to Akhenaten, Moran 1992: 86–99.

24. Amarna Letter EA 22, lines 43–49; translation following Moran 1992: 51–61, esp. 57. Such royal marriages were not uncommon in the ancient Near East; see Liverani 1990.

25. Cline 1998: 248.

26. Amarna Letter EA 4; translation following Moran 1992: 8–10.

27. Amarna Letter EA 1; translation following Moran 1992: 1–5.

28. Amarna Letters EA 2–3, 5; Moran 1992: 6–8, 10–11.

29. E.g., Amarna Letters EA 19; translation following Moran 1992: 4.

30. Amarna Letter EA 3; translation following Moran 1992: 7.

31. Amarna Letters EA 7 and 10; translations following Moran 1992: 12–16, 19–20. See also Podany 2010: 249–52.

32. Amarna Letter EA 7; translation following Moran 1992: 14.

33. Amarna Letter EA 7; Moran 1992: 14. See also Amarna Letter 8, in which Burna-Buriash complains to Akhenaten about yet another attack on his merchants, during which they were killed; Moran 1992: 16–17.

34. Malinowski 1922; see also Uberoi 1962; Leach and Leach 1983; Mauss 1990: 27–29; and previous discussion in Cline 1995a.

35. This has been pointed out previously elsewhere, in Cline 1995a: 149–50, with further references and bibliography cited there.

36. Again, this has been pointed out previously, in Cline 1995a: 150. The further references and bibliography cited there include Zaccagnini 1983: 250–54; Liverani 1990: 227–29; Niemeier 1991; Bietak 1992: 26–28. See now also Niemeier and Niemeier 1998; Pfälzner 2008a, 2008b; Hitchcock 2005, 2008; Cline and Yasur-Landau 2013.

37. Amarna Letters EA 33–40. The equation of Cyprus with Alashiya has a long, and convoluted, scholarly history. For an irreverent brief discussion of the equation, see now Cline 2005.

38. Amarna Letter EA 35; Moran 1992: 107–9. The word "talents" is reconstructed, but seems most logical here.

39. See brief note by Moran 1992: 39.

40. Amarna Letter EA 15; translation following Moran 1992: 37–38.

41. Amarna Letter EA 16; translation following Moran 1992: 38–41.

42. Van De Mieroop 2007: 131, 138, 175; Bryce 2012: 182–83.

43. The bust is listed among *Time* magazine's Top 10 Plundered Artifacts: see http://www.time.com/time/specials/packages/article/0,28804,1883142_1883129_1883119,00.html (last accessed January 18, 2011). See also the *New York Times* article: http://www.nytimes.com/2009/10/19/world/europe/19iht-germany.html?_r=2 (last accessed January 18, 2011).

44. See the lyrics to the song, sung by comedian Steve Martin on *Saturday Night Live* during the days of Tut-mania in the United States in the late 1970s. Numerous copies of the clip can now be found on the Internet, including at http://www.hulu.com/watch/55342 and http://www.nbc.com/saturday-night-live/digital-shorts/video/king-tut/1037261/ (both last accessed on May 23, 2013).

45. Hawass 2005: 263–72.

46. Hawass 2010; Hawass et al. 2010.

47. Reeves 1990: 44.

48. Reeves 1990: 40–46.

49. Reeves 1990: 48–51.

50. Reeves 1990: 10.

51. See photographs in Reeves 1990: 52–53.

52. Bryce 2005: 148–59; Podany 2010: 267–71.

53. Cline 1998: 248–49. On Amenhotep III's dynastic marriages, see also Schulman 1979: 183–85, 189–90; Schulman 1988: 59–60; Moran 1992: 101–3.

54. Translation following Singer 2002: 62; cited and discussed by Bryce 2005: 154–55 (see also 188).

55. See Yener 2013a, with previous references.

56. See Bryce 2005: 155–59, 161–63, 175–80; Bryce 2012: 14.

57. Richter 2005; Merola 2007; Pfälzner 2008a, 2008b. See now Richter and Lange 2012 for the full publication of the archive and Ahrens, Dohmann-Pfälzner, and Pfälzner 2012 for the clay sealing of Akhenaten, and Morandi Bonacossi 2013 on the final crisis ca. 1340 BC.

58. See discussion in Beckman, Bryce, and Cline 2011: 158–61.

59. Translation following Bryce 2005: 178. The following is heavily indebted to the account found in Bryce 2005: 178–83. See also, though, Cline 2006, in an account written for children.

60. Translation following Bryce 2005: 180–81; the letter is KBo xxviii 51.

61. Translation following Bryce 2005: 181.

62. Translation following Bryce 2005: 182.

63. For examples of scholarly differences of opinion, Bryce 2005: 179 says that the widowed queen was Ankhsenamen, but Reeves 1990: 23 says that the queen was Nefertiti. See also Podany 2010: 285–89, who believes that it was Ankhsenamen.

64. See Bryce 2005: 183 and n. 130, with references.

65. See discussions in Cline 1991a: 133–43; Cline 1991b: 1–9; Cline 1994: 68–74.

66. Cline 1998: 249.

67. See Bryce 1989a: 1–21; Bryce 1989b: 297–310.

CHAPTER THREE

1. Sources for this and the details and discussion that follow below are many and varied, but see especially Bass 1986, 1987, 1997, 1998; Pulak 1988, 1998, 1999, 2005; Bachhuber 2006; Cline and Yasur-Landau 2007. See now also Podany 2010: 256–58.

2. Bass 1967; Bass 1973.

3. Pulak 1998: 188.

4. Pulak 1998: 213.

5. In addition to the articles by Pulak, Bass, and Bachhuber, see the list in Monroe 2009: 11–12, with additional discussion on 13–15, 234–38; also Monroe 2010. Information now updated slightly courtesy of lecture by Cemal Pulak, delivered at an academic conference in Freiburg, Germany, in May 2012.

6. Weinstein 1989.

7. See, most recently, Manning et al. 2009.

8. Payton 1991.

9. RS 16.238+254; translation following Heltzer 1988: 12. See also, among many discussions, Caubet and Matoian 1995: 100; Monroe 2009: 165–66.

10. RS 16.386; translation following Monroe 2009: 164–65.

11. Singer 1999: 634–35. For some of the correspondence exchanged between the kings at this time, see Nougayrol 1956.

12. Bryce 2005: 234.

13. Bryce 2005: 277.

14. Bryce 2005: 236, with earlier references.

15. Bryce 2005: 236–37.

16. Translation following Bryce 2005: 237–38, following Gardiner.

17. Bryce 2005: 235.

18. Bryce 2005: 238–39.

19. Bryce 2005: 277–78.

20. Translation following Bryce 2005: 277, following Kitchen.

21. Bryce 2005: 277, 282, 284–85.

22. Translation following Bryce 2005: 283, following Kitchen.

23. A lengthier version of the discussion in this section on Troy and the Trojan War, as well as in the next chapter, can be found in Cline 2013, which was written at the same time as this book and contains some of the same material and language, albeit in different order and with a more detailed discussion in places. In both cases, the discussions

represent an edited version of material first published, with additional references, by the present author in the Course Guide accompanying the fourteen-lecture recorded audio series entitled *Archaeology and the Iliad: The Trojan War in Homer and History* (Recorded Books/The Modern Scholar, 2006) and is reproduced here by permission of the publisher.

24. See discussion in Beckman, Bryce, and Cline 2011: 140–44.

25. Beckman, Bryce, and Cline 2011: 101–22.

26. Beckman, Bryce, and Cline 2011: 101–22.

27. Beckman, Bryce, and Cline 2011: 101–22.

28. Beckman, Bryce, and Cline 2011: 101–22.

29. See now the discussion, with further references, in Cline 2013. See also, in general, Strauss 2006.

30. See, e.g., Wood 1996; Allen 1999; now Cline 2013.

31. Mountjoy 1999a: 254–56, 258; see also Mountjoy 1999b: 298–99; Mountjoy 2006: 244–45; Cline 2013: 90.

32. See now discussion in Cline 2013: 87–90.

33. See, e.g., Loader 1998; also Shelmerdine 1998b: 87; Deger-Jalkotzy 2008: 388; Maran 2009: 248–50; Kostoula and Maran 2012: 217, citing Maran 2004.

34. Hirschfeld 1990, 1992, 1996, 1999, 2010; Cline 1994: 54, 61; Cline 1999b; Cline 2007a: 195; Maran 2004; Maran 2009: 246–47.

35. Cline 1994: 50, 128–30. See now also recent mentions in Monroe 2009: 196–97, 226–27.

36. Cline 1994: 60, 130 (Cat. nos. E13–14); Palaima 1991: 280–81, 291–95; Shelmerdine 1998b.

37. Cline 1994: 60, 130; see also Palaima 1991: 280–81, 291–95; Knapp 1991. See now Yasur-Landau 2010a: 40, table 2.1, conveniently itemizing in a single table these and the following names, which are then placed on a map in his fig. 2.3.

38. Cline 1994: 50, 68–69, 128–31 (Cat. nos. E3, E7, E15–18); see most recently Latacz 2004: 280–81, who cites Niemeier 1999: 154 for additional occurrences of mentions in the Pylos tablets of women from Lemnos and Chios, as well as perhaps Troy or the Troad.

39. Cline 1994: 50, 129 (Cat. nos. E8–11); previously Astour 1964: 194, 1967: 336–44; now also Bell 2009: 32.

40. Cline 1994: 35, 128 (Cat. nos. E1–2); Shelmerdine 1998a.

41. Zivie 1987.

42. The discussion below of the Exodus is an edited version of material first published, with additional references, by the present author in Cline 2007b and is reproduced here by permission of the publisher.

43. Diodorus Siculus 1.47; translated by Oldfather 1961.

44. See discussion in Cline 2007b: 61–92, with further references; also Miller and Hayes 2006: 39–41; Bryce 2012: 187–88.

45. Translation following Pritchard 1969: 378.

46. See discussion in Cline 2007b: 83–85, with further references; also Hoffmeier 2005, as well as Ben-Tor and Rubiato 1999.

47. See discussion in Cline 2007b: 85–87, with further references.

48. Such claims are mostly, but easily, found on the Internet; see, e.g., http://www .discoverynews.us/DISCOVERY%20MUSEUM/BibleLandsDisplay/Red_Sea_Chariot _Wheels/Red_Sea_Chariot_Wheels_1.html (last accessed May 27, 2013).

49. On the dating of the eruption, which has generated much scholarly debate over the past several decades, see Manning 1999, 2010, with further references.

50. Cline 2007b, 2009a, 2009b, with references.

51. Zuckerman 2007a: 17, citing and quoting from earlier publications by Garstang, Yadin, and Ben-Tor. See now also Ben-Tor 2013.

52. Zuckerman 2007a: 24.

53. Ben-Tor and Zuckerman 2008: 3–4, 6.

54. Ben-Tor 1998, 2006, 2013; Ben-Tor and Rubiato 1999; Zuckerman 2006, 2007a, 2007b, 2009, 2010; Ben-Tor and Zuckerman 2008; see now Ashkenazi 2012; Zeiger 2012; Marom and Zuckerman 2012.

55. See discussions, with further references, in Cline 2007b: 86–92; Cline 2009a: 76–78; and see also Cline 2009b.

56. Bryce 2009: 85.

57. Kuhrt 1995: 353–54; Bryce 2012: 182–83.

58. Bryce 2005: 314.

59. Porada 1992: 182–83; Kuhrt 1995: 355–58; Singer 1999: 688–90; Potts 1999: 231; Bryce 2005: 314–19; Bryce 2009: 86; Bryce 2012: 182–85. Note that Singer places the beginning of Tukulti-Ninurta's reign at 1233 BC, rather than 1244 BC.

60. On the battle against the Hittites, at Nihriya in northern Mesopotamia, see Bryce 2012: 54, 183–84, among others. On the possible gift sent to Boeotian Thebes, see initial discussion in Porada 1981, briefly discussed in Cline 1994: 25–26.

61. Translation following Beckman, Bryce, and Cline 2011: 61; previously Bryce 2005: 315–19.

62. Translation following Beckman, Bryce, and Cline 2011: 63.

63. I have discussed this in a number of my previous publications; see most recently Cline 2007a: 197, with further references.

64. Translation following Beckman, Bryce, and Cline 2011: 61; previously Bryce 2005: 309–10.

65. See discussion in Beckman, Bryce, and Cline 2011: 101–22; previously Bryce 1985, 2005: 306–8.

66. Bryce 2005: 321–22; Demand 2011: 195. See now also Kaniewski et al. 2013 on a possible drought in Cyprus itself at this time, on which more below.

67. Translation following Bryce 2005: 321, after Güterbock, as well as discussion on 321–22 and 333; see also similar translation by Beckman 1996b: 32 and the discussion by Hoffner 1992: 48–49.

68. Translation following Beckman 1996b: 33; see also Bryce 2005: 332; Singer 2000: 27; Singer 1999: 719, 721–22; Hoffner 1992: 48–49; Sandars 1985: 141–42.

69. Bryce 2005: 323, 327–33; Singer 2000: 25–27; Hoffner 1992: 48–49.

70. Singer 2000: 27.

71. Phelps, Lolos, and Vichos 1999; Lolos 2003.

72. Bass 1967; Bass 1973.

73. Bass 1988; Bass 2013.

74. Cline 1994: 100–101.

Chapter Four

1. Yon 2006: 7. The scholarly literature on these sites is immense, but Yon 2006 is fairly brief and very accessible, as is previously Curtis 1999. On the political and

economic history of Ugarit, see also the good overview and summation in Singer 1999. See also Podany 2010: 273–75.

2. Caubet 2000; Yon 2003, 2006: 7–8.

3. See Yon 2006: 142–43, for a picture of these Canaanite jars in situ, with brief discussion and further references.

4. Dietrich and Loretz 1999; Yon 2006: 7–8, 44, with further references.

5. Yon 2006: 7–8, 19, 24; Lackenbacher 1995a: 72; Singer 1999: 623–27, 641–42, 680–81, 701–4. The Amarna Letters sent by the kings of Ugarit are EA 45 and 49, and others may include EA 46–48; see Moran 1992.

6. Van Soldt 1991; Lackenbacher 1995a: 69–70; Millard 1995: 121; Huehnergard 1999: 375; Singer 1999: 704. See now, more recently, Singer 2006: esp. 256–58; Bell 2006: 17; McGeough 2007: 325–32.

7. Singer 1999: 657–60, 668–73; Pitard 1999: 48–51; Bell 2006: 2, 17; McGeough 2007; Bell 2012: 180.

8. Yon 2006: 20–21, with specific objects illustrated and discussed on 129–72, including 168–69 for the sword; Singer 1999: 625, 676; McGeough 2007: 297–305.

9. Documented on tablet RS 17.382 + RS 17.380; see Singer 1999: 635; McGeough 2007: 325.

10. Lackenbacher 1995a; Bordreuil and Malbran-Labat 1995; Malbran-Labat 1995. Previous discussions about the end of Ugarit include those by Astour 1965 and Sandars 1985.

11. Yon 2006: 51, 54; McGeough 2007: 183–84, 254–55, 333–35; Bell 2012: 182–83. On Cypro-Minoan, see Hirschfeld 2010, with references.

12. Yon 2006: 73–77, with references; van Soldt 1999: 33–34; Bell 2006: 65; McGeough 2007: 247–49; Bell 2012: 182.

13. Ugaritic text RS 20.168; see Singer 1999: 719–20; original publication in Nougayrol et al. 1968: 80–83.

14. Malbran-Labat 1995; Bordreuil and Malbran-Labat 1995; Singer 1999: 605; van Soldt 1999: 35–36; Yon 2006: 22, 87–88; Bell 2006: 67; McGeough 2007: 257–59; Bell 2012: 183–84. See now also Bordreuil, Pardee, and Hawley 2012.

15. RS 34.165. Lackenbacher in Bordreuil 1991: 90–100; Hoffner 1992: 48; Singer 1999: 689–90.

16. Singer 1999: 658–59; see now also Cohen and Singer 2006; McGeough 2007: 184, 335.

17. Singer 1999: 719–20, summarizing previous reports; Bordreuil and Malbran-Labat 1995: 445.

18. Lackenbacher and Malbran-Labat 2005: 237–38 and nn. 69, 76; Singer 2006: 256–58; Cline and Yasur-Landau 2007: 130; Bryce 2010; Bell 2012: 184. The letter from the Hittite king (probably Suppiluliuma II) is RS 94.2530; that from the top Hittite official is RS 94.2523.

19. RS 88.2158. Lackenbacher 1995b: 77–83; Lackenbacher in Yon and Arnaud 2001: 239–47; see discussion in Singer 1999: 708–712; Singer 2000: 22.

20. RS 34.153; Bordreuil 1991: 75–76; translation following Monroe 2009: 188–89.

21. RS 17.450A; see discussion in Monroe 2009: 180, 188–89.

22. Malbran-Labat 1995: 107.

23. Millard 1995: 121.

24. Singer 1999: 729–30 and n. 427; Caubet 1992: 123; Yon 2006: 22; Kaniewski et al. 2011: 4–5.

25. Yon 1992: 111, 117, 120; Singer 1999: 730; Bell 2006: 12, 101–2.

26. Ugarit text RS 86.2230. See Yon 1992: 119; Hoffner 1992: 49; Drews 1993: 13; Singer 1999: 713–15; Arnaud in Yon and Arnaud 2001: 278–79 Yasur-Landau 2003d: 236; Bell 2006: 12; Yon 2006: 127; Yasur-Landau 2010a: 187; Kaniewski et al. 2010: 212; Kaniewski et al. 2011: 5.

27. KTU 1.78 (RS 12.061); see now Kaniewski et al. 2010: 212 and Kaniewski et al. 2011: 5, citing Dietrich and Loretz 2002. Contra Demand 2011: 199, citing an earlier publication by Lipinski, the destruction is unlikely to have been as late as 1160 BC.

28. See, e.g., Sandars 1985.

29. See Millard 1995: 119 and Singer 1999: 705, with earlier references; also van Soldt 1999: 32; Yon 2006: 44; Van De Mieroop 2007: 245; McGeough 2007: 236–37; McGeough 2011: 225.

30. Yon 1992: 117; Caubet 1992: 129; McClellan 1992: 165–67; Drews 1993: 15, 17; Singer 2000: 25.

31. Courbin 1990, quoted in Caubet 1992: 127; see also Lagarce and Lagarce 1978.

32. Bounni, Lagarce, and Saliby 1976; Bounni, Lagarce, and Saliby 1978, cited by Caubet 1992: 124; see also Drews 1993: 14; Singer 2000: 24; Yasur-Landau 2010a: 165–66; Killebrew and Lehmann 2013: 12.

33. Kaniewski et al. 2011: 1 and see fig. 2. For earlier discussions of the discoveries made at this site, see Maqdissi et al. 2008; Bretschneider and Van Lerberghe 2008, 2011; Vansteenhuyse 2010; Bretschneider, Van Vyve, and Jans 2011.

34. Kaniewski et al. 2011: 1–2.

35. Kaniewski et al. 2011: 1.

36. See Badre 2003 and the discussion following; also Badre et al. 2005; Badre 2006, 2011; Jung 2009; Jung 2010: 177–78.

37. Jung 2012: 115–16.

38. Drews 1993: 7 n. 11, 15–16; cf. previously Franken 1961; Dothan, T. 1983: 101, 104; Dever 1992: 104. See now also Gilmour and Kitchen 2012.

39. See brief discussion by Weinstein 1992: 143, with earlier references.

40. See brief overview and discussion in Dever 1992: 101–2.

41. Loud 1948: 29 and figs 70–71; cf. also Kempinski 1989: 10, 76–77, 160; Finkelstein 1996: 171–72; Nur and Ron 1997: 537–39; Nur and Cline 2000: 59.

42. Ussishkin 1995; also personal communication, May 2013.

43. Weinstein 1992: 144–45; Ussishkin 1995: 214; Finkelstein 1996: 171; cf. Loud 1939: pl. 62 no. 377.

44. See most recently Feldman 2002, 2006, and 2009; Steel 2013: 162–69. Previously, Loud 1939; Kantor 1947.

45. Weinstein 1992: 144–45; Ussishkin 1995: 214; Finkelstein 1996: 171; see now also Yasur-Landau 2003d: 237–38; Zwickel 2012: 599–600.

46. Information from Israel Finkelstein, Eran Arie, and Michael Toffolo; I am indebted to them for permission to mention their ongoing studies, which are unpublished at the moment.

47. Ussishkin 1995: 215.

48. Ussishkin 2004b: tables 2.1 and 3.3.

49. Ussishkin 2004b: 60–69.

50. Ussishkin 2004b: 60–62.

51. Ussishkin 2004b: 62, 65–68.

52. Ussishkin 2004b: 71; Barkay and Ussishkin 2004: 357.

53. Zuckerman 2007a: 10, citing Barkay and Ussishkin 2004: 353, 358–61 and Smith 2004: 2504–7.

54. Barkay and Ussishkin 2004: 361; Zuckerman 2007a: 10.

55. Ussishkin 2004b: 70; also Ussishkin 1987.

56. Ussishkin 2004b: 69–70, with references to the earlier publications.

57. Ussishkin 1987; Ussishkin 2004b: 64 and color plates on p. 136; see also Weinstein 1992: 143–44; Giveon, Sweeney, and Lalkin. 2004: 1626–28; Ussishkin 2004d, with plates. See now also Zwickel 2012: 597–98.

58. Ussishkin 1987.

59. Carmi and Ussishkin 2004: 2508–13, with table 35.1; Barkay and Ussishkin 2004: 361; Ussishkin 2004b: 70; Giveon, Sweeney, and Lalkin 2004: 1627–28, with earlier references. Ussishkin, personal communication, May 14, 2013, writes: "As to dating the destruction of Lachish VI to 1130—I suggested it not on the basis of C14 dates but on the basis of the assumption that the Egyptians must have held Lachish as long as they held Megiddo and Beth Shan located further north, and based on the statue of Rameses VI in Megiddo these cities must have existed till about 1130. I still hold to this view."

60. Zwickel 2012: 598, with previous references.

61. Ussishkin 2004b: 70.

62. Ussishkin 2004b: 70.

63. Ussishkin 2004b: 69–72, with references to the earlier publications.

64. Ussishkin 1987; Ussishkin 2004b: 71–72; Zuckerman 2007a: 10. See now also Zwickel 2012: 597–98.

65. Ussishkin 2004b: 71 and color plates on p. 127; see also Barkay and Ussishkin 2004: 358, 363; Smith 2004: 2504–7.

66. See previously Nur and Ron 1997; Nur and Cline 2000, 2001; Nur and Burgess 2008; Cline 2011.

67. Ussishkin 2004c: 216, 267, 270–71.

68. Weinstein 1992: 147.

69. Master, Stager, and Yasur-Landau 2011: 276; see previously Dothan, M. 1971: 25; Dothan, T. 1982: 36–37; Dever 1992: 102–3; Dothan and Dothan 1992: 160–61; Dothan, M. 1993: 96; Dothan and Porath 1993: 47; Dothan, T. 1990, 2000; Stager 1995; Killebrew 1998: 381–82; Killebrew 2000; Gitin 2005; Barako 2013: 41. See also now brief discussion in Demand 2011: 208–10 and the detailed debate and discussion, with full references, as to what constitutes Philistine culture and how the Philistines might have interacted with the local Canaanite population in Killebrew 2005: 197–245; Killebrew 2006–7; Killebrew 2013; Yasur-Landau 2010a: esp. 216–334; Faust and Lev-Tov 2011; Yasur-Landau 2012a; Killebrew and Lehmann 2013: 16; Sherratt 2013; and Maeir, Hitchcock, and Horwitz 2013.

70. Dothan, T. 2000: 147; see also the very similar statement in Dothan, T. 1998: 151. See also Yasur-Landau 2010a: 223–24.

71. Master, Stager, and Yasur-Landau 2011: 261, 274–76, and passim; see also previously Dothan, T. 1982: 36.

72. Stager 1995: 348, cited specifically by Yasur-Landau 2012a: 192. See also Middleton 2010: 85, 87.

73. Potts 1999: 206, 233, and tables 7.5–7.6. See also discussion in Zettler 1992: 174–76.

74. Translation following Potts 1999: 233 and table 7.6.

75. Potts 1999: 188, 233, and table 7.9; Bryce 2012: 185–87.

76. Yener 2013a; Yener 2013b: 144.

77. Drews 1993: 9.

78. See comments on precisely this matter by Güterbock 1992: 55, with references to earlier publications by Kurt Bittel, Heinrich Otten, and others. See now also the discussion by Bryce 2012: 14–15.

79. Neve 1989: 9; Hoffner 1992: 48; Güterbock 1992: 53; Bryce 2005: 269–71, 319–21; Genz 2013: 469–72.

80. Hoffner 1992: 49, 51.

81. Hoffner 1992: 46–47, with references to earlier publications by Kurt Bittel, Heinrich Otten, and others; also now Singer 2001; Middleton 2010: 56.

82. Muhly 1984: 40–41.

83. Bryce 2012: 12; Genz 2013: 472.

84. Seeher 2001; Bryce 2005: 345–46; Van De Mieroop 2007: 240–41; Demand 2011: 195; Bryce 2012: 11; Genz 2013: 469–72.

85. Drews 1993: 9, 11, with references; Yasur-Landau 2010a: 159–61, 186–87, with references. On Tarsus, see now Yalçin 2013.

86. Drews 1993: 9, with references.

87. Bryce 2005: 347–48. Others had noticed this before Bryce; see, for example, Güterbock 1992: 53, citing Bittel; see now also Genz 2013.

88. As with the section in the previous chapter on Troy and the Trojan War, this brief discussion of Troy VIIa and its destruction repeats material that was presented in Cline 2013, which was written at the same time as this book. Again, the discussion represents an edited version of material first published, with additional references, by the present author in the Course Guide accompanying the fourteen-lecture recorded audio series entitled *Archaeology and the Iliad: The Trojan War in Homer and History* (Recorded Books/The Modern Scholar, 2006) and is reproduced here by permission of the publisher.

89. Mountjoy 1999b: 300–301 and table 1 on p. 298; Mountjoy 2006: 245–48; see now Cline 2013: 91.

90. Mountjoy 1999b: 296–97; see now Cline 2013: 93–94.

91. See, e.g., Blegen et al. 1958: 11–12.

92. Transcript of the BBC documentary *The Truth of Troy*, http://www.bbc.co.uk /science/horizon/2004/troytrans.shtml (last accessed April 17, 2012); see now also discussion in Cline 2013: 94–101.

93. See Mountjoy 1999b: 333–34 and now Cline 2013: 94.

94. See, e.g., Deger-Jalkotzy 2008: 387, 390 and the list of sites in Shelmerdine 2001: 373 n. 275.

95. Middleton 2010: 14–15. See now further discussion in Middleton 2012: 283–85.

96. Blegen and Lang 1960: 159–60.

97. Rutter 1992: 70; see now also Deger-Jalkotzy 2008: 387.

98. See originally Blegen and Rawson 1966: 421–22. For the redating of the destruction of Pylos, see now Mountjoy 1997; Shelmerdine 2001: 381.

99. Blegen and Kourouniotis 1939: 561.

100. Davis 2010: 687. See also the discussion in Davis 1998: 88, 97.

101. Blegen 1955: 32 and see also mentions throughout Blegen and Rawson 1966.

102. See most recently Deger-Jalkotzy 2008: 389, with references to the pros and cons of this discussion, which include Hooker 1982, Baumbach 1983, and Palaima 1995; see also Shelmerdine 1999 and Maran 2009: 245, with references.

103. Iakovidis 1986: 259.

104. Taylour 1969: 91–92, 95; Iakovidis 1986: 244–45, as cited in Nur and Cline 2000: 50.

105. Wardle, Crouwel, and French. 1973: 302.

106. French 2009: 108; see also French 2010: 676–77.

107. Iakovidis 1986: 259; see also Middleton 2010: 100.

108. Iakovidis 1986: 260.

109. See Yasur-Landau 2010a: 69–71; see now also the Ph.D. thesis by Murray 2013 and the M.A. thesis by Enverova 2012.

110. Maran 2009: 246–47; Cohen, Maran, and Vetters 2010; Kostoula and Maran 2012.

111. Maran 2010: 729, citing Kilian 1996.

112. See full references in Nur and Cline 2000: 51–52, where this material was initially published; see also Nur and Cline 2001.

113. Kilian 1996: 63, cited in Nur and Cline 2000: 52.

114. See Yasur-Landau 2010a: 58–59, 66–69, with further references; Maran 2010; Middleton 2010: 97–99; Middleton 2012: 284.

115. Karageorghis 1982: 82.

116. Karageorghis 1982: 82–87; subsequently updated in Karageorghis 1992: 79–86; see now also Karageorghis 2011. See also Sandars 1985: 144–48; Drews 1993: 11–12; Bunimovitz 1998; Yasur-Landau 2010a: 150–51; Middleton 2010: 83; Jung 2011.

117. Karageorghis 1982: 86–88, 91.

118. Karageorghis 1982: 88; see now brief discussion in Demand 2011: 205–6.

119. Karageorghis 1982: 89.

120. On the destruction at Enkomi, see Steel 2004: 188, citing earlier excavation reports; also now Mountjoy 2005. On the text from Ugarit—RS 20.18 (*Ugaritica* 5.22)—see Karageorghis 1982: 83; original publication in Nougayrol et al. 1968: 83–85 and with a new translation quoted in Bryce 2005: 334; see also Sandars 1985: 142.

121. Drews 1993: 11–12; Muhly 1984; Karageorghis 1992.

122. Steel 2004: 187. See now also Iacovou 2008 and Iacovou 2013 (the latter was written/presented in 2001 and updated in 2008, but not since then, according to the author).

123. Steel 2004: 188.

124. Steel 2004: 188–90; see now also the discussion of the pottery at these sites in Jung 2011.

125. Voskos and Knapp 2008; Middleton 2010: 84; Knapp 2012; see now also Karageorghis 2011 for his thoughts on the topic.

126. Åström 1998: 83.

127. Kaniewski et al. 2013.

128. Karageorghis 1982: 89–90. For a translation of "The Report of Wenamun," see Wente 2003b.

129. Steel 2004: 186–87, 208–13; see also discussion in Iacovou 2008.

130. Kitchen 2012: 7–11.

131. Snape 2012: 412–13; previously Clayton 1994: 164–65. For the full story, see Redford, S. 2002.

132. Clayton 1994: 165; Redford, S. 2002: 131.

133. See Zink et al. 2012, with further media reports in the *Los Angeles Times*, *USA Today*, and elsewhere, available at http://articles.latimes.com/2012/dec/18/science/la-sci -sn-egypt-mummy-pharoah-ramses-murder-throat-slit-20121218, http://www.usatoday .com/story/tech/sciencefair/2012/12/17/ramses-ramesses-murdered-bmj/1775159/, and http://www.pasthorizonspr.com/index.php/archives/12/2012/ramesses-iii-and-the -harem-conspiracy-murder (all last accessed on May 29, 2013).

134. See again Zink et al. 2012, with further media reports in the *Los Angeles Times*, *USA Today*, and elsewhere, available at http://articles.latimes.com/2012/dec/18/science/la-sci -sn-egypt-mummy-pharoah-ramses-murder-throat-slit-20121218, http://www.usatoday .com/story/tech/sciencefair/2012/12/17/ramses-ramesses-murdered-bmj/1775159/, and http://www.pasthorizonspr.com/index.php/archives/12/2012/ramesses-iii-and-the -harem-conspiracy-murder (all last accessed on May 29, 2013).

135 Cf. Singer 2000: 24 and Caubet 1992: 124 on the resettlement of sites like Ras Ibn Hani by people making and using LH IIIC1 pottery. See now also Sherratt 2013: 627–28.

136. Caubet 1992: 127; see also now Yasur-Landau 2010a: 166; Killebrew and Lehmann 2013: 12, with additional references.

137. Steel 2004: 188–208, citing many earlier studies; see also Yasur-Landau 2010a passim.

Chapter Five

1. As written by Sir Arthur Conan Doyle in "The Hound of the Baskervilles."

2. See, e.g., Sandars 1985; Drews 1993; and the papers in conference volumes edited by Ward and Joukowsky (1992) (especially the overview by Muhly [1992]) and by Oren (1997).

3. See again, e.g., Monroe 2009; Middleton 2010; Yasur-Landau 2010a; and the papers in the conference volumes edited by Bachhuber and Roberts (2009), Galil et al. (2012), and Killebrew and Lehmann (2013); also the brief summaries and lengthier discussions in Killebrew 2005: 33–37; Bell 2006: 12–17; Dickinson 2006: 46–57; Friedman 2008: 163–202; Dickinson 2010; Jung 2010; Wallace 2010: 13, 49–51; Kaniewski et al. 2011: 1; and Strobel 2013.

4. Davis 2010: 687.

5. Deger-Jalkotzy 2008: 390–91; Maran 2009: 242. See also Shelmerdine 2001: 374–76, 381 and especially the detailed examination of possible causes in the Bronze Age Aegean in Middleton 2010 and elsewhere in Middleton 2012, as well as the discussions in Murray 2013 and Enverova 2012.

6. Schaeffer 1948: 2; Schaeffer 1968: 756, 761, 763–765, 766, 768; Drews 1993: 33–34; Nur and Cline 2000: 58; Bryce 2005: 340–41; Bell 2006: 12.

7. Callot 1994: 203; Callot and Yon 1995: 167; Singer 1999: 730.

8. See Nur and Cline 2001, with full discussion and references in Nur and Cline 2000.

9. Kochavi 1977: 8, cited and quoted in Nur and Cline 2001: 34; Nur and Cline 2000: 60. See now also discussion in Cline 2011.

10. See Nur and Cline 2000; Nur and Cline 2001; now also Nur and Burgess 2008.

11. See Nur and Cline 2001: 33–35, with full discussion in Nur and Cline 2000, enlarging upon and disputing the discussion in Drews 1993: 33–47; see also now the discussion in Middleton 2010: 38–41; Middleton 2012: 283–84; Demand 2011: 198. For the addition of Enkomi, see Steel 2004: 188 and n. 13, with earlier references.

12. For all examples, see Nur and Cline 2000: 50–53 and figs. 12–13, with original references cited there.

13. Stiros and Jones 1996; see again Nur and Cline 2000; Nur and Cline 2001; also Shelmerdine 2001: 374–77; Nur and Burgess 2008. On the continued occupation of Tiryns, see Muhlenbruch 2007, 2009; also comments by Dickinson 2010: 486–87 and Jung 2010: 171–73, 175.

14. See Anthony 1990, 1997; Yakar 2003: 13; Yasur-Landau 2007: 610–11; Yasur-Landau 2010a: 30–32; Middleton 2010: 73.

15. See Carpenter 1968.

16. See discussion in Drews 1992: 14–16 and Drews 1993: 77–84; but see now also Drake 2012, which may breathe new life into Carpenter's theory, but from a different aspect. For a recent reexamination of the impact of the end of the Bronze Age on the population and trade in Iron Age Greece, see Murray 2013 as well as Enverova 2012.

17. See Singer 1999: 661–62; Demand 2011: 195; Kahn 2012: 262–63.

18. Hittite text KUB 21.38; translation following Singer 1999: 715; see also Demand 2011: 195.

19. Egyptian text KRI VI 5, 3; translation following Singer 1999: 707–8; see also Hoffner 1992: 49; Bryce 2005: 331; now Kaniewski et al. 2010: 213.

20. Hittite text KBo 2810; translation following Singer 1999: 717–18.

21. RS 20.212; translation following Monroe 2009: 83; McGeough 2007: 331–32; see previously Nougayrol et al. 1968: 105–7, 731; also Hoffner 1992: 49; Singer 1999: 716–17, with further references; Bryce 2005: 331–32; Kaniewski et al. 2010: 213.

22. RS 26.158; discussed by Nougayrol et al. 1968: 731–33; see Lebrun 1995: 86; Singer 1999: 717 n. 381.

23. The version of the letter found had been translated into Ugaritic: KTU 2.39/RS 18.038; Singer 1999: 707–8, 717; Pardee 2003: 94–95. On initial comments, see Nougayrol et al. 1968: 722. See, most recently, Kaniewski et al. 2010: 213.

24. Singer 1999: 717.

25. Ugarit text RS 34.152; Bordreuil 1991: 84–86; translation following Cohen and Singer 2006: 135. See Cohen and Singer 2006: 123, 134–35, with reference to the earlier primary publication by Lackenbacher 1995a; see also Singer 1999: 719, 727; Singer 2000: 24; and, most recently, Kaniewski et al. 2010: 213.

26. On the letter from the House of Urtenu (RS 94.2002+2003), see Singer 1999: 711–12; also Hoffner 1992: 49.

27. RS 18.147; translation following Pardee 2003: 97. The original letter, with this statement, has not been found, but is quoted verbatim in this letter sent in reply.

28. KTU 2.38/RS 18.031; translation following Monroe 2009: 98 and Pardee 2003: 93–94; see also Singer 1999: 672–73, 716, with earlier references.

29. See, e.g., Carpenter 1968; also Shrimpton 1987; Drews 1992; Drews 1993: 58; most recently Dickinson 2006: 54–56; Middleton 2010: 36–38; Demand 2011: 197–98; Kahn 2012: 262–63; Drake 2012.

30. See, e.g., Weiss 2012.

31. See Kaniewski et al. 2010 and now Kaniewski, Van Campo, and Weiss 2012; also Kaniewski et al. 2013.

32. Kaniewski et al. 2010: 207. Other studies have previously utilized ice cores and sediment cores; see, e.g., Rohling et al. 2009 and also others cited in Drake 2012.

33. Kaniewski et al. 2013.

34. Kaniewski et al. 2013: 6.

35. Kaniewski et al. 2013: 9.

36. Drake 2012: 1862–65.

37. Drake 2012: 1868; he says specifically, "Bayesian change-point analysis suggests that the change occurred before 1250–1197 BCE based on the high posterior probabilities from dinocyst/formaniferal records."

38. Drake 2012: 1862, 1866, 1868.

39. See the press release at http://www.imra.org.il/story.php3?id=62135 and the official publication by Langgut, Finkelstein, and Litt 2013. There may have been a similar dry period in Egypt at approximately this same time; see Bernhardt, Horton, and Stanley 2012.

40. Drake 2012: 1866, 1868.

41. Carpenter 1968: 53; see also previously Andronikos 1954 and now Drake 2012: 1867.

42. Zuckerman 2007a: 25–26.

43. Zuckerman 2007a: 26. But see now Ben-Tor 2013, who disagrees.

44. Bell 2012: 180.

45. See discussions in Carpenter 1968: 40–53; Drews 1993: 62–65; Dickinson 2006: 44–45; Middleton 2010: 41–45.

46. Carpenter 1968: 52–53; Sandars 1985: 184–86.

47. See, most recently, Murray 2013.

48. Singer 1999: 733; Monroe 2009: 361–63; both cited and quoted in Bell 2006: 1.

49. RS L 1 (*Ugaritica* 5.23); translation following Singer 1999: 728 and Bryce 2005: 334; see also Sandars 1985: 142–43 and the original publication in Nougayrol et al. 1968: 85–86; see also Yon 1992: 119. Note that van Soldt 1999: 33 n. 40 says that this text was actually purchased on the antiquities market.

50. RS 20.18 (*Ugaritica* 5.22), following the translation quoted in Bryce 2005: 334 and the discussion in Singer 1999: 721; see also Sandars 1985: 142 and the original publication in Nougayrol et al. 1968: 83–85.

51. RS 88.2009; publication by Malbran-Labat in Yon and Arnaud 2001: 249–50; further discussion in Singer 1999: 729.

52. RS 19.011; translation following Singer 1999: 726.

53. Singer 1999: 730.

54. See specific listing of hoard locations in Singer 1999: 731.

55. Singer 1999: 733.

56. RS 34.137; see Monroe 2009: 147.

57. Sherratt 1998: 294.

58. Sherratt 1998: 307; see also related discussion in Middleton 2010: 32–36.

59. Kilian 1990: 467.

60. Artzy 1998. See now also Killebrew and Lehmann 2013: 12 and Artzy 2013 in the volume edited by Killebrew and Lehmann.

61. Bell 2006: 112.

62. Routledge and McGeough 2009: 22, citing also Artzy 1998 and Liverani 2003.

63. Routledge and McGeough 2009: 22, 29.

64. Muhly 1992: 10, 19.

65. Liverani 1995: 114–15.

66. RS 34.129; Bordreuil 1991: 38–39; see Yon 1992: 116; Singer 1999: 722, 728, with earlier references; also Sandars 1985: 142; Singer 2000: 24; Strobel 2013: 511.

67. See Singer 2000: 27, citing Hoffner 1992: 48–51.

68. Yasur-Landau 2003a; Yasur-Landau 2010a: 114–18; Yasur-Landau 2012b. See now also Singer 2012 and, contra, Strobel 2013: 512–13.

69. Genz 2013: 477.

70. Kaniewski et al. 2011.

71. Kaniewski et al. 2011: 1.

72. Kaniewski et al. 2011: 4.

73. Kaniewski et al. 2011: 4.

74. Harrison 2009, 2010; Hawkins 2009, 2011; Yasur-Landau 2010a: 162–63; Bryce 2012: 128–29; Singer 2012; Killebrew and Lehmann 2013: 11. See also previously Janeway 2006–7 on Ta'yinat and the Aegean.

75. Yasur-Landau 2003a; see also Yasur-Landau 2003b, 2003c, and 2010a with previous references; Bauer 1998; Barako 2000, 2001; Gilboa 2005; Ben-Shlomo et al. 2008; Maeir, Hitchcock, and Horwitz 2013.

76. See now discussions by Demand 2011: 210–12, Stern 2012, Artzy 2013, and Strobel 2013: 526–27. See also Gilboa 1998, 2005, and 2006–7, with further bibliography; Dothan, T. 1982: 3–4; Dever 1992: 102–3; Stern 1994, 1998, 2000; Cline and O'Connor 2003, esp. 112–16, 138; Killebrew 2005: 204–5; Killebrew and Lehmann 2013: 13; Barakao 2013; Sharon and Gilboa 2013; Mountjoy 2013; Killebrew 2013; Lehmann 2013; Sherratt 2013. Zertal's claim to have found a site associated with the Shardana near Megiddo in Israel has been thoroughly refuted by Finkelstein; see Zertal 2002 and Finkelstein 2002. For a translation of "The Report of Wenamun," see Wente 2003b.

77. Bell 2006: 110–11.

78. Finkelstein 2000: 165; see also similar statements in Finkelstein 1998 and see now Finkelstein 2007. Weinstein 1992: 147 had earlier proposed a similar scenario, in which he saw the collapse of the Egyptian empire in Canaan as taking place in two phases, the first during the time of Ramses III and the second during the time of Ramses VI. See now also Yasur-Landau 2007: 612–13, 616 and Yasur-Landau 2010a: 340–41, for similar conclusions.

79. See Killebrew 2005: 230–31 for a summation of previous views.

80. Yasur-Landau 2003a; see now also discussion in Yasur-Landau 2010a: 335–45; Yasur-Landau 2012b; Bryce 2012: 33; Killebrew and Lehmann 2013: 17.

81. Yasur-Landau, personal communication, July 2012.

82. Yasur-Landau 2012a: 193–94; see also now Yasur-Landau 2012b and previously Yasur-Landau 2007: 615–16.

83. Yasur-Landau 2012a: 195.

84. Hitchcock and Maeir 2013: 51–56, esp. 53; also Maeir, Hitchcock, and Horwitz 2013.

85. See again Hitchcock and Maeir 2013: 51–56, esp. 53; also Maeir, Hitchcock, and Horwitz 2013.

86. See also the relevant discussion in Strobel 2013: 525–26.

87. Sandars 1985: 11, 19. Apart from Sandars, who was considered the expert on the topic, only a few other authors have attempted to write books specifically on the Sea Peoples and the collapse of the Bronze Age, including Nibbi 1975 and Robbins 2003. See now, however, Roberts's 2008 dissertation, which has the same title as Nibbi's earlier book.

88. Sandars 1985: 11.

89. Demand 2011: 193, citing Renfrew 1979.

90. See, e.g., Lorenz 1969, 1972. See now Yasur-Landau 2010a: 334, who (independently) also invokes the butterfly metaphor in connection with these events at the end of the Late Bronze Age.

91. Renfrew 1979: 482–87.

92. Diamond 2005; see now also Middleton 2010 and 2012, as well as previously the volume by Tainter (1988) and the edited volume by Yoffee and Cowgill (1988), besides the additional references in n. 2 to the preface, above.

93. Drews 1993: 85–90, esp. 88; see also Deger-Jalkotzy 2008: 391.

94. See the brief discussion by Dever 1992: 106–7 of the systems collapse that he sees occurring in Canaan at this time. See also Middleton 2010: 118–21 on the many contributing causes in the Aegean and now Drake 2012: 1866–68.

95. Liverani 1987: 69; also Drews 1993: 86 and Monroe 2009: 293, both citing Liverani.

96. Liverani 1987: 69; see now Monroe 2009: 292–96 for a critique of Liverani's views.

97. Monroe 2009: 294–96.

98. Monroe 2009: 297.

99. Monroe 2009: 297.

100. Monroe 2009: 297.

101. Drake 2012: 1866–68; Kaniewski et al. 2013.

102. Drews 1993; see my own review of Drews's book: Cline 1997b.

103. See now the recent discussion regarding collapse and the potential reasons for such in Middleton 2012.

104. Johnson 2007: 3–5.

105. Bell 2006: 14–15.

106. Johnson 2007: 13.

107. Johnson 2007: 13–16.

108. Johnson 2007: 14–15; Sherratt 2003: 53–54.

109. Johnson 2007: 15.

110. Johnson 2007: 17.

111. Bell 2006: 15, citing Dark 1998: 65, 106, and 120.

112. Dark 1998: 120.

113. Dark 1998: 120–21.

114. Bell 2006: 15. See now also Killebrew and Lehmann 2013: 16–17.

115. See most recently Langgut, Finkelstein, and Litt 2013: 166.

Epilogue

1. See now the dissertation by Murray 2013.

2. Davis 2010: 687.

3. Maran 2009: 242.

4. Cf. Millard 1995: 122–24; Bryce 2012: 56–57; Millard 2012; Lemaire 2012; Killebrew and Lehmann 2013: 5–6.

5. Van De Mieroop 2007: 252–53.

6. Sherratt 2003: 53–54; Bryce 2012: 195.

7. See the volumes edited by Schwartz and Nichols (2006) and McAnany and Yoffee (2010), at least partially in response to Diamond's 2005 book. A conference on this topic was recently held at Southern Illinois University in March 2013: "Beyond Collapse: Archaeological Perspectives on Resilience, Revitalization & Reorganization in Complex Societies."

8. Dever 1992: 108.

9. Monroe 2009: 292.

10. Cho and Appelbaum 2008, A1.

Abt, J. 2011. *American Egyptologist: The Life of James Henry Breasted and the Creation of His Oriental Institute.* Chicago: University of Chicago Press.

Adams, M. J., and M. E. Cohen. 2013. Appendix: The "Sea Peoples" in Primary Sources. In *The Philistines and Other "Sea Peoples" in Text and Archaeology,* ed. A. E. Killebrew and G. Lehmann, 645–64. Atlanta: Society of Biblical Literature.

Ahrens, A., H. Dohmann-Pfälzner, and P. Pfälzner. 2012. New Light on the Amarna Period from the Northern Levant. A Clay Sealing with the Throne Name of Amenhotep IV/Akhenaten from the Royal Palace at Tall Misrife/Qatna. *Zeitschrift für Orient-Archäologie* 5: 232–48.

Allen, J. P. 2005. After Hatshepsut: The Military Campaigns of Thutmose III. In *Hatshepsut: From Queen to Pharaoh,* ed. C. Roehrig, 261–62. New Haven: Yale University Press.

Allen, S. H. 1999. *Finding the Walls of Troy: Frank Calvert and Heinrich Schliemann at Hisarlik.* Berkeley: University of California Press.

Andronikos, M. 1954. E 'dorike Eisvole' kai ta archaiologika Euremata. *Hellenika* 13: 221–40. (in Greek)

Anthony, D. W. 1990. Migration in Archaeology: The Baby and the Bathwater. *American Anthropologist* 92: 895–914.

Anthony, D. W. 1997. Prehistoric Migrations as a Social Process. In *Migrations and Invasions in Archaeological Explanation,* ed. J. Chapman and H. Hamerow, 21–32. Oxford: Tempus Reparatum.

Artzy, M. 1998. Routes, Trade, Boats and "Nomads of the Sea." In *Mediterranean Peoples in Transition: Thirteenth to Early Tenth Centuries BCE,* ed. S. Gitin, A. Mazar, and E. Stern, 439–48. Jerusalem: Israel Exploration Society.

Artzy, M. 2013. On the Other "Sea Peoples." In *The Philistines and Other "Sea Peoples" in Text and Archaeology,* ed. A. E. Killebrew and G. Lehmann, 329–44. Atlanta: Society of Biblical Literature.

Aruz, J., ed. 2008. *Beyond Babylon: Art, Trade, and Diplomacy in the Second Millennium B.C. Catalogue of an Exhibition at the Metropolitan Museum of Art, New York.* New York: Metropolitan Museum of Art.

Ashkenazi, E. 2012. A 3,400-Year-Old Mystery: Who Burned the Palace of Canaanite Hatzor? Archaeologists Take on the Bible during Tel Hatzor Excavations, When Disagreements Arise over the Destroyer of the City. *Haaretz,* July 23, 2012, http://www .haaretz.com/news/national/a-3-400-year-old-mystery-who-burned-the-palace-of -canaanite-hatzor.premium-1.453095 (last accessed August 6, 2012).

Astour, M. C. 1964. Greek Names in the Semitic World and Semitic Names in the Greek World. *Journal of Near Eastern Studies* 23: 193–201.

Astour, M. C. 1965. New Evidence on the Last Days of Ugarit. *American Journal of Archaeology* 69: 253–58.

Astour, M. C. 1967. *HellenoSemitica.* 2nd Edition. Leiden: E. J. Brill.

Åström, P. 1998. Continuity or Discontinuity: Indigenous and Foreign Elements in Cyprus around 1200 BCE. In *Mediterranean Peoples in Transition: Thirteenth to Early*

Tenth Centuries BCE, ed. S. Gitin, A. Mazar, and E. Stern, 80–86. Jerusalem: Israel Exploration Society.

Bachhuber, C. 2006. Aegean Interest on the Uluburun Ship. *American Journal of Archaeology* 110: 345–63.

Bachhuber, C., and R. G. Roberts. 2009. *Forces of Transformation: The End of the Bronze Age in the Mediterranean*. Oxford: Oxbow Books.

Badre, L. 2003. Handmade Burnished Ware and Contemporary Imported Pottery from Tell Kazel. In *Sea Routes . . . : Interconnections in the Mediterranean 16th–6th c. BC. Proceedings of the International Symposium Held at Rethymnon, Crete in September 29th–October 2nd 2002*, ed. N. Chr. Stampolidis and V. Karageorghis, 83–99. Athens: University of Crete and the A. G. Leventis Foundation.

Badre, L. 2006. Tell Kazel-Simyra: A Contribution to a Relative Chronological History in the Eastern Mediterranean during the Late Bronze Age. *Bulletin of the American Schools of Oriental Research* 343: 63–95.

Badre, L. 2011. Cultural Interconnections in the Eastern Mediterranean: Evidence from Tell Kazel in the Late Bronze Age. In *Intercultural Contacts in the Ancient Mediterranean. Proceedings of the International Conference at the Netherlands-Flemish Institute in Cairo, 25th to 29th October 2008*, ed. K. Duistermaat and I. Regulski, 205–23. Leuven: Uitgeveru Peeters.

Badre, L., M.-C. Boileau, R. Jung, and H. Mommsen. 2005. The Provenance of Aegean- and Surian-type Pottery Found at Tell Kazel (Syria). *Egypt and the Levant* 15: 15–47.

Bakry, H. 1973. The Discovery of a Temple of Mernptah at On. *Aegyptus* 53: 3–21.

Barako, T. J. 2000. The Philistine Settlement as Mercantile Phenomenon? *American Journal of Archaeology* 104/3: 513–30.

Barako, T. J. 2001. *The Seaborne Migration of the Philistines*. Ph.D. Dissertation, Harvard University.

Barako, T. J. 2003a. One If by Sea . . . Two If by Land: How Did the Philistines Get to Canaan? One: by Sea—A Hundred Penteconters Could Have Carried 5,000 People Per Trip. *Biblical Archaeology Review* 29/2: 26–33, 64–66.

Barako, T. J. 2003b. The Changing Perception of the Sea Peoples Phenomenon: Migration, Invasion or Cultural Diffusion? In *Sea Routes . . . : Interconnections in the Mediterranean 16th–6th c. BC. Proceedings of the International Symposium Held at Rethymnon, Crete in September 29th–October 2nd 2002*, ed. N. Chr. Stampolidis and V. Karageorghis, 163–69. Athens: University of Crete and the A. G. Leventis Foundation.

Barako, T. J. 2013. Philistines and Egyptians in Southern Coastal Canaan during the Early Iron Age. In *The Philistines and Other "Sea Peoples" in Text and Archaeology*, ed. A. E. Killebrew and G. Lehmann, 37–51. Atlanta: Society of Biblical Literature.

Barkay, G., and D. Ussishkin. 2004. Area S: The Late Bronze Age Strata. In *The Renewed Archaeological Excavations at Lachish (1973-1994)*, ed. D. Ussishkin, 316–407. Tel Aviv: Tel Aviv University.

Bass, G. F. 1967. *Cape Gelidonya*. Transactions of the American Philosophical Society, vol. 57, pt. 8. Philadelphia: American Philosophical Society.

Bass, G. F. 1973. Cape Gelidonya and Bronze Age Maritime Trade. In *Orient and Occident*, ed. H. A. Hoffner, Jr., 29–38. Neukirchener-Vluyn: Neukirchener Verlag.

Bass, G. F. 1986. A Bronze Age Shipwreck at Ulu Burun (Kas): 1984 Campaign. *American Journal of Archaeology* 90/3: 269–96.

Bass, G. F. 1987. Oldest Known Shipwreck Reveals Splendors of the Bronze Age. *National Geographic* 172/6: 693–733.

Bass, G. F. 1988. Return to Cape Gelidonya. *INA Newsletter* 15/2: 3–5.

Bass, G. F. 1997. Prolegomena to a Study of Maritime Traffic in Raw Materials to the Aegean during the Fourteenth and Thirteenth Centuries B.C. In *Techne: Craftsmen, Craftswomen and Craftsmanship in the Aegean Bronze Age. Proceedings of the 6th International Aegean Conference, Philadelphia, Temple University, 18–21 April 1996*, ed. R. Laffineur and P. P. Betancourt, 153–70. Liège: Université de Liège.

Bass, G. F. 1998. Sailing between the Aegean and the Orient in the Second Millennium BC. In *The Aegean and the Orient in the Second Millennium. Proceedings of the 50th Anniversary Symposium, Cincinnati, 18–20 April 1997*, ed. E. H. Cline and D. H. Cline, 183–91. Liège: Université de Liège.

Bass, G. F. 2013. Cape Gelidonya Redux. In *Cultures in Contact: From Mesopotamia to the Mediterranean in the Second Millennium B.C.*, ed. J. Aruz, S. B. Graff, and Y. Rakic, 62–71. New York: Metropolitan Museum of Art.

Bauer, A. A. 1998. Cities of the Sea: Maritime Trade and the Origin of Philistine Settlement in the Early Iron Age Southern Levant. *Oxford Journal of Archaeology* 17/2: 149–68.

Baumbach, L. 1983. An Examination of the Evidence for a State of Emergency at Pylos c. 1200 BC from the Linear B Tablets. In *Res Mycenaeae*, ed. A. Heubeck and G. Neumann, 28–40. Göttingen: Vandenhoeck and Ruprecht.

Beckman, G. 1996a. Akkadian Documents from Ugarit. In *Sources for the History of Cyprus*, vol. 2, *Near Eastern and Aegean Texts from the Third to the First Millennia BC*, ed. A. B. Knapp, 26–28. Altamont, NY: Greece and Cyprus Research Center.

Beckman, G. 1996b. Hittite Documents from Hattusa. In *Sources for the History of Cyprus*, vol. 2, *Near Eastern and Aegean Texts from the Third to the First Millennia BC*, ed. A. B. Knapp, 31–35. Altamont, NY: Greece and Cyprus Research Center.

Beckman, G., T. Bryce, and E. H. Cline. 2011. *The Ahhiyawa Texts*. Atlanta: Society of Biblical Literature. Reissued in hardcopy, Leiden: Brill, 2012.

Bell, C. 2006. *The Evolution of Long Distance Trading Relationships across the LBA/Iron Age Transition on the Northern Levantine Coast: Crisis, Continuity and Change.* BAR International Series 1574. Oxford: Archaeopress.

Bell, C. 2009. Continuity and Change: The Divergent Destinies of Late Bronze Age Ports in Syria and Lebanon across the LBA/Iron Age Transition. In *Forces of Transformation: The End of the Bronze Age in the Mediterranean*, ed. C. Bachhuber and R. G. Roberts, 30–38. Oxford: Oxbow Books.

Bell, C. 2012. The Merchants of Ugarit: Oligarchs of the Late Bronze Age Trade in Metals? In *Eastern Mediterranean Metallurgy and Metalwork in the Second Millennium BC: A Conference in Honour of James D. Muhly; Nicosia, 10th–11th October 2009*, ed. V. Kassianidou and G. Papasavvas, 180–87. Oxford: Oxbow Books.

Ben Dor Evian, S. 2011. Shishak's Karnak Relief—More Than Just Name-Rings. In *Egypt, Canaan and Israel: History, Imperialism, Ideology and Literature: Proceedings of a Conference at the University of Haifa, 3–7 May 2009*, ed. S. Bar, D. Kahn, and J. J. Shirley, 11–22. Leiden: Brill.

Ben-Shlomo, D., I. Shai, A. Zukerman, and A. M. Maeir. 2008. Cooking Identities: Aegean-Style Cooking Jugs and Cultural Interaction in Iron Age Philistia and Neighboring Regions. *American Journal of Archaeology* 112/2: 225–46.

Ben-Tor, A. 1998. The Fall of Canaanite Hazor—The "Who" and "When" Questions. In *Mediterranean Peoples in Transition: Thirteenth to Early Tenth Centuries BCE*, ed. S. Gitin, A. Mazar, and E. Stern, 456–68. Jerusalem: Israel Exploration Society.

Ben-Tor, A. 2006. The Sad Fate of Statues and the Mutilated Statues of Hazor. In *Confronting the Past: Archaeological and Historical Essays on Ancient Israel in Honor of William G. Dever*, ed. S. Gitin, J. E. Wright, and J. P. Dessel, 3–16. Winona Lake, IN: Eisenbrauns.

Ben-Tor, A. 2013. Who Destroyed Canaanite Hazor? *Biblical Archaeology Review* 39/4: 26–36, 58–60.

Ben-Tor, A., and M. T. Rubiato. 1999. Excavating Hazor, Part Two: Did the Israelites Destroy the Canaanite City? *Biblical Archaeology Review* 25/3: 22–39.

Ben-Tor, A., and S. Zuckerman. 2008. Hazor at the End of the Late Bronze Age: Back to Basics. *Bulletin of the American Schools of Oriental Research* 350: 1–6.

Bernhardt, C. E., B. P. Horton, and J.-D. Stanley. 2012. Nile Delta Vegetation Response to Holocene Climate Variability. *Geology* 40/7: 615–18.

Bietak, M. 1992. Minoan Wall-Paintings Unearthed at Ancient Avaris. *Egyptian Archaeology* 2: 26–28

Bietak, M. 1996. *Avaris: The Capital of the Hyksos. Recent Excavations at Tell el-Dab'a*. London: British Museum Press.

Bietak, M. 2005. Egypt and the Aegean: Cultural Convergence in a Thutmoside Palace at Avaris. In *Hatshepsut: From Queen to Pharaoh*, ed. C. Roehrig, 75–81. New Haven: Yale University Press.

Bietak, M., N. Marinatos, and C. Palyvou. 2007. *Taureador Scenes in Tell El-Dab'a (Avaris) and Knossos*. Vienna: Austrian Academy of Sciences.

Blegen, C. W. 1955. The Palace of Nestor Excavations of 1954. *American Journal of Archaeology* 59/1: 31–37.

Blegen, C. W., C. G. Boulter, J. L. Caskey, and M. Rawson. 1958. *Troy IV: Settlements VIIa, VIIb and VIII*. Princeton, NJ: Princeton University Press.

Blegen, C. W., and K. Kourouniotis. 1939. Excavations at Pylos, 1939. *American Journal of Archaeology* 43/4: 557–76.

Blegen, C. W., and M. Lang. 1960. The Palace of Nestor Excavations of 1959. *American Journal of Archaeology* 64/2: 153–64.

Blegen, C. W., and M. Rawson. 1966. *The Palace of Nestor at Pylos in Western Messenia*. Vol. 1, *The Buildings and Their Contents*. Pt. 1, *Text*. Princeton, NJ: Princeton University Press.

Bordreuil, P., ed. 1991. *Une bibliothèque au sud de la ville: Les textes de la 34ᵉ campagne (1973)*. Ras Shamra-Ougarit VII. Paris: Éditions Recherche sur les Civilisations.

Bordreuil, P., and F. Malbran-Labat. 1995. Les archives de la maison d'Ourtenou. *Comptes-rendus des séances de l'Académie des Inscriptions et Belles-Lettres* 139/2: 443–51.

Bordreuil, P., D. Pardee, and R. Hawley. 2012. *Une bibliothèque au sud de la ville***. Textes 1994–2002 en cunéiforme alphabétique de la maison d'Ourtenou Ras Shamra-Ougarit XVIII*. RSO 18. Lyon: Maison de l'Orient et de la Méditerranée–Jean Pouilloux.

Bounni, A., A. and J. Lagarce, and N. Saliby. 1976. Rapport préliminaire sur la première campagne de fouilles (1975) à Ibn Hani (Syrie). *Syria* 55: 233–79.

Bounni, A., A. and J. Lagarce, and N. Saliby. 1978. Rapport préliminaire sur la deuxième campagne de fouilles (1976) à Ibn Hani (Syrie). *Syria* 56: 218–91.

Bouzek, J. 2011. Bird-Shaped Prows of Boats, Sea Peoples and the Pelasgians. In *Exotica in the Prehistoric Mediterranean*, ed. A. Vianello, 188–93. Oxford: Oxbow Books.

Braudel, F. 2001. *The Mediterranean in the Ancient World*. London: Allen Lane, Penguin Books.

Breasted, J. H. 1906. *Ancient Records of Egypt*. Urbana: University of Illinois Press. Reprinted 2001.

Breasted, J. H. 1930. Foreword. In *Medinet Habu*, vol. 1, *Earlier Historical Records of Ramses III*, ed. The Epigraphic Survey, ix–xi. Chicago: University of Chicago Press.

Bretschneider J., and K. Van Lerberghe, eds. 2008. *In Search of Gibala: An Archaeological and Historical Study Based on Eight Seasons of Excavations at Tell Tweini (Syria) in the A and C Fields (1999-2007)*. Aula Orientalis–Supplementa 24. Barcelona: Sabadell.

Bretschneider, J., and K. Van Lerberghe. 2011. The Jebleh Plain through History: Tell Tweini and Its Intercultural Contacts in the Bronze and Early Iron Age. In *Intercultural Contacts in the Ancient Mediterranean. Proceedings of the International Conference at the Netherlands-Flemish Institute in Cairo, 25th to 29th October 2008*, ed. K. Duistermaat and I. Regulski, 183–203. Leuven: Uitgeveru Peeters.

Bretschneider, J., A.-S. Van Vyve,, and G. Jans. 2011. Tell Tweini: A Multi-Period Harbour Town at the Syrian Coast. In *Egypt and the Near East—the Crossroads: Proceedings of an International Conference on the Relations of Egypt and the Near East in the Bronze Age, Prague, September 1-3, 2010*, ed. J. Mynářová, 73–87. Prague: Charles University in Prague.

Bryce, T. R. 1985. A Reinterpretation of the Milawata Letter in the Light of the New Join Piece. *Anatolian Studies* 35: 13–23.

Bryce, T. R. 1989a. The Nature of Mycenaean Involvement in Western Anatolia. *Historia* 38: 1–21.

Bryce, T. R. 1989b. Ahhiyawans and Mycenaeans—An Anatolian Viewpoint. *Oxford Journal of Archaeology* 8: 297–310.

Bryce, T. R. 2002. *Life and Society in the Hittite World*. Oxford: Oxford University Press.

Bryce, T. R. 2005. *The Kingdom of the Hittites*. New Edition. Oxford: Oxford University Press.

Bryce, T. R. 2009. *The Routledge Handbook of the Peoples and Places of Ancient Western Asia: From the Early Bronze Age to the Fall of the Persian Empire*. London: Routledge.

Bryce, T. R. 2010. The Hittite Deal with the Hiyawa-Men. In *Pax Hethitica: Studies on the Hittites and Their Neighbours in Honor of Itamar Singer*, ed. Y. Cohen, A. Gilan, and J. L. Miller, 47–53. Wiesbaden: Harrassowitz Verlag.

Bryce, T. R. 2012. *The World of the Neo-Hittite Kingdoms*. Oxford: Oxford University Press.

Bunimovitz, S. 1998. Sea Peoples in Cyprus and Israel: A Comparative Study of Immigration Processes. In *Mediterranean Peoples in Transition: Thirteenth to Early Tenth Centuries BCE*, ed. S. Gitin, A. Mazar, and E. Stern, 103–13. Jerusalem: Israel Exploration Society.

Butzer, K. W. 2012. Collapse, Environment, and Society. *Proceedings of the National Academy of Sciences* 109/10: 3632–39.

Butzer, K. W., and G. H. Endfield. 2012. Critical Perspectives on Historical Collapse. *Proceedings of the National Academy of Sciences* 109/10: 3628–31.

Callot, O. 1994. *Ras Shamra-Ougarit X: La tranchée «Ville sud». Études d'architecture domestique*. Paris: Éditions Recherche sur les Civilisations.

Callot, O., and M. Yon. 1995. Urbanisme et architecture. In *Le Pays d'Ougarit autour de 1200 av. J.-C.: Historie et archéologie. Actes du Colloque International; Paris, 28 juin-1ᵉʳ juillet 1993*, ed. M. Yon, M. Sznycer, and P. Bordreuil, 155–68. Paris: Éditions Recherche sur les Civilisations.

Carmi, I., and D. Ussishkin. 2004. ¹⁴C Dates. In *The Renewed Archaeological Excavations at Lachish (1973–1994)*, ed. D. Ussishkin, 2508–13. Tel Aviv: Tel Aviv University.

Carpenter, R. 1968. *Discontinuity in Greek Civilization*. New York: W. W. Norton & Co.

Carruba, O. 1977. Beitrage zur mittelhethitischen Geschichtc, I: Die Tuthalijas und die Arnuwandas. *Studi micenei ed egeo-anatolici* 18: 137–74.

Castleden, R. 1993. *Minoan Life in Bronze Age Crete*. London: Routledge.

Caubet, A. 1992. Reoccupation of the Syrian Coast after the Destruction of the "Crisis Years." In *The Crisis Years: The 12th Century B.C.*, ed. W. A. Ward and M. S. Joukowsky, 123–30. Dubuque, IA: Kendall/Hunt Publishing Co.

Caubet, A. 2000. Ras Shamra-Ugarit before the Sea Peoples. In *The Sea Peoples and Their World: A Reassessment*, ed. E. D. Oren, 35–49. Philadelphia: University of Pennsylvania.

Caubet, A., and V. Matoian. 1995. Ougarit et l'Égée. In *Le Pays d'Ougarit autour de 1200 av. J.-C.: Historie et archéologie. Actes du Colloque International; Paris, 28 juin-1ᵉʳ juillet 1993*, ed. M. Yon, M. Sznycer, and P. Bordreuil, 99–112. Paris: Éditions Recherche sur les Civilisations.

Cho, D., and B. Appelbaum. 2008. Unfolding Worldwide Turmoil Could Reverse Years of Prosperity. *Washington Post*, October 7, 2008, A1.

Cifola, B. 1991. The Terminology of Ramses III's Historical Records with a Formal Analysis of the War Scenes. *Orientalia* 60: 9–57.

Cifola, B. 1994. The Role of the Sea Peoples at the End of the Late Bronze Age: A Reassessment of Textual and Archaeological Evidence. *Oriens Antiqvi Miscellanea* 1: 1–57.

Clayton, P. A. 1994. *Chronicle of the Pharaohs: The Reign-by-Reign Record of the Rulers and Dynasties of Ancient Egypt*. London: Thames and Hudson.

Cline, E. H. 1987. Amenhotep III and the Aegean: A Reassessment of Egypto-Aegean Relations in the 14th Century BC. *Orientalia* 56/1: 1–36.

Cline, E. H. 1990. An Unpublished Amenhotep III Faience Plaque from Mycenae. *Journal of the American Oriental Society* 110/2: 200–212.

Cline, E. H. 1991a. Hittite Objects in the Bronze Age Aegean. *Anatolian Studies* 41: 133–43.

Cline, E. H. 1991b. A Possible Hittite Embargo against the Mycenaeans. *Historia* 40/1: 1–9.

Cline, E. H. 1994. *Sailing the Wine-Dark Sea: International Trade and the Late Bronze Age Aegean*. Oxford: Tempus Reparatum. Republished 2009.

Cline, E. H. 1995a. 'My Brother, My Son': Rulership and Trade between the LBA Aegean, Egypt and the Near East. In *The Role of the Ruler in the Prehistoric Aegean*, ed. P. Rehak, 143–50. Aegaeum 11. Liège: Université de Liège.

Cline, E. H. 1995b. Tinker, Tailor, Soldier, Sailor: Minoans and Mycenaeans Abroad. In *Politeia: Society and State in the Aegean Bronze Age*, ed. W.-D. Niemeier and R. Laffineur, 265–87. Aegaeum 12. Liège: Université de Liège.

Cline, E. H. 1996. Aššuwa and the Achaeans: The 'Mycenaean' Sword at Hattušas and Its Possible Implications. *Annual of the British School at Athens* 91: 137–51.

Cline, E. H. 1997a. Achilles in Anatolia: Myth, History, and the Aššuwa Rebellion. In *Crossing Boundaries and Linking Horizons: Studies in Honor of Michael Astour on His 80th Birthday*, ed. G. D. Young, M. W. Chavalas, and R. E. Averbeck, 189–210. Bethesda, MD: CDL Press.

Cline, E. H. 1997b. Review of R. Drews, *The End of the Bronze Age* (Princeton 1993). *Journal of Near Eastern Studies* 56/2: 127–29.

Cline, E. H. 1998. Amenhotep III, the Aegean and Anatolia. In *Amenhotep III: Perspectives on His Reign*, ed. D. O'Connor and E. H. Cline, 236–50. Ann Arbor: University of Michigan Press.

Cline, E. H. 1999a. The Nature of the Economic Relations of Crete with Egypt and the Near East during the Bronze Age. In *From Minoan Farmers to Roman Traders: Sidelights on the Economy of Ancient Crete*, ed. A. Chaniotis. 115–43. Munich: G. B. Steiner.

Cline, E. H. 1999b. Coals to Newcastle, Wallbrackets to Tiryns: Irrationality, Gift Exchange, and Distance Value. In *Meletemata: Studies in Aegean Archaeology Presented to Malcolm H. Wiener As He Enters His 65th Year*, ed. P. P. Betancourt, V. Karageorghis, R. Laffineur, and W.-D. Niemeier, 119–23. Aegaeum 20. Liège: Université de Liège.

Cline, E. H. 2000. *The Battles of Armageddon: Megiddo and the Jezreel Valley from the Bronze Age to the Nuclear Age*. Ann Arbor: University of Michigan Press.

Cline, E. H. 2005. Cyprus and Alashiya: One and the Same! *Archaeology Odyssey* 8/5: 41–44.

Cline, E. H. 2006. A Widow's Plea and a Murder Mystery. *Dig* magazine, January 2006, 28–30.

Cline, E. H. 2007a. Rethinking Mycenaean International Trade. In *Rethinking Mycenaean Palaces*, ed. W. Parkinson and M. Galaty, 190–200. 2nd Edition. Los Angeles: Cotsen Institute of Archaeology.

Cline, E. H. 2007b. *From Eden to Exile: Unraveling Mysteries of the Bible*. Washington, DC: National Geographic Books.

Cline, E. H. 2009a. *Biblical Archaeology: A Very Short Introduction*. New York: Oxford University Press.

Cline, E. H. 2009b. The Sea Peoples' Possible Role in the Israelite Conquest of Canaan. In *Doron: Festschrift for Spyros E. Iakovidis*, ed. D. Danielidou, 191–98. Athens: Athens Academy.

Cline, E. H. 2010. Bronze Age Interactions between the Aegean and the Eastern Mediterranean Revisited: Mainstream, Margin, or Periphery? In *Archaic State Interaction: The Eastern Mediterranean in the Bronze Age*, ed. W. Parkinson and M. Galaty, 161–80. Santa Fe, NM: School for Advanced Research.

Cline, E. H., ed. 2010. *The Oxford Handbook of the Bronze Age Aegean*. New York: Oxford University Press.

Cline, E. H. 2011. Whole Lotta Shakin' Going On: The Possible Destruction by Earthquake of Megiddo Stratum VIA. In *The Fire Signals of Lachish: Studies in the Archaeology and History of Israel in the Late Bronze Age, Iron Age, and Persian Period in Honor of David Ussishkin*, ed. I. Finkelstein and N. Na'aman, 55–70. Tel Aviv: Tel Aviv University.

Cline, E. H. 2013. *The Trojan War: A Very Short Introduction*. Oxford: Oxford University Press.

Cline, E. H., and M. J. Cline. 1991. Of Shoes and Ships and Sealing Wax: International Trade and the Late Bronze Age Aegean. *Expedition* 33/3: 46–54.

Cline, E. H., and D. Harris-Cline, eds. 1998. *The Aegean and the Orient in the Second Millennium. Proceedings of the 50th Anniversary Symposium, Cincinnati, 18–20 April 1997*. Aegaeum 18. Liège: Université de Liège.

Cline, E. H., and D. O'Connor. 2003. The Mystery of the 'Sea Peoples'. In *Mysterious Lands*, ed. D. O'Connor and S. Quirke, 107–38. London: UCL Press.

Cline, E. H., and D. O'Connor, eds. 2006. *Thutmose III: A New Biography*. Ann Arbor: University of Michigan Press.

Cline, E. H., and D. O'Connor, eds. 2012. *Ramesses III: The Life and Times of Egypt's Last Hero*. Ann Arbor: University of Michigan Press.

Cline, E. H., and S. M. Stannish. 2011. Sailing the Great Green Sea: Amenhotep III's "Aegean List" from Kom el-Hetan, Once More. *Journal of Ancient Egyptian Interconnections* 3/2: 6–16.

Cline, E. H., and A. Yasur-Landau. 2007. Musings from a Distant Shore: The Nature and Destination of the Uluburun Ship and Its Cargo. *Tel Aviv* 34/2: 125–41.

Cline, E. H., and A. Yasur-Landau. 2013. Aegeans in Israel: Minoan Frescoes at Tel Kabri. *Biblical Archaeology Review* 39/4 (July/August 2013) 37–44, 64, 66.

Cline, E. H., A. Yasur-Landau, and N. Goshen. 2011. New Fragments of Aegean-Style Painted Plaster from Tel Kabri, Israel. *American Journal of Archaeology* 115/2: 245–61.

Cohen, C., J. Maran, and M. Vetters, 2010. An Ivory Rod with a Cuneiform Inscription, Most Probably Ugaritic, from a Final Palatial Workshop in the Lower Citadel of Tiryns. *Archäologischer Anzeiger* 2010/2: 1–22.

Cohen, R., and R. Westbrook., eds. 2000. *Amarna Diplomacy: The Beginnings of International Relations*. Baltimore: Johns Hopkins University Press.

Cohen, Y., and I. Singer. 2006. A Late Synchronism between Ugarit and Emar. In *Essays on Ancient Israel in Its Near Eastern Context: A Tribute to Nadav Na'aman*: 123–39, ed. Y. Amit, E. Ben Zvi, I. Finkelstein, and O. Lipschits. Winona Lake, IN: Eisenbrauns.

Collins, B. J. 2007. *The Hittites and Their World*. Atlanta: Society of Biblical Literature.

Courbin, P. 1990. Bassit Poidaeion in the Early Iron Age. In *Greek Colonists and Native Populations. First Australian Congress of Classical Archaeology in Honour of A. D. Trendall*, ed. J.-P. Descoeudres, 504–9. Oxford: Clarendon Press.

Curtis, A.H.W. 1999. Ras Shamra, Minet el-Beida and Ras Ibn Hani: The Material Sources. In *Handbook of Ugaritic Studies*, ed. W.G.E. Watson and N. Wyatt, 5–27. Leiden: Brill.

Dalley, S. 1984. *Mari and Karana: Two Old Babylonian Cities*. London: Longman.

Dark, K. R. 1998. *Waves of Time: Long Term Change and International Relations*. New York: Continuum.

Darnell, J. C., and C. Manassa. 2007. *Tutankhamun's Armies: Battle and Conquest during Ancient Egypt's Late Eighteenth Dynasty*. Hoboken, NJ: John Wiley & Sons.

Davies, N. de G. 1943. *The Tombs of Rekh-mi-Re' at Thebes* (= PMMA, 11). New York: Metropolitan Museum of Art.

Davis, J. L., ed. 1998. *Sandy Pylos. An Archaeological History from Nestor to Navarino*. Austin: University of Texas Press.

Davis, J. L. 2010. Pylos. In *The Oxford Handbook of the Bronze Age Aegean*, ed. E. H. Cline, 680–89. New York: Oxford University Press.

Deger-Jalkotzy, S. 2008. Decline, Destruction, Aftermath. In *The Cambridge Companion to the Aegean Bronze Age*, ed. C. W. Shelmerdine, 387–415. Cambridge: Cambridge University Press.

Demand, N. H. 2011. *The Mediterranean Context of Early Greek History*. Oxford: Wiley-Blackwell.

Dever, W. G. 1992. The Late Bronze–Early Iron I Horizon in Syria-Palestine: Egyptians, Canaanites, 'Sea Peoples,' and Proto-Israelites. In *The Crisis Years: The 12th Century B.C.*, ed. W. A. Ward and M. S. Joukowsky, 99–110. Dubuque, IA: Kendall/Hunt Publishing Co.

Diamond, J. 2005. *Collapse: How Societies Choose to Fail or Succeed*. New York: Viking.

Dickinson, O. 2006. *The Aegean from Bronze Age to Iron Age. Continuity and Change between the Twelfth and Eighth Centuries BC*. New York: Routledge.

Dickinson, O. 2010. The Collapse at the End of the Bronze Age. In *The Oxford Handbook of the Bronze Age Aegean*, ed. E. H. Cline, 483–90. New York: Oxford University Press.

Dietrich, M., and O. Loretz. 1999. Ugarit, Home of the Oldest Alphabets. In *Handbook of Ugaritic Studies*, ed. W.G.E. Watson and N. Wyatt, 81–90. Leiden: Brill.

Dietrich, M., and O. Loretz. 2002. Der Untergang von Ugarit am 21. Januar 1192 v. Chn? Der astronomisch-hepatoskopische Bericht KTU 1.78 (RS 12.061). *Ugarit-Forschungen* 34: 53–74.

Dorman, P. F. 2005a. Hatshepsut: Princess to Queen to Co-Ruler. In *Hatshepsut: From Queen to Pharaoh*, ed. C. Roehrig, 87–89. New Haven: Yale University Press.

Dorman, P. F. 2005b. The Career of Senenmut. In *Hatshepsut: From Queen to Pharaoh*, ed. C. Roehrig, 107–9. New Haven: Yale University Press.

Dothan, M. 1971. *Ashdod II–III. The Second and Third Season of Excavations 1963, 1965, Sounding in 1967. Text and Plates.* 'Atiqot 9–10. Jerusalem: Israel Antiquities Authority.

Dothan, M. 1993. Ashdod. In *The New Encyclopedia of Archaeological Excavations in the Holy Land*, ed. E. Stern, 93–102. Jerusalem: Carta.

Dothan, M., and Y. Porath. 1993. *Ashdod V. Excavations of Area G. The Fourth–Sixth Season of Excavations 1968–1970.* 'Atiqot 23. Jerusalem: Israel Antiquities Authority.

Dothan, T. 1982. *The Philistines and Their Material Culture*. New Haven: Yale University Press.

Dothan, T. 1983. Some Aspects of the Appearance of the Sea Peoples and Philistines in Canaan. In *Griechenland, die Ägäis und die Levante während der "Dark Ages,"* ed. S. Deger-Jalkotzy, 99–117. Vienna: Österreichische Akademie der Wissenschaft.

Dothan, T. 1990. Ekron of the Philistines, Part 1: Where They Came From, How They Settled Down and the Place They Worshiped In. *Biblical Archaeology Review* 18/1: 28–38.

Dothan, T. 1998. Initial Philistine Settlement: From Migration to Coexistence. In *Mediterranean Peoples in Transition: Thirteenth to Early Tenth Centuries BCE*, ed. S. Gitin, A. Mazar, and E. Stern, 148–61. Jerusalem: Israel Exploration Society.

Dothan, T. 2000. Reflections on the Initial Phase of Philistine Settlement. In *The Sea Peoples and Their World: A Reassessment*, ed. E. D. Oren, 146–58. Philadelphia: University of Pennsylvania.

Dothan, T., and M. Dothan. 1992. *People of the Sea: The Search for the Philistines*. New York: Macmillan Publishing Company.

Drake, B. L. 2012. The Influence of Climatic Change on the Late Bronze Age Collapse and the Greek Dark Ages. *Journal of Archaeological Science* 39: 1862–70.

Drews, R. 1992. Herodotus 1.94, the Drought ca. 1200 B.C., and the Origin of the Etruscans. *Historia* 41: 14–39.

Drews, R. 1993. *The End of the Bronze Age: Changes in Warfare and the Catastrophe ca. 1200 B.C.* Princeton, NJ: Princeton University Press.

Drews, R. 2000. Medinet Habu: Oxcarts, Ships, and Migration Theories. *Journal of Near Eastern Studies* 59: 161–90.

Durard, J.-M. 1983. *Textes administratifs des salles 134 et 160 du Palais de Mari*. ARMT XX. Paris: Librairie Orientaliste Paul Geuthner.

Edel, E. 1961. Ein kairener fragment mit einem Bericht über den libyerkrieg Merneptahs, *Zeitschrift für Ägyptische Sprache und Altertumskunde* 86: 101–3.

Edel, E. 1966. *Die Ortsnamenlisten aus dem Totentempel Amenophis III.* Bonn: Peter Hanstein Verlag.

Edel, E., and M. Görg. 2005. *Die Ortsnamenlisten im nördlichen Säulenhof des Totentempels Amenophis' III.* Wiesbaden: Harrassowitz Verlag.

Edgerton, W. F., and J. A. Wilson. 1936. *Historical Records of Ramses III: The Texts in Medinet Habu.* Vols. 1 and 2. Chicago: University of Chicago Press.

Emanuel, J. P. 2013. 'ŠRDN from the Sea': The Arrival, Integration, and Acculturation of a 'Sea People.' *Journal of Ancient Egyptian Interconnections* 5/1: 14–27.

Enverova, D. A. 2012. *The Transition from Bronze Age to Iron Age in the Aegean: An Heterarchical Approach.* M.A. Thesis, Bilkent University http://www.thesis.bilkent.edu.tr /0006047.pdf (last accessed September 11, 2013).

Ertekin, A., and I. Ediz. 1993. The Unique Sword from Bogazkoy/Hattusa. In *Aspects of Art and Iconography: Anatolia and Its Neighbors. Studies in Honor of Nonet Ozguc,* ed. M. J. Mellink, E. Porada, and T. Ozguc, 719–25. Ankara: Türk Tarih Kurumu Basimevi.

Evans, A. J. 1921–35. *The Palace of Minos at Knossos.* Vols. 1–4. London: Macmillan and Co.

Fagles, R. 1990. *Homer: The Iliad.* New York: Penguin.

Faust, A., and J. Lev-Tov. 2011. The Constitution of Philistine Identity: Ethnic Dynamics in Twelfth to Tenth Century Philistia. *Oxford Journal of Archaeology* 30: 13–31.

Feldman, M. 2002. Luxurious Forms: Redefining a Mediterranean "International Style," 1400–1200 B.C.E. *Art Bulletin* 84/1: 6–29.

Feldman, M. 2006. *Diplomacy by Design: Luxury Arts and an "International Style" in the Ancient Near East, 1400–1200 BCE.* Chicago: University of Chicago Press.

Feldman, M. 2009. Hoarded Treasures: The Megiddo Ivories and the End of the Bronze Age. *Levant* 41/2: 175–94.

Finkelstein, I. 1996. The Stratigraphy and Chronology of Megiddo and Beth-Shean in the 12th–11th Centuries BCE. *Tel Aviv* 23: 170–84.

Finkelstein, I. 1998. Philistine Chronology: High, Middle or Low? In *Mediterranean Peoples in Transition: Thirteenth to Early Tenth Centuries BCE,* ed. S. Gitin, A. Mazar, and E. Stern, 140–47. Jerusalem: Israel Exploration Society.

Finkelstein, I. 2000. The Philistine Settlements: When, Where and How Many? In *The Sea Peoples and Their World: A Reassessment,* ed. E. D. Oren, 159–80. Philadelphia: University of Pennsylvania.

Finkelstein, I. 2002. El-Aḥwat: A Fortified Sea People City? *Israel Exploration Journal* 52/2: 187–99.

Finkelstein, I. 2007. Is the Philistine Paradigm Still Viable? In *The Synchronisation of Civilisations in the Eastern Mediterranean in the Second Millennium B.C. III, Proceedings of the SCIEM 2000—2nd EuroConference, Vienna, 28th of May–1st of June 2003,* ed. M. Bietak and E. Czerny, 517–23. Vienna: Verlag der Österreichischen Akademie der Wissenschaften.

Fitton, J. L. 2002. *Minoans.* London: British Museum Press.

Frank. A. G. 1993. Bronze Age World System and Its Cycles. *Current Anthropology* 34: 383–429.

Frank, A. G., and B. K. Gillis. 1993. *The World System: Five Hundred Years or Five Thousand?* London: Routledge.

Frank, A. G., and W. R. Thompson. 2005. Afro-Eurasian Bronze Age Economic Expansion and Contraction Revisited. *Journal of World History* 16: 115–72.

Franken, H. J. 1961. The Excavations at Deir ʿAlla, Jordan. *Vetus Testamentum* 11: 361–72.

French, E. 2009. The Significance of Changes in Spatial Usage at Mycenae. In *Forces of Transformation: The End of the Bronze Age in the Mediterranean*, ed. C. Bachhuber and R. G. Roberts, 108–10. Oxford: Oxbow Books.

French, E. 2010. Mycenae. In *The Oxford Handbook of the Bronze Age Aegean*, ed. E. H. Cline, 671–79. New York: Oxford University Press.

Friedman, K. E. 2008. Structure, Dynamics, and the Final Collapse of Bronze Age Civilizations in the Second Millennium. In *Historical Transformations: The Anthropology of Global Systems*, ed. K. E. Friedman and J. Friedman, 163–202. Lanham, MD: Altamira Press.

Galil, G., A. Gilboa, A. M. Maeir, and D. Kahn, eds. 2012. *The Ancient Near East in the 12th–10th Centuries BCE: Culture and History. Proceedings of the International Conference Held at the University of Haifa, 2–5 May, 2010*. AOAT 392. Münster: Ugarit-Verlag.

Genz, H. 2013. "No Land Could Stand before Their Arms, from Hatti . . . On . . ."? New Light on the End of the Hittite Empire and the Early Iron Age in Central Anatolia. In *The Philistines and Other "Sea Peoples" in Text and Archaeology*, ed. A. E. Killebrew and G. Lehmann, 469–77. Atlanta: Society of Biblical Literature.

Gilboa, A. 1998. Iron I–IIA Pottery Evolution at Dor—Regional Contexts and the Cypriot Connection. In *Mediterranean Peoples in Transition: Thirteenth to Early Tenth Centuries BCE*, ed. S. Gitin, A. Mazar, and E. Stern, 413–25. Jerusalem: Israel Exploration Society.

Gilboa, A. 2005. Sea Peoples and Phoenicians along the Southern Phoenician Coast—A Reconciliation: An Interpretation of Šikila (SKL) Material Culture. *Bulletin of the American Schools of Oriental Research* 337: 47–78.

Gilboa, A. 2006–7. Fragmenting the Sea Peoples, with an Emphasis on Cyprus, Syria and Egypt: A Tel Dor Perspective. *Scripta Mediterranea* 27–28: 209–44.

Gillis, C. 1995. Trade in the Late Bronze Age. In *Trade and Production in Premonetary Greece: Aspects of Trade*, ed. C. Gillis, C. Risberg, and B. Sjöberg, 61–86. Jonsered: Paul Åström Förlag.

Gilmour, G., and K. A. Kitchen. 2012. Pharaoh Sety II and Egyptian Political Relations with Canaan at the End of the Late Bronze Age. *Israel Exploration Journal* 62/1: 1–21.

Gitin, S. 2005. Excavating Ekron. Major Philistine City Survived by Absorbing Other Cultures. *Biblical Archaeology Review* 31/6: 40–56, 66–67.

Giveon, R., D. Sweeney, and N. Lalkin. 2004. The Inscription of Ramesses III. In *The Renewed Archaeological Excavations at Lachish (1973–1994)*, ed. D. Ussishkin, 1626–28. Tel Aviv: Tel Aviv University.

Grundon, I. 2007. *The Rash Adventurer: A Life of John Pendlebury*. London: Libri Publications.

Güterbock, H. G. 1992. Survival of the Hittite Dynasty. In *The Crisis Years: The 12th Century B.C.*, ed. W. A. Ward and M. S. Joukowsky, 53–55. Dubuque, IA: Kendall/ Hunt Publishing Co.

Habachi, L. 1972. *The Second Stele of Kamose*. Gluckstadt: J. J. Augustin.

Halpern, B. 2006–7. The Sea-Peoples and Identity. *Scripta Mediterranea* 27–28: 15–32.

Hankey, V. 1981. The Aegean Interest in El Amarna. *Journal of Mediterranean Anthropology and Archaeology* 1: 38–49.

Harrison, T. P. 2009. Neo-Hittites in the "Land of Palistin." Renewed Investigations at Tell Taʾyinat on the Plain of Antioch. *Near Eastern Archaeology* 72/4: 174–89.

Harrison, T. P. 2010. The Late Bronze/Early Iron Age Transition in the North Orontes Valley. In *Societies in Transition: Evolutionary Processes in the Northern Levant between Late Bronze Age II and Early Iron Age. Papers Presented on the Occasion of the 20th Anniversary of the New Excavations in Tell Afis. Bologna, 15th November 2007,* ed. F. Venturi, 83–102. Bologna: Clueb.

Hawass, Z. 2005. *Tutankhamun and the Golden Age of the Pharaohs.* Washington, DC: National Geographic Society.

Hawass, Z. 2010. King Tut's Family Secrets. *National Geographic,* September 2010, 34–59.

Hawass, Z., et al. 2010. Ancestry and Pathology in King Tutankhamun's Family. *Journal of the American Medical Association* 303/7 (2010): 638–47.

Hawkins, J. D. 2009. Cilicia, the Amuq and Aleppo: New Light in a Dark Age. *Near Eastern Archaeology* 72/4: 164–73.

Hawkins, J. D. 2011. The Inscriptions of the Aleppo Temple. *Anatolian Studies* 61: 35–54.

Heimpel, W. 2003. *Letters to the King of Mari: A New Translation, with Historical Introduction, Notes, and Commentary.* Winona Lake, IN: Eisenbrauns.

Heltzer, M. 1988. Sinaranu, Son of Siginu, and the Trade Relations between Ugarit and Crete. *Minos* 23: 7–13.

Heltzer, M. 1989. The Trade of Crete and Cyprus with Syria and Mesopotamia and Their Eastern Tin-Sources in the XVIII–XVII Centuries B.C. *Minos* 24: 7–28.

Hirschfeld, N. 1990. *Incised Marks on LH/LM III Pottery.* M.A. Thesis, Institute of Nautical Archaeology, Texas A&M University.

Hirschfeld, N. 1992. Cypriot Marks on Mycenaean Pottery. In *Mykenaïka: Actes du IXe Colloque international sur les textes mycéniens et égéens, Athènes, 2–6 octobre 1990,* ed. J.-P. Olivier, 315–19. Paris: Diffusion de Bocard.

Hirschfeld, N. 1996. Cypriots in the Mycenaean Aegean. In *Atti e Memorie del Secondo Congresso Internazionale di Micenologia, Roma-Napoli, 14–20 Ottobre 1991,* ed. E. De Miro, L. Godart, and A. Sacconi, 1:289–97. Rome/Naples: Gruppo Editoriale Internatzionale.

Hirschfeld, N. 1999. *Potmarks of the Late Bronze Age Eastern Mediterranean.* Ph.D. Dissertation, University of Texas at Austin.

Hirschfeld, N. 2010. Cypro-Minoan. In *The Oxford Handbook of the Bronze Age Aegean,* ed. E. H. Cline, 373–84. New York: Oxford University Press.

Hitchcock, L. A. 2005. 'Who will personally invite a foreigner, unless he is a craftsman?': Exploring Interconnections in Aegean and Levantine Architecture. In *Emporia. Aegeans in the Central and Eastern Mediterranean. Proceedings of the 10th International Aegean Conference. Athens, Italian School of Archaeology, 14–18 April 2004,* ed. R. Laffineur and E. Greco, 691–99. Aegaeum 25. Liège: Université de Liège.

Hitchcock, L. A. 2008. 'Do you see a man skillful in his work? He will stand before kings': Interpreting Architectural Influences in the Bronze Age Mediterranean. *Ancient West and East* 7: 17–49.

Hitchcock, L. A. 2011. 'Transculturalism' as a Model for Examining Migration to Cyprus and Philistia at the End of the Bronze Age. *Ancient West and East* 10: 267–80.

Hitchcock, L. A. In press. 'All the Cherethites, and all the Pelethites, and all the Gittites': A Current Assessment of the Evidence for the Minoan Connection with the Philistines. To be published in the *Proceedings of the 11th International Congress of Cretan Studies, 21–27 October 2011, Rethymnon, Crete.*

Hitchcock, L. A., and A. M. Maeir. 2013. Beyond Creolization and Hybridity: Entangled and Transcultural Identities in Philistia. *Archaeological Review from Cambridge* 28/1: 51–74.

Hoffmeier, J. K. 2005. *Ancient Israel in Sinai: The Evidence for the Authenticity of the Wilderness Tradition.* Oxford: Oxford University Press.

Hoffner, H. A., Jr. 1992. The Last Days of Khattusha. In *The Crisis Years: The 12th Century B.C.*, ed. W. A. Ward and M. S. Joukowsky, 46–52. Dubuque, IA: Kendall/Hunt Publishing Co.

Hoffner, H. A., Jr. 2007. Hittite Laws. In *Law Collections from Mesopotamia and Asia Minor*, ed. M. T. Roth, 213–40. 2nd Edition. Atlanta: Scholars Press.

Hooker, J. T. 1982. The End of Pylos and the Linear B Evidence. *Studi micenei ed egeoanatolici* 23: 209–17.

Houwink ten Cate, P.H.J. 1970. *The Records of the Early Hittite Empire (c. 1450–1380 B.C.).* Istanbul: Nederlands Historisch-Archaeologisch Instituut in het Nabije Oosten.

Huehnergard, J. 1999. The Akkadian Letters. In *Handbook of Ugaritic Studies*, ed. W.G.E. Watson and N. Wyatt, 375–89. Leiden: Brill.

Iacovou, M. 2008. Cultural and Political Configurations in Iron Age Cyprus: The Sequel to a Protohistoric Episode. *American Journal of Archaeology* 112/4: 625–57.

Iacovou, M. 2013. Aegean-Style Material Culture in Late Cypriot III: Minimal Evidence, Maximal Interpretation. In *The Philistines and Other "Sea Peoples" in Text and Archaeology*, ed. A. E. Killebrew and G. Lehmann, 585–618. Atlanta: Society of Biblical Literature.

Iakovidis, Sp. E. 1986. Destruction Horizons at Late Bronze Age Mycenae. In *Philia Epi eis Georgion E. Mylonan, v. A*, 233–60. Athens: Library of the Archaeological Society of Athens.

Janeway, B. 2006–7. The Nature and Extent of Aegean Contact at Tell Ta'yinat and Vicinity in the Early Iron Age: Evidence of the Sea Peoples? *Scripta Mediterranea* 27–28: 123–46.

Jennings, J. 2011. *Globalizations and the Ancient World.* Cambridge: Cambridge University Press.

Johnson, N. 2007. *Simply Complexity: A Clear Guide to Complexity Theory.* Oxford: OneWorld Publications.

Jung, R. 2009. "'Sie vernichteten sie, als ob sie niemals existiert hätten'—Was blieb von den Zerstörungen der Seevölker?' In *Schlachtfeldarchäologie / Battlefield Archaeology. 1. Mitteldeutscher Archäologentag vom 09. Bis 11. Oktober 2008 in Halle (Saale) (Tagungen des Landesmuseums für Vorgeschichte Halle 2)*, ed. H. Meller, 31–48. Halle (Saale): Landesmuseum für Vorgeschichte.

Jung, R. 2010. End of the Bronze Age. In *The Oxford Handbook of the Bronze Age Aegean*, ed. E. H. Cline, 171–84. New York: Oxford University Press.

Jung, R. 2011. Innovative Cooks and New Dishes: Cypriote Pottery in the 13th and 12th Centuries BC and Its Historical Interpretation. In *On Cooking Pots, Drinking Cups, Loomweights and Ethnicity in Bronze Age Cyprus and Neighbouring Regions. An International Archaeological Symposium Held in Nicosia, November 6th–7th 2010*, ed. V. Karageorghis and O. Kouka, 57–85. Nicosia: A. G. Leventis Foundation.

Jung, R. 2012. Can We Say, What's behind All Those Sherds? Ceramic Innovations in the Eastern Mediterranean at the End of the Second Millennium. In *Materiality and Social Practice: Transformative Capacities of Intercultural Encounters*, ed. J. Maran and P. W. Stockhammer, 104–20. Oxford: Oxbow Books.

Kahn, D. 2011. One Step Forward, Two Steps Backward: The Relations between Amenhotep III, King of Egypt and Tushratta, King of Mitanni. In *Egypt, Canaan and Israel:*

History, Imperialism, Ideology and Literature: Proceedings of a Conference at the University of Haifa, 3–7 May 2009, ed. S. Bar, D. Kahn, and J. J. Shirley, 136–54. Leiden: Brill.

Kahn, D. 2012. A Geo-Political and Historical Perspective of Merneptah's Policy in Canaan. In *The Ancient Near East in the 12th–10th Centuries BCE: Culture and History. Proceedings of the International Conference Held at the University of Haifa, 2–5 May, 2010*, ed. G. Galil, A. Gilboa, A. M. Maeir, and D. Kahn, 255–68. AOAT 392. Münster: Ugarit-Verlag.

Kammenhuber, A. 1961. *Hippologia hethitica*. Wiesbaden: O. Harrassowitz.

Kamrin, J. 2013. The Procession of "Asiatics" at Beni Hasan. In *Cultures in Contact: From Mesopotamia to the Mediterranean in the Second Millennium B.C.*, ed. J. Aruz, S. B. Graff, and Y. Rakic, 156–69. New York: Metropolitan Museum of Art.

Kaniewski, D., E. Paulissen, E. Van Campo, H. Weiss, T. Otto, J. Bretschneider, and K. Van Lerberghe. 2010. Late Second–Early First Millennium BC Abrupt Climate Changes in Coastal Syria and Their Possible Significance for the History of the Eastern Mediterranean. *Quaternary Research* 74: 207–15.

Kaniewski, D., E. Van Campo, K. Van Lerberghe, T. Boiy, K. Vansteenhuyse, G. Jans, K. Nys, H. Weiss, C. Morhange, T. Otto, and J. Bretschneider. 2011. The Sea Peoples, from Cuneiform Tablets to Carbon Dating. *PloS ONE* 6/6: e20232, http://www.plosone.org/article/info%3Adoi%2F10.1371%2Fjournal.pone.0020232 (last accessed August 25, 2013).

Kaniewski, D., E. Van Campo, J. Guiot, S. Le Burel, T. Otto, and C. Baeteman. 2013. Environmental Roots of the Late Bronze Age Crisis. *PloS ONE* 8/8: e71004, http://www.plosone.org/article/info%3Adoi%2F10.1371%2Fjournal.pone.0071004 (last accessed August 25, 2013).

Kaniewski, D., E. Van Campo, and H. Weiss. 2012. Drought Is a Recurring Challenge in the Middle East. *Proceedings of the National Academy of Sciences* 109/10: 3862–67.

Kantor, H. J. 1947. *The Aegean and the Orient in the Second Millennium BC*. AIA Monograph no. 1. Bloomington, IN: Principia Press.

Karageorghis, V. 1982. *Cyprus: From the Stone Age to the Romans*. London: Thames and Hudson.

Karageorghis, V. 1992. The Crisis Years: Cyprus. In *The Crisis Years: The 12th Century B.C.*, ed. W. A. Ward and M. S. Joukowsky, 79–86. Dubuque, IA: Kendall/Hunt Publishing Co.

Karageorghis, V. 2011. What Happened in Cyprus c. 1200 BC: Hybridization, Creolization or Immigration? An Introduction. In *On Cooking Pots, Drinking Cups, Loomweights and Ethnicity in Bronze Age Cyprus and Neighbouring Regions. An International Archaeological Symposium Held in Nicosia, November 6th–7th 2010*, ed. V. Karageorghis and O. Kouka, 19–28. Nicosia: A. G. Leventis Foundation.

Kelder, J. M. 2010. *The Kingdom of Mycenae: A Great Kingdom in the Late Bronze Age Aegean*. Bethesda, MD: CDL Press.

Kelder, J. M. 2012. Ahhiyawa and the World of the Great Kings: A Re-evaluation of Mycenaean Political Structures. *Talanta* 44: 1–12.

Keller, C. A. 2005. The Joint Reign of Hatshepsut and Thutmose III. In *Hatshepsut: From Queen to Pharaoh*, ed. C. Roehrig, 96–98. New Haven: Yale University Press.

Kempinski, A. 1989. *Megiddo: A City-State and Royal Centre in North Israel*. Munich: Verlag C. H. Beck.

Kilian, K. 1990. Mycenaean Colonization: Norm and Variety. In *Greek Colonists and Native Populations: Proceedings of the First Australian Congress of Classical Archaeology Held in Honour of Emeritus Professor A. D. Trendall*, ed. J.-P. Descoeudres, 445–67. Oxford: Clarendon Press.

Kilian, K. 1996. Earthquakes and Archaeological Context at 13th Century BC Tiryns. In *Archaeoseismology*, ed. S. Stiros and R. E. Jones, 63–68. Fitch Laboratory Occasional Papers 7. Athens: British School at Athens.

Killebrew, A. E. 1998. Ceramic Typology and Technology of Late Bronze II and Iron I Assemblages from Tel Miqne-Ekron: The Transition from Canaanite to Philistine Culture. In *Mediterranean Peoples in Transition: Thirteenth to Early Tenth Centuries BCE*, ed. S. Gitin, A. Mazar, and E. Stern, 379–405. Jerusalem: Israel Exploration Society.

Killebrew, A. E. 2000. Aegean-Style Early Philistine Pottery in Canaan during the Iron I Age: A Stylistic Analysis of Mycenaean IIIC:1b Pottery and Its Associated Wares. In *The Sea Peoples and Their World: A Reassessment*, ed. E. D. Oren, 233–53. Philadelphia: University of Pennsylvania.

Killebrew, A. E. 2005. *Biblical Peoples and Ethnicity. An Archaeological Study of Egyptians, Canaanites, Philistines, and Early Israel 1300–1100 B.C.E.* Atlanta: Society of Biblical Literature.

Killebrew, A. E. 2006-7. The Philistines in Context: The Transmission and Appropriation of Mycenaean-Style Culture in the East Aegean, Southeastern Coastal Anatolia, and the Levant. *Scripta Mediterranea* 27–28: 245–66.

Killebrew, A. E. 2013. Early Philistine Pottery Technology at Tel Miqne-Ekron: Implications for the Late Bronze–Early Iron Age Transition in the Eastern Mediterranean. In *The Philistines and Other "Sea Peoples" in Text and Archaeology*, ed. A. E. Killebrew and G. Lehmann, 77–129. Atlanta: Society of Biblical Literature.

Killebrew, A. E. and G. Lehmann. 2013. Introduction: The World of the Philistines and Other "Sea Peoples." In *The Philistines and Other "Sea Peoples" in Text and Archaeology*, ed. A. E. Killebrew and G. Lehmann, 1–17. Atlanta: Society of Biblical Literature.

Killebrew, A. E. and Lehmann, G., eds. 2013. *The Philistines and Other "Sea Peoples" in Text and Archaeology*. Atlanta: Society of Biblical Literature.

Kitchen, K. A. 1965. Theban Topographical Lists, Old and New. *Orientalia* 34: 5–6.

Kitchen, K. A. 1966. Aegean Place Names in a List of Amenophis III. *Bulletin of the American Schools of Oriental Research* 191: 23–24.

Kitchen, K. A. 1982. *Pharaoh Triumphant: The Life and Times of Ramesses II.* Warminster: Aris & Phillips.

Kitchen, K. A. 2012. Ramesses III and the Ramesside Period. In *Ramesses III: The Life and Times of Egypt's Last Hero*, ed. E. H. Cline and D. O'Connor, 1–26. Ann Arbor: University of Michigan Press.

Knapp, A. B. 1991. Spice, Drugs, Grain and Grog: Organic Goods in Bronze Age East Mediterranean Trade. In *Bronze Age Trade in the Aegean*, ed. N. H. Gale, 21–68. Jonsered: Paul Åström Förlag.

Knapp, A. B. 2012. Matter of Fact: Transcultural Contacts in the Late Bronze Age Eastern Mediterranean. In *Materiality and Social Practice: Transformative Capacities of Intercultural Encounters*, ed. J. Maran and P. W. Stockhammer, 32–50. Oxford: Oxbow Books.

Kochavi, M. 1977. *Aphek-Antipatris: Five Seasons of Excavation at Tel Aphek-Antipatris (1972–1976)*. Tel Aviv: The Israel Exploration Society.

Kostoula, M., and J. Maran. 2012. A Group of Animal-Headed Faience Vessels from Tiryns. In *All the Wisdom of the East: Studies in Near Eastern Archaeology and History in Honor of Eliezer D. Oren*, ed. M. Gruber, S. Ahituv, G. Lehmann, and Z. Talshir, 193–234. Orbis Biblicus et Orientalis 255. Fribourg: Vandenhoeck & Ruprecht Göttingen.

Kuhrt, A. 1995. *The Ancient Near East c. 3000–330 BC*. Vol. 1. London: Routledge.

Lackenbacher, S. 1995a. La correspondence international dans les archives d'Ugarit. *Revue d'assyriologie et d'archéologie orientale* 89: 67–75.

Lackenbacher, S. 1995b. Une correspondance entre l'Administration du Pharaon Merneptah et le Roi d'Ougarit. In *Le Pays d'Ougarit autour de 1200 av. J.-C.: Historie et archéologie. Actes du Colloque International; Paris, 28 juin–1er juillet 1993*, ed. M. Yon, M. Sznycer, and P. Bordreuil, 77–83. Paris: Éditions Recherche sur les Civilisations.

Lackenbacher, S., and F. Malbran-Labat. 2005. Ugarit et les Hittites dans les archives de la "Maison d'Urtenu." *Studi micenei ed egeo-anatolici* 47: 227–40.

Lagarce, J., and E. Lagarce. 1978. Découvertes archéologiques à Ras Ibn Hani près de Ras Shamra: un palais du roi d'Ugarit, des tablettes inscrites en caractères cuneiforms, un petit établissement des peoples de la mer et une ville hellénistique. *Comptes rendus de l'Académie des inscriptions et belles-lettres* 1978: 45–64.

Langgut, D., I. Finkelstein, and T. Litt. 2013. Climate and the Late Bronze Collapse: New Evidence from the Southern Levant. *Tel Aviv* 40: 149–75.

Latacz, J. 2004. *Troy and Homer: Towards a Solution of an Old Mystery*. Oxford: Oxford University Press.

Leach, J. W., and E. Leach, eds. 1983. *The Kula: New Perspectives on Massim Exchange*. Cambridge: Cambridge University Press.

Lebrun, R. 1995. Ougarit et le Hatti à la fin du XIIIe siècle av. J.-C. In *Le Pays d'Ougarit autour de 1200 av. J.-C.: Historie et archéologie. Actes du Colloque International; Paris, 28 juin–1er juillet 1993*, ed. M. Yon, M. Sznycer, and P. Bordreuil, 85–88. Paris: Éditions Recherche sur les Civilisations.

Lehmann, G. 2013. Aegean-Style Pottery in Syria and Lebanon during Iron Age I. In *The Philistines and Other "Sea Peoples" in Text and Archaeology*, ed. A. E. Killebrew and G. Lehmann, 265–328. Atlanta: Society of Biblical Literature.

Lemaire, A. 2012. West Semitic Epigraphy and the History of the Levant during the 12th–10th Centuries BCE. In *The Ancient Near East in the 12th–10th Centuries BCE: Culture and History. Proceedings of the International Conference Held at the University of Haifa, 2–5 May, 2010*, ed. G. Galil, A. Gilboa, A. M. Maeir, and D. Kahn, 291–307. AOAT 392. Münster: Ugarit-Verlag.

Liverani, M. 1987. The Collapse of the Near Eastern Regional System at the End of the Bronze Age: The Case of Syria. In *Centre and Periphery in the Ancient World*, ed. M. Rowlands, M. Larsen, and K. Kristiansen, 66–73. Cambridge: Cambridge University Press.

Liverani, M. 1990. *Prestige and Interest: International Relations in the Near East ca. 1600–1100 B.C.*. Padua: Sargon Press.

Liverani, M. 1995. La Fin d'Ougarit: Quand? Pourquoi? Comment? In *Le Pays d'Ougarit autour de 1200 av. J.-C.: Historie et archéologie. Actes du Colloque International; Paris, 28 juin–1er juillet 1993*, ed. M. Yon, M. Sznycer, and P. Bordreuil, 113–17. Paris: Éditions Recherche sur les Civilisations.

Liverani, M. 2001. *International Relations in the Ancient Near East, 1600–1100 BC*. London: Palgrave.

Liverani, M. 2003. The Influence of Political Institutions on Trade in the Ancient Near East (Late Bronze to Early Iron Ages). In *Mercanti e politica nel Mondo Antico*, ed. C. Zaccagnini, 119–37. Rome: L'Erma di Bretschneider.

Liverani, M. 2009. Exploring Collapse. In *Scienze dell'antichità: Storia Archeologia Antropologia* 15: 15–22.

Loader, N. C. 1998. *Building in Cyclopean Masonry: With Special Reference to the Mycenaean Fortifications on Mainland Greece*. Jonsered: Paul Åströms Förlag.

Lolos, Y. G. 2003. Cypro-Mycenaean Relations ca. 1200 BC: Point Iria in the Gulf of Argos and Old Salamis in the Saronic Gulf. In *Sea Routes . . . : Interconnections in the Mediterranean 16th–6th c. BC. Proceedings of the International Symposium Held at Rethymnon, Crete in September 29th–October 2nd 2002*, ed. N. Chr. Stampolidis and V. Karageorghis, 101–16. Athens: University of Crete and the A. G. Leventis Foundation.

Lorenz, E. N. 1969. Atmospheric Predictability as Revealed by Naturally Occurring Analogues. *Journal of the Atmospheric Sciences* 26/4: 636–46.

Lorenz, E. N. 1972. Predictability: Does the Flap of a Butterfly's Wings in Brazil Set Off a Tornado in Texas? Paper presented at the annual meeting of the American Association for the Advancement of Science.

Loud, G. 1939. *Megiddo Ivories*. Chicago: University of Chicago Press.

Loud, G. 1948. *Megiddo II: Season of 1935–39*. Chicago: University of Chicago Press.

Maeir, A. M., L. A. Hitchcock, and L. K. Horwitz. 2013. On the Constitution and Transformation of Philistine Identity. *Oxford Journal of Archaeology* 32/1: 1–38.

Malbran-Labat, F. 1995. La découverte épigraphique de 1994 à Ougarit (Les textes Akkadiens). *Studi micenei ed egeo-anatolici* 36: 103–11.

Malinowski, B. 1922. *Argonauts of the Western Pacific*. New York: Dutton.

Mallowan, A. C. (Agatha Christie). 1976. *Come, Tell Me How You Live*. New York: HarperCollins.

Manning, S. W. 1999. *A Test of Time: The Volcano of Thera and the Chronology and History of the Aegean and East Mediterranean in the Mid-second Millennium BC*. Oxford: Oxbow Books.

Manning, S. W. 2010. Eruption of Thera/Santorini. In *The Oxford Handbook of the Bronze Age Aegean*, ed. E. H. Cline, 457–74. New York: Oxford University Press.

Manning S. W., C. Pulak, B. Kromer, S. Talamo, C. Bronk Ramsey, and M. Dee. 2009. Absolute Age of the Uluburun Shipwreck: A Key Late Bronze Age Time-Capsule for the East Mediterranean. In *Tree-Rings, Kings, and Old World Archaeology and Environment*, ed. S. W. Manning and M. J. Bruce, 163–87. Oxford: Oxbow Books.

Maqdissi, al-, M., M. Badawy, J. Bretschneider, H. Hameeuw, G. Jans, K. Vansteenhuyse, G. Voet, and K. Van Lerberghe. 2008. The Occupation Levels of Tell Tweini and Their Historical Implications. In *Proceedings of the 51st Rencontre Assyriologique Internationale Held at the Oriental Institute of the University of Chicago, July 18–22, 2005*, ed. R. D. Biggs, J. Myers, and M. T. Roth, 341–50. Chicago: University of Chicago Press.

Maran, J. 2004. The Spreading of Objects and Ideas in the Late Bronze Age Eastern Mediterranean: Two Case Examples from the Argolid of the 13th and 12th Centuries B.C. *Bulletin of the American Schools of Oriental Research* 336: 11–30.

Maran, J. 2009. The Crisis Years? Reflections on Signs of Instability in the Last Decades of the Mycenaean Palaces. In *Scienze dell'antichità: Storia Archeologia Antropologia* 15: 241–62.

Maran, J. 2010. Tiryns. In *The Oxford Handbook of the Bronze Age Aegean*, ed. E. H. Cline, 722–34. New York: Oxford University Press.

Marom, N., and S. Zuckerman. 2012. The Zooarchaeology of Exclusion and Expropriation: Looking Up from the Lower City in Late Bronze Age Hazor. *Journal of Anthropological Archaeology* 31: 573–85.

Master, D. M., L. E. Stager, and A. Yasur-Landau. 2011. Chronological Observations at the Dawn of the Iron Age in Ashkelon. *Egypt and the Levant* 21: 261–80.

Mauss, M. 1990. *The Gift: The Form and Reason for Exchange in Archaic Societies.* New York: W. W. Norton.

McAnany, P. A., and N. Yoffee. 2010. *Questioning Collapse: Human Resilience, Ecological Vulnerability, and the Aftermath of Empire.* Cambridge: Cambridge University Press.

McCall, H. 2001. *The Life of Max Mallowan: Archaeology and Agatha Christie.* London: British Museum Press.

McClellan, T. L. 1992. Twelfth Century B.C. Syria: Comments on H. Sader's Paper. In *The Crisis Years: The 12th Century B.C.*, ed. W. A. Ward and M. S. Joukowsky, 164–73. Dubuque, IA: Kendall/Hunt Publishing Co.

McGeough, K. M. 2007. *Exchange Relationships at Ugarit.* Leuven: Peeters.

McGeough, K. M. 2011. *Ugaritic Economic Tablets: Text, Translation and Notes.* Edited by Mark S. Smith. Leuven: Peeters.

Merola, M. 2007. Messages from the Dead. *Archaeology* 60/1: 20–27.

Middleton, G. D. 2010. *The Collapse of Palatial Society in LBA Greece and the Postpalatial Period.* BAR International Series 2110. Oxford: Archaeopress.

Middleton, G. D. 2012. Nothing Lasts Forever: Environmental Discourses on the Collapse of Past Societies. *Journal of Archaeological Research* 20: 257–307.

Millard, A. 1995. The Last Tablets of Ugarit. In *Le Pays d'Ougarit autour de 1200 av. J.-C.: Historie et archéologie. Actes du Colloque International; Paris, 28 juin–1er juillet 1993*, ed. M. Yon, M. Sznycer, and P. Bordreuil, 119–24. Paris: Éditions Recherche sur les Civilisations.

Millard, A. 2012. Scripts and Their Uses in the 12th–10th Centuries BCE. In *The Ancient Near East in the 12th–10th Centuries BCE: Culture and History. Proceedings of the International Conference Held at the University of Haifa, 2–5 May, 2010*, ed. G. Galil, A. Gilboa, A. M. Maeir, and D. Kahn, 405–12. AOAT 392. Münster: Ugarit-Verlag.

Miller, J. M., and J. H. Hayes. 2006. *A History of Ancient Israel and Judah.* 2nd Edition. Louisville, KY: Westminster John Knox Press.

Momigliano, N. 2009. *Duncan Mackenzie: A Cautious Canny Highlander and the Palace of Minos at Knossos.* Bulletin of the Institute of Classical Studies Supplement no. 72. London: University of London.

Monroe, C. M. 2009. *Scales of Fate: Trade, Tradition, and Transformation in the Eastern Mediterranean ca. 1350–1175 BCE.* Münster: Ugarit-Verlag.

Monroe, C. M. 2010. Sunk Costs at Late Bronze Age Uluburun. *Bulletin of the American Schools of Oriental Research* 357: 19–33.

Moran, W. L. 1992. *The Amarna Letters.* Baltimore: Johns Hopkins University Press.

Morandi Bonacossi, D. 2013. The Crisis of Qatna at the Beginning of the Late Bronze Age II and the Iron Age II Settlement Revival Towards the Collapse of the Late Bronze Age Palace System in the Northern Levant. In *Across the Border: Late Bronze–Iron Age Relations between Syria and Anatolia. Proceedings of a Symposium Held at the Research Center of Anatolian Studies, Koç University, Istanbul May 31–June 1, 2010*, ed. K.A. Yener, 113–46. Leuven: Peeters.

Mountjoy, P. A. 1997. The Destruction of the Palace at Pylos Reconsidered. *Annual of the British School at Athens* 92: 109–37.

Mountjoy, P.A. 1999a. The Destruction of Troia VIh. *Studia Troica* 9: 253–93.

Mountjoy, P. A. 1999b. Troia VII Reconsidered. *Studia Troica* 9: 295–346.

Mountjoy, P. A. 2005. The End of the Bronze Age at Enkomi, Cyprus: The Problem of Level IIIB. *Annual of the British School at Athens* 100: 125–214.

Mountjoy, P. A. 2006. Mykenische Keramik in Troia—Ein Überblick. In *Troia: Archäologie eines Siedlungshügels und seiner Landschaft*, ed. M. O. Korfman, 241–52. Mainz am Rhein: Philipp von Zabern.

Mountjoy, P. A. 2013. The Mycenaean IIIC Pottery at Tel Miqne-Ekron. In *The Philistines and Other "Sea Peoples" in Text and Archaeology*, ed. A. E. Killebrew and G. Lehmann, 53–75. Atlanta: Society of Biblical Literature.

Muhlenbruch, T. 2007. The Post-Palatial Settlement in the Lower Citadel of Tiryns. In *LH IIIC Chronology and Synchronisms II: LH IIIC Middle. Proceedings of the International Workshop Held at the Austrian Academy of Sciences at Vienna, October 29th and 30th, 2004*, ed. S. Deger-Jalkotzy and M. Zavadil, 243–51. Vienna: Verlag der Österreichischen Akademie der Wissenschaften.

Muhlenbruch, T. 2009. Tiryns—The Settlement and Its History in LH IIIC. In *LH IIIC Chronology and Synchronisms III: LH IIIC Late and the Transition to the Early Iron Age. Proceedings of the International Workshop Held at the Austrian Academy of Sciences at Vienna, February 23rd and 24th, 2007*, ed. S. Deger-Jalkotzy and E. Bächle, 313–26. Vienna: Verlag der Österreichischen Akademie der Wissenschaften.

Muhly, J. D. 1984. The Role of the Sea Peoples in Cyprus during the LC III Period. In *Cyprus at the Close of the Late Bronze Age*, ed. V. Karageorghis and J. D. Muhly, 39–56. Nicosia: Leventis.

Muhly, J. D. 1992. The Crisis Years in the Mediterranean World: Transition or Cultural Disintegration? In *The Crisis Years: The 12th Century B.C.*, ed. W. A. Ward and M. S. Joukowsky, 10–22. Dubuque, IA: Kendall/Hunt Publishing Co.

Murray, Sarah C. 2013. *Trade, Imports and Society in Early Greece*. Ph.D. Dissertation, Stanford University.

Mynářová, J. 2007. *Language of Amarna—Language of Diplomacy: Perspectives on the Amarna Letters*. Prague: Czech Institute of Egyptology.

Neve, P. J. 1989. Bogazkoy-Hattusha. New Results of the Excavations in the Upper City. *Anatolica* 16: 7–19.

Newberry, P. E. 1893. *Beni Hasan*, vol. 1. *Archaeological Survey of Egypt* 1. London: Egypt Exploration Fund.

Nibbi, A. 1975. *The Sea Peoples and Egypt*. Park Ridge, NJ: Noyes Press.

Niemeier, W.-D. 1991. Minoan Artisans Travelling Overseas: The Alalakh Frescoes and the Painted Plaster Floor at Tel Kabri (Western Galilee). In *Thalassa: L'Égée prehistorique et la mer*, ed. R. Laffineur and L. Basch, 189–201. Aegaeum 7. Liège: Université de Liège.

Niemeier, W.-D. 1999. Mycenaeans and Hittites in War in Western Asia Minor. In *Polemos: Le contexte guerrier en Égée a l'âge du Bronze*, ed. R. Laffineur, 141–55. Liège: Université de Liège.

Niemeier, W.-D., and B. Niemeier. 1998. "Minoan Frescoes in the Eastern Mediterranean." In *The Aegean and the Orient in the Second Millennium*, ed. E. H. Cline and D. Harris-Cline, 69–97. Aegaeum 18. Liège: Université de Liège; Austin: University of Texas at Austin.

Nougayrol, J. 1956. *Textes accadiens des archives Sud*. Le Palais Royal d'Ugarit 4. Paris: Librairie C. Klincksieck.

Nougayrol, J., E. Laroche, C. Virolleaud, and C.F.A. Schaeffer. 1968. *Ugaritica* 5. Mission de Ras Shamra 16. Paris: Geuthner.

Nur, A., and D. Burgess. 2008. *Apocalypse: Earthquakes, Archaeology, and the Wrath of God*. Princeton, NJ: Princeton University Press.

Nur, A., and E. H. Cline. 2000. Poseidon's Horses: Plate Tectonics and Earthquake Storms in the Late Bronze Age Aegean and Eastern Mediterranean. *Journal of Archaeological Science* 27: 43–63.

Nur, A., and E. H. Cline. 2001. What Triggered the Collapse? Earthquake Storms. *Archaeology Odyssey* 4/5: 31–36, 62–63.

Nur, A., and H. Ron. 1997. Armageddon's Earthquakes. *International Geology Review* 39: 532–41.

Nyland, A. 2009. *The Kikkuli Method of Horse Training*. 2009 Revised Edition. Sydney: Maryannu Press.

O'Connor, D., and E. H. Cline, eds. 1998. *Amenhotep III: Perspectives on His Reign*. Ann Arbor: University of Michigan Press.

Oldfather, C. H. 1961. *Diodorus Siculus: Library of History*. Loeb Classical Library, vol. 303. Cambridge, MA: Harvard University Press.

Oren, E. D., ed. 1997. *The Hyksos: New Historical and Archaeological Perspectives*. Philadelphia: University of Pennsylvania.

Oren, E. D., ed. 2000. *The Sea Peoples and Their World: A Reassessment*. Philadelphia: University of Pennsylvania.

Palaima, T. G. 1991. Maritime Matters in the Linear B Tablets. In *Thalassa: L'Égée préhistorique et la mer*, ed. R. Laffineur and L. Basch, 273–310. Aegaeum 7. Liège: Université de Liège.

Palaima, T. G. 1995. The Last Days of the Pylos Polity. In *Politeia: Society and State in the Aegean Bronze Age*, ed. W.-D. Niemeier and R. Laffineur, 265–87. Aegaeum 12. Liège: Université de Liège.

Panagiotopoulos, D. 2006. Foreigners in Egypt in the Time of Hatshepsut and Thutmose III. In *Thutmose III: A New Biography*, ed. E. H. Cline and D. O'Connor, 370–412. Ann Arbor: University of Michigan Press.

Pardee, D. 2003. Ugaritic Letters. In *The Context of Scripture*, vol. 3, *Archival Documents from the Biblical World*, ed. W. W. Hallo, 87–116. Leiden: E. J. Brill.

Paul, K. A. 2011. *Bronze Age Aegean Influence in the Mediterranean: Dissecting Reflections of Globalization in Prehistory*. MA Thesis, George Washington University.

Payton, R. 1991. The Ulu Burun Writing-Board Set. *Anatolian Studies* 41: 99–106.

Pendlebury, J.D.S. 1930. *Aegyptiaca: A Catalogue of Egyptian Objects in the Aegean Area*. Cambridge: Cambridge University Press.

Pfälzner, P. 2008a. Between the Aegean and Syria: The Wall Paintings from the Royal Palace of Qatna. In *Fundstellen Gesammelte Schriften zur Archäologie und Geschichte Altvorderasiens ad honorem Hartmut Kühne*, ed. D. Bonatz, R. M. Czichon, and F. J. Kreppner, 95–118. Wiesbaden: Harrassowitz.

Pfälzner, P. 2008b. The Royal Palace at Qatna: Power and Prestige in the Late Bronze Age. In *Beyond Babylon: Art, Trade, and Diplomacy in the Second Millennium B.C. Catalogue of an Exhibition at the Metropolitan Museum of Art, New York*, ed. J. Aruz, 219–21. New York: Metropolitan Museum of Art.

Phelps, W., Y. Lolos, and Y. Vichos, eds. 1999. *The Point Iria Wreck: Interconnections in the Mediterranean ca. 1200 BC.* Athens: Hellenic Institute of Marine Archaeology.

Phillips, J. 2008. *Aegyptiaca on the Island of Crete in Their Chronological Context: A Critical Review.* Vols.1 and 2. Vienna: Verlag der Österreichischen Akademie der Wissenschaften/Austrian Academy of Sciences Press.

Phillips, J., and E. H. Cline. 2005. Amenhotep III and Mycenae: New Evidence. In *Autochthon: Papers Presented to O.T.P.K. Dickinson on the Occasion of His Retirement*, ed. A. Dakouri-Hild and E. S. Sherratt, 317–28. BAR International Series 1432. Oxford: Archaeopress.

Pitard, W. T. 1999. The Written Sources: 2. The Alphabetic Ugaritic Tablets. In *Handbook of Ugaritic Studies*, ed. W.G.E. Watson and N. Wyatt, 46–57. Leiden: Brill.

Podany, A. H. 2010. *Brotherhood of Kings: How International Relations Shaped the Ancient Near East.* New York: Oxford University Press.

Porada, E. 1981. The Cylinder Seals Found at Thebes in Boeotia. *Archiv für Orientforschung* 28: 1–70, 77.

Porada, E. 1992. Sidelights on Life in the 13th and 12th Centuries B.C. in Assyria. In *The Crisis Years: The 12th Century B.C.*, ed. W. A. Ward and M. S. Joukowsky, 182–87. Dubuque, IA: Kendall/Hunt Publishing Co.

Potts, D. T. 1999. *The Archaeology of Elam: Formation and Transformation of an Ancient Iranian State.* Cambridge: Cambridge University Press.

Pritchard, J. B., ed. 1969. *Ancient Near Eastern Texts Relating to the Old Testament.* Princeton, NJ: Princeton University Press.

Pulak, C. 1988. The Bronze Age Shipwreck at Ulu Burun, Turkey: 1985 Campaign. *American Journal of Archaeology* 92: 1–37.

Pulak, C. 1998. The Uluburun Shipwreck: An Overview. *International Journal of Nautical Archaeology* 27/3: 188–224.

Pulak, C. 1999. Shipwreck! Recovering 3,000-Year-Old Cargo. *Archaeology Odyssey* 2/4: 18–29, 59.

Pulak, C. 2005. Who Were the Mycenaeans Aboard the Uluburun Ship? In *Emporia. Aegeans in the Central and Eastern Mediterranean. Proceedings of the 10th International Aegean Conference. Athens, Italian School of Archaeology, 14–18 April 2004*, ed. R. Laffineur and E. Greco, 295–310. Aegaeum 25. Liège: Université de Liège.

Raban, A., and R. R. Stieglitz. 1991. The Sea Peoples and Their Contributions to Civilization. *Biblical Archaeology Review* 17/6: 35–42, 92–93.

Redford, D. B. 1967. *History and Chronology of the Eighteenth Dynasty of Egypt: Seven Studies.* Toronto: University of Toronto Press.

Redford, D. B. 1992. *Egypt, Canaan, and Israel in Ancient Times.* Princeton, NJ: Princeton University Press.

Redford, D. B. 1997. Textual Sources for the Hyksos Period. In *The Hyksos: New Historical and Archaeological Perspectives*, ed. E. Oren, 1–44. Philadelphia: University of Pennsylvania.

Redford, D. B. 2006. The Northern Wars of Thutmose III. In *Thutmose III: A New Biography*, ed. E. H. Cline and D. O'Connor, 325–41. Ann Arbor: University of Michigan Press.

Redford, S. 2002. *The Harem Conspiracy: The Murder of Ramesses III.* DeKalb: Northern Illinois University Press.

Reeves, N. 1990. *The Complete Tutankhamun.* London: Thames and Hudson.

Rehak, P. 1998. Aegean Natives in the Theban Tomb Paintings: The Keftiu Revisited. In *The Aegean and the Orient in the Second Millennium*, ed. E. H. Cline and D. Harris-Cline, 39–49. Aegaeum 18. Liège: Université de Liège.

Renfrew, C. 1979. Systems Collapse as Social Transformation. In *Transformations, Mathematical Approaches to Culture Change*, ed. C. Renfrew and K. L. Cooke, 481–506. New York: Academic Press.

Richter, T. 2005. Qatna in the Late Bronze Age: Preliminary Remarks. In *Studies on the Civilization and Culture of Nuzi and the Hurrians*, vol. 15, ed. D. L. Owen and G. Wilhelm, 109–26. Bethesda, MD: CDL Press.

Richter, T., and S. Lange. 2012. *Das Archiv des Idadda: Die Keilschrifttexte aus den deutsch-syrischen Ausgrabungen 2001–2003 im Königspalast von Qaṭna*. Qatna-Studien. Ergebnisse der Ausgrabungen 3. Wiesbaden: Harrassowitz.

Robbins, M. 2003. *Collapse of the Bronze Age: The Story of Greece, Troy, Israel, Egypt, and the Peoples of the Sea*. San Jose, CA: Authors Choice Press.

Roberts, R. G. 2008. *The Sea Peoples and Egypt*. Ph.D. Dissertation, University of Oxford.

Roberts, R. G. 2009. Identity, Choice, and the Year 8 Reliefs of Ramesses III at Medinet Habu. In *Forces of Transformation: The End of the Bronze Age in the Mediterranean*, ed. C. Bachhuber and R. G. Roberts, 60–68. Oxford: Oxbow Books.

Roehrig, C., ed. 2005. *Hatshepsut: From Queen to Pharaoh*, 75–81. New Haven: Yale University Press.

Rohling, E. J., A. Hayes, P. A. Mayewski, and M. Kucera. 2009. Holocene Climate Variability in the Eastern Mediterranean, and the End of the Bronze Age. In *Forces of Transformation: The End of the Bronze Age in the Mediterranean*, ed. C. Bachhuber and R. G. Roberts, 2–5. Oxford: Oxbow Books.

Roth, A. M. 2005. Hatshepsut's Mortuary Temple at Deir el-Bahri. In *Hatshepsut: From Queen to Pharaoh*, ed. C. Roehrig, 147–51. New Haven: Yale University Press.

Routledge, B., and K. McGeough. 2009. Just What Collapsed? A Network Perspective on 'Palatial' and 'Private' Trade at Ugarit. In *Forces of Transformation: The End of the Bronze Age in the Mediterranean*, ed. C. Bachhuber and R. G. Roberts, 22–29. Oxford: Oxbow Books.

Rubalcaba, J., and E. H. Cline. 2011. *Digging for Troy: From Homer to Hisarlik*. Watertown, MA: Charlesbridge.

Rutter, J. B. 1992. Cultural Novelties in the Post-Palatial Aegean: Indices of Vitality or Decline? In *The Crisis Years: The 12th Century B.C.*, ed. W. A. Ward and M. S. Joukowsky, 61–78. Dubuque, IA: Kendall/Hunt Publishing Co.

Ryan, D. P. 2010. *Beneath the Sands of Egypt: Adventures of an Unconventional Archaeologist*. New York: HarperCollins Publishers.

Sandars, N. K. 1985. *The Sea Peoples: Warriors of the Ancient Mediterranean*. Revised Edition. London: Thames and Hudson.

Schaeffer, C.F.A. 1948. *Stratigraphie comparée et chronologie de l'Asie occidentale*. London: Oxford University Press.

Schaeffer, C.F.A. 1962. *Ugaritica* 4. Mission de Ras Shamra 15. Paris: Geuthner.

Schaeffer, C.F.A. 1968. Commentaires sur les lettres et documents trouvés dans les bibliothèques privées d'Ugarit. In *Ugaritica* 5, 607–768. Paris: Geuthner.

Schliemann, H. 1878. *Mycenae*. Leipzig: F. A. Brockhaus.

Schulman, A. R. 1979. Diplomatic Marriage in the Egyptian New Kingdom. *Journal of Near Eastern Studies* 38: 177–93.

Schulman, A. R. 1988. Hittites, Helmets and Amarna: Akhenaten's First Hittite War. In *The Akhenaten Temple Project*, vol. 2, *Rwd-Mnw, Foreigners and Inscriptions*, ed. D. B. Redford, 54–79. Toronto: Akhenaten Temple Project.

Schwartz, G. M., and J. J. Nichols. 2006. *After Collapse: The Regeneration of Complex Societies*. Tucson: University of Arizona Press.

Seeher, J. 2001. Die Zerstörung der Stadt Hattusa. In *Akten IV. Internationalen Kongresses für Hethitologie. Würzburg, 4.–8. Oktober 1999*, ed. G. Wilhelm, 623–34. Wiesbaden: Harrassowitz.

Sharon, I., and A. Gilboa. 2013. The SKL Town: Dor in the Early Iron Age. In *The Philistines and Other "Sea Peoples" in Text and Archaeology*, ed. A. E. Killebrew and G. Lehmann, 393–468. Atlanta: Society of Biblical Literature.

Shelmerdine, C. W. 1998a. Where Do We Go from Here? And How Can the Linear B Tablets Help Us Get There? In *The Aegean and the Orient in the Second Millennium. Proceedings of the 50th Anniversary Symposium, Cincinnati, 18–20 April 1997*, ed. E. H. Cline and D. Harris-Cline, 291–99. Aegaeum 18. Liège: Université de Liège.

Shelmerdine, C. W. 1998b. The Palace and Its Operations. In *Sandy Pylos. An Archaeological History from Nestor to Navarino*, ed. J. L. Davis, 81–96. Austin: University of Texas Press.

Shelmerdine, C. W. 1999. Pylian Polemics: the Latest Evidence on Military Matters. In *Polemos: Le contexte en Égée à l'âge du Bronze. Actes la 7ᵉ Rencontre égéenne internationale (Liège 1998)*, ed. R. Laffineur, 403–8. Aegaeum 19. Liège: Université de Liège.

Shelmerdine, C. W. 2001. The Palatial Bronze Age of the Southern and Central Greek Mainland. In *Aegean Prehistory: A Review*, ed. T. Cullen, 329–82. Boston: Archaeological Institute of America.

Shelmerdine, C. W., ed. 2008. *The Cambridge Companion to the Aegean Bronze Age*. Cambridge: Cambridge University Press.

Sherratt, S. 1998. "Sea Peoples" and the Economic Structure of the Late Second Millennium in the Eastern Mediterranean. In *Mediterranean Peoples in Transition: Thirteenth to Early Tenth Centuries BCE*, ed. S. Gitin, A. Mazar, and E. Stern, 292–313. Jerusalem: Israel Exploration Society.

Sherratt, S. 2003. The Mediterranean Economy: "Globalization" at the End of the Second Millennium B.C.E. In *Symbiosis, Symbolism, and the Power of the Past: Canaan, Ancient Israel, and Their Neighbors from the Late Bronze Age through Roman Palaestina. Proceedings of the Centennial Symposium W. F. Albright Institute of Archaeological Research and American Schools of Oriental Research, Jerusalem, May 29–31, 2000*, ed. W. G. Dever and S. Gitin, 37–54. Winona Lake, IN: Eisenbrauns.

Sherratt, S. 2013. The Ceramic Phenomenon of the "Sea Peoples": An Overview. In *The Philistines and Other "Sea Peoples" in Text and Archaeology*, ed. A. E. Killebrew and G. Lehmann, 619–44. Atlanta: Society of Biblical Literature.

Shrimpton, G. 1987. Regional Drought and the Economic Decline of Mycenae. *Echos du monde classique* 31: 133–77.

Silberman, N. A. 1998. The Sea Peoples, the Victorians, and Us: Modern Social Ideology and Changing Archaeological Interpretations of the Late Bronze Age Collapse. In *Mediterranean Peoples in Transition: Thirteenth to Early Tenth Centuries BCE*, ed. S. Gitin, A. Mazar, and E. Stern, 268–75. Jerusalem: Israel Exploration Society.

Singer, I. 1999. A Political History of Ugarit. In *Handbook of Ugaritic Studies*, ed. W.G.E. Watson and N. Wyatt, 603–733. Leiden: Brill.

Singer, I. 2000. New Evidence on the End of the Hittite Empire. In *The Sea Peoples and Their World: A Reassessment*, ed. E. D. Oren, 21–33. Philadelphia: University of Pennsylvania.

Singer, I. 2001. The Fate of Hattusa during the Period of Tarhuntassa's Supremacy. In *Kulturgeschichten: altorientalistische Studien für Volkert Haas zum 65. Geburtstag*, 395–403. Saarbrücken: Saarbücker Druckerei und Verlag.

Singer, I. 2002. *Hittite Prayers*. Atlanta: Society of Biblical Literature.

Singer, I. 2006. Ships Bound for Lukka: A New Interpretation of the Companion Letters RS 94.2530 and RS 94.2523. *Altorientalische Forschungen* 33: 242–62.

Singer, I. 2012. The Philistines in the North and the Kingdom of Taita. In *The Ancient Near East in the 12th–10th Centuries BCE: Culture and History. Proceedings of the International Conference Held at the University of Haifa, 2–5 May, 2010*, ed. G. Galil, A. Gilboa, A. M. Maeir, and D. Kahn, 451–72. AOAT 392. Münster: Ugarit-Verlag.

Smith, P. 2004. Skeletal Remains from Level VI. In *The Renewed Archaeological Excavations at Lachish (1973–1994)*, ed. D. Ussishkin, 2504–7. Tel Aviv: Tel Aviv University.

Snape, S. R. 2012. The Legacy of Ramesses III and the Libyan Ascendancy. In *Ramesses III: The Life and Times of Egypt's Last Hero*, ed. E. H. Cline and D. O'Connor, 404–41. Ann Arbor: University of Michigan Press.

Sørensen, A. H. 2009. Approaching Levantine Shores. Aspects of Cretan Contacts with Western Asia during the MM–LM I Periods. In *Proceedings of the Danish Institute at Athens 6*, ed. E. Hallager and S. Riisager, 9–55. Athens: Danish Institute at Athens.

Sourouzian, H. 2004. Beyond Memnon: Buried for More Than 3,300 Years, Remnants of Amenhotep III's Extraordinary Mortuary Temple at Kom el-Hettan Rise from beneath the Earth. *ICON* magazine, Summer 2004, 10–17.

Sourouzian, H., R. Stadelmann, N. Hampikian, M. Seco Alvarez, I. Noureddine, M. Elesawy, M. A. López Marcos, and C. Perzlmeier. 2006. Three Seasons of Work at the Temple of Amenhotep III at Kom El Hettan. Part III: Works in the Dewatered Area of the Peristyle Court and the Hypostyle Hall. *Annales du Service des antiquités de l'Egypte* 80: 401–88.

Stager, L. E. 1995. The Impact of the Sea Peoples in Canaan. In *The Archaeology of Society in the Holy Land*, ed. T. E. Levy, 332–48. London: Leicester University Press.

Steel, L. 2004. *Cyprus before History: From the Earliest Settlers to the End of the Bronze Age*. London: Gerald Duckworth & Co.

Steel, L. 2013. *Materiality and Consumption in the Bronze Age Mediterranean*. New York: Routledge.

Stern, E. 1994. *Dor, Ruler of the Seas: Twelve Years of Excavations at the Israelite-Phoenician Harbor Town on the Carmel Coast*. Jerusalem: Israel Exploration Society.

Stern, E. 1998. The Relations between the Sea Peoples and the Phoenicians in the Twelfth and Eleventh Centuries BCE. In *Mediterranean Peoples in Transition: Thirteenth to Early Tenth Centuries BCE*, ed. S. Gitin, A. Mazar, and E. Stern, 345–52. Jerusalem: Israel Exploration Society.

Stern, E. 2000. The Settlement of the Sea Peoples in Northern Israel. In *The Sea Peoples and Their World: A Reassessment*, ed. E. D. Oren, 197–212. Philadelphia: University of Pennsylvania.

Stern, E. 2012. Archaeological Remains of the Northern Sea People along the Sharon and Carmel Coasts and the Acco and Jezreel Valleys. In *The Ancient Near East in the 12th–10th Centuries BCE: Culture and History. Proceedings of the International Conference Held at the University of Haifa, 2–5 May, 2010*, ed. G. Galil, A. Gilboa, A. M. Maeir, and D. Kahn, 473–507. AOAT 392. Münster: Ugarit-Verlag.

Stiros, S. C., and R. E. Jones, eds. 1996. *Archaeoseismology*. Fitch Laboratory Occasional Paper no. 7. Athens: British School at Athens.

Stockhammer, P. W. 2013. From Hybridity to Entanglement, from Essentialism to Practice. *Archaeological Review from Cambridge* 28/1: 11–28.

Strange, J. 1980. *Caphtor/Keftiu*. Leiden: E. J. Brill.

Strauss, B. 2006. *The Trojan War: A New History*. New York : Simon & Schuster.

Strobel, K. 2013. Qadesh, Sea Peoples, and Anatolian-Levantine Interactions. In *Across the Border: Late Bronze–Iron Age Relations between Syria and Anatolia. Proceedings of a Symposium Held at the Research Center of Anatolian Studies, Koç University, Istanbul May 31–June 1, 2010*, ed. K. A. Yener, 501–38. Leuven: Peeters.

Tainter, J. A. 1988. *The Collapse of Complex Societies*. Cambridge: Cambridge University Press.

Taylour, W. D. 1969. Mycenae, 1968. *Antiquity* 43: 91–97.

Troy, L. 2006. Religion and Cult during the Time of Thutmose III. In *Thutmose III: A New Biography*, ed. E. H. Cline and D. O'Connor, 123–82. Ann Arbor: University of Michigan Press.

Trumpler, C. 2001. *Agatha Christie and Archaeology*. London: British Museum Press.

Tsountas, C., and J. I. Manatt. 1897. *The Mycenaean Age*. London: Macmillan and Co.

Tyldesley, J. 1998. *Hatchepsut: The Female Pharaoh*. London: Penguin Books.

Uberoi, J. P. Singh. 1962. *Politics of the Kula Ring*. Manchester: Manchester University Press.

Unal, A., A. Ertekin, and I. Ediz. 1991. The Hittite Sword from Bogazkoy—Hattusa, Found 1991, and Its Akkadian Inscription. *Muze* 4: 46–52.

Ussishkin, D. 1987. Lachish: Key to the Israelite Conquest of Canaan? *Biblical Archaeology Review* 13/1: 18–39.

Ussishkin, D. 1995. The Destruction of Megiddo at the End of the Late Bronze Age and Its Historical Significance. In *Mediterranean Peoples in Transition: Thirteenth to Early Tenth Centuries BCE*, ed. S. Gitin, A. Mazar, and E. Stern, 197–219. Jerusalem: Israel Exploration Society.

Ussishkin, D. 2004a. *The Renewed Archaeological Excavations at Lachish (1973–1994)*. Tel Aviv: Tel Aviv University.

Ussishkin, D. 2004b. A Synopsis of the Stratigraphical, Chronological and Historical Issues. In *The Renewed Archaeological Excavations at Lachish (1973–1994)*, ed. D. Ussishkin, 50–119. Tel Aviv: Tel Aviv University.

Ussishkin, D. 2004c. Area P: The Level VI Temple. In *The Renewed Archaeological Excavations at Lachish (1973–1994)*, ed. D. Ussishkin, 215–81. Tel Aviv: Tel Aviv University.

Ussishkin, D. 2004d. A Cache of Bronze Artefacts from Level VI. In *The Renewed Archaeological Excavations at Lachish (1973–1994)*, ed. D. Ussishkin, 1584–88. Tel Aviv: Tel Aviv University.

Vagnetti, L. 2000. Western Mediterranean Overview: Peninsular Italy, Sicily and Sardinia at the Time of the Sea Peoples. In *The Sea Peoples and Their World: A Reassessment*, ed. E. D. Oren, 305–26. Philadelphia: University of Pennsylvania.

Van De Mieroop, Marc. 2007. *A History of the Ancient Near East ca. 3000–323 BC*. 2nd Edition. Malden, MA: Blackwell Publishing.

van Soldt, W. 1991. *Studies in the Akkadian of Ugarit: Dating and Grammar*. Neukirchen: Neukirchener Verlag.

van Soldt, W. 1999. The Written Sources: 1. The Syllabic Akkadian Texts. In *Handbook of Ugaritic Studies*, ed. W.G.E. Watson and N. Wyatt, 28–45. Leiden: Brill.

Vansteenhuyse, K. 2010. The Bronze to Iron Age Transition at Tell Tweini (Syria). In *Societies in Transition: Evolutionary Processes in the Northern Levant between Late Bronze Age II and Early Iron Age. Papers Presented on the Occasion of the 20th Anniversary of the New Excavations in Tell Afis. Bologna, 15th November 2007*, ed. F. Venturi, 39–52. Bologna: Clueb.

Voskos, I., and A. B. Knapp. 2008. Cyprus at the End of the Late Bronze Age: Crisis and Colonization, or Continuity and Hybridization? *American Journal of Archaeology* 112: 659–84.

Wachsmann, S. 1987. *Aegeans in the Theban Tombs*. Orientalia Lovaniensia Analecta 20. Leuven: Uitgeverij Peeters.

Wachsmann, S. 1998. *Seagoing Ships & Seamanship in the Bronze Age Levant*. College Station: Texas A&M University Press.

Wallace, S. 2010. *Ancient Crete. From Successful Collapse to Democracy's Alternatives, Twelfth to Fifth Centuries BC*. Cambridge: Cambridge University Press.

Ward, W. A., and M. S. Joukowsky, eds. 1992. *The Crisis Years: The 12th century B.C. from beyond the Danube to the Tigris*. Dubuque, IA: Kendall/Hunt Publishing Co.

Wardle, K. A., J. Crouwel, and E. French. 1973. A Group of Late Helladic IIIB 2 Pottery from within the Citadel at Mycenae: 'The Causeway Deposit'. *Annual of the British School at Athens* 68: 297–348.

Weinstein, J. 1989. The Gold Scarab of Nefertiti from Ulu Burun: Its Implications for Egyptian History and Egyptian-Aegean Relations. *American Journal of Archaeology* 93: 17–29.

Weinstein, J. 1992. The Collapse of the Egyptian Empire in the Southern Levant. In *The Crisis Years: The 12th Century B.C.*, ed. W. A. Ward and M. S. Joukowsky, 142–50. Dubuque, IA: Kendall/Hunt Publishing Co.

Weiss, H. 2012. Quantifying Collapse: The Late Third Millennium BC. In *Seven Generations since the Fall of Akkad*, ed. H. Weiss, vii–24. Wiesbaden: Harrassowitz.

Wente, E. F. 2003a. The Quarrel of Apophis and Seknenre. In *The Literature of Ancient Egypt*, ed. W. K. Simpson, 69–71. New Haven: Yale University Press.

Wente, E. F. 2003b. The Report of Wenamun. In *The Literature of Ancient Egypt*, ed. W. K. Simpson, 116–24. New Haven: Yale University Press.

Wilson, J. 1969. The War against the Peoples of the Sea. In *Ancient Near Eastern Texts Relating to the Old Testament*, 3rd Edition with Supplement, ed. J. Pritchard, 262–63. Princeton, NJ: Princeton University Press.

Wood, M. 1996. *In Search of the Trojan War*. 2nd Edition. Berkeley: University of California Press.

Yakar, J. 2003. Identifying Migrations in the Archaeological Records of Anatolia. In *Identifying Changes: The Transition from Bronze to Iron Ages in Anatolia and Its Neighbouring Regions. Proceedings of the International Workshop, Istanbul, November 8–9, 2002*, ed. B. Fischer, H. Genz, E. Jean, and K. Köroğlu, 11–19. Istanbul: Türk Eskiçağ Bilimleri Enstitüsü Yayınları.

Yalçin, S. 2013. A Re-evaluation of the Late Bronze to Early Iron Age Transitional Period: Stratigraphic Sequence and Plain Ware of Tarsus-Gözlükule. *In Across the Border: Late Bronze–Iron Age Relations between Syria and Anatolia. Proceedings of a Symposium held at the Research Center of Anatolian Studies, Koç University, Istanbul May 31–June 1, 2010*, ed. K. A. Yener, 195–211. Leuven: Peeters.

Yasur-Landau, A. 2003a. One If by Sea . . . Two If by Land: How Did the Philistines Get to Canaan? Two: By Land—the Trek through Anatolia Followed a Well-Trod Route. *Biblical Archaeology Review* 29/2: 34–39, 66–67.

Yasur-Landau, A. 2003b. The Many Faces of Colonization: 12th Century Aegean Settlements in Cyprus and the Levant. *Mediterranean Archaeology and Archaeometry* 3/1: 45–54.

Yasur-Landau, A. 2003c. Why Can't We Find the Origin of the Philistines? In Search of the Source of a Peripheral Aegean Culture. In *The 2nd International Interdisciplinary Colloquium: The Periphery of the Mycenaean World. 26–30 September, Lamia 1999*, ed. N. Kyparissi-Apostolika and M. Papakonstantinou, 578–98. Athens: Ministry of Culture.

Yasur-Landau, A. 2003d. The Absolute Chronology of the Late Helladic IIIC Period: A View from the Levant. In *LH IIIC Chronology and Synchronisms. Proceedings of the International Workshop Held at the Austrian Academy of Sciences at Vienna, May 7th and 8th, 2001*, ed. S. Deger-Jalkotzy and M. Zavadil, 235–44. Vienna: Verlag der Österreichischen Akademie der Wissenschaften.

Yasur-Landau, A. 2007. Let's Do the Time Warp Again: Migration Processes and the Absolute Chronology of the Philistine Settlement. In *The Synchronisation of Civilisations in the Eastern Mediterranean in the Second Millennium B.C. III, Proceedings of the SCIEM 2000—2nd EuroConference, Vienna, 28th of May–1st of June 2003*, ed. M. Bietak and E. Czerny, 610–17. Vienna: Verlag der Österreichischen Akademie der Wissenschaften.

Yasur-Landau, A. 2010a. *The Philistines and Aegean Migration at the End of the Late Bronze Age*. Cambridge: Cambridge University Press.

Yasur-Landau, A. 2010b. On Birds and Dragons: A Note on the Sea Peoples and Mycenaean Ships. In *Pax Hethitica. Studies on the Hittites and Their Neighbours in Honor of Itamar Singer*, ed. Y. Cohen, A. Gilan, and J. L. Miller, 399–410. Wiesbaden: Harrassowitz Verlag.

Yasur-Landau, A. 2012a. The Role of the Canaanite Population in the Aegean Migration to the Southern Levant in the Late Second Millennium BCE. In *Materiality and Social Practice: Transformative Capacities of Intercultural Encounters*, ed. J. Maran and P. W. Stockhammer, 191–97. Oxford: Oxbow Books.

Yasur-Landau, A. 2012b. Chariots, Spears and Wagons: Anatolian and Aegean Elements in the Medinet Habu Land Battle Relief. In *The Ancient Near East in the 12th–10th Centuries BCE: Culture and History. Proceedings of the International Conference Held at the University of Haifa, 2–5 May, 2010*, ed. G. Galil, A. Gilboa, A. M. Maeir, and D. Kahn, 549–67. AOAT 392. Münster: Ugarit-Verlag.

Yener, K. A. 2013a. New Excavations at Alalakh: the 14th–12th Centuries BC. In *Across the Border: Late Bronze–Iron Age Relations between Syria and Anatolia. Proceedings of a Symposium held at the Research Center of Anatolian Studies, Koç University, Istanbul May 31–June 1, 2010*, ed. K.A. Yener, 11-35. Leuven: Peeters.

Yener, K. A. 2013b. Recent Excavations at Alalakh: Throne Embellishments in Middle Bronze Age Level VII. In *Cultures in Contact: From Mesopotamia to the Mediterranean in the Second Millennium B.C.*, ed. J. Aruz, S. B. Graff, and Y. Rakic, 142–53. New York: Metropolitan Museum of Art.

Yoffee, N., and G. L. Cowgill, eds. 1988. *The Collapse of Ancient States and Civilization*. Tucson: University of Arizona.

Yon, M. 1992. The End of the Kingdom of Ugarit. In *The Crisis Years: The 12th Century B.C.*, ed. W. A. Ward and M. S. Joukowsky, 111–22. Dubuque, IA: Kendall/Hunt Publishing Co.

Yon, M. 2003. The Foreign Relations of Ugarit. In *Sea Routes . . . : Interconnections in the Mediterranean 16th–6th c. BC. Proceedings of the International Symposium Held at*

Rethymnon, Crete in September 29th–October 2nd 2002, ed. N. Chr. Stampolidis and V. Karageorghis, 41–51. Athens: University of Crete and the A. G. Leventis Foundation.

Yon, M. 2006. *The City of Ugarit at Tell Ras Shamra*. Winona Lake, IN: Eisenbrauns.

Yon, M., and D. Arnaud. 2001. *Études Ougaritiques I: Travaux 1985–1995*. Paris: Éditions Recherche sur les Civilisations.

Yon, M., M. Sznycer, and P. Bordreuil. 1955. *Le Pays d'Ougarit autour de 1200 av. J.-C.: Historie et archéologie. Actes du Colloque International; Paris, 28 juin–1er juillet 1993*. Paris: Éditions Recherche sur les Civilisations.

Zaccagnini, C. 1983. Patterns of Mobility among Ancient Near Eastern Craftsmen. *Journal of Near Eastern Studies* 42: 250–54.

Zeiger, A. 2012. 3,000-Year-Old Wheat Traces Said to Support Biblical Account of Israelite Conquest; Archaeologist Amnon Ben-Tor Claims Find at Tel Hazor Is a Remnant of Joshua's Military Campaign in 13th Century BCE. *Times of Israel*, July 23, 2012, http://www.timesofisrael.com/3000-year-old-wheat-corroborates-biblical-narrative-archaeologist-claims/ (last accessed August 6, 2012).

Zertal, A. 2002. Philistine Kin Found in Early Israel. *Biblical Archaeology Review* 28/3: 18–31, 60–61.

Zettler, R. L. 1992. 12th Century B.C. Babylonia: Continuity and Change. In *The Crisis Years: The 12th Century B.C.*, ed. W. A. Ward and M. S. Joukowsky, 174–81. Dubuque, IA: Kendall/Hunt Publishing Co.

Zink, A. R., et al. 2012. Revisiting the Harem Conspiracy and Death of Ramesses III: Anthropological, Forensic, Radiological, and Genetic Study. *British Medical Journal* 345 (2012): 345:e8268, http://www.bmj.com/content/345/bmj.e8268 (last accessed August 25, 2013).

Zivie, A. 1987. *The Lost Tombs of Saqqara*. Cairo: American University in Cairo Press.

Zuckerman, S. 2006. Where Is the Hazor Archive Buried? *Biblical Archaeology Review* 32/2 (2006): 28–37.

Zuckerman, S. 2007a. Anatomy of a Destruction: Crisis Architecture, Termination Rituals and the Fall of Canaanite Hazor. *Journal of Mediterranean Archaeology* 20/1: 3–32.

Zuckerman, S. 2007b. Dating the Destruction of Canaanite Hazor *without* Mycenaean Pottery? In *The Synchronisation of Civilisations in the Eastern Mediterranean in the Second Millennium B.C. III, Proceedings of the SCIEM 2000—2nd EuroConference, Vienna, 28th of May–1st of June 2003*, ed. M. Bietak and E. Czerny, 621–29. Vienna: Verlag der Österreichischen Akademie der Wissenschaften.

Zuckerman, S. 2009. The Last Days of a Canaanite Kingdom: A View from Hazor. In *Forces of Transformation: The End of the Bronze Age in the Mediterranean*, ed. C. Bachhuber and R. G. Roberts, 100–107. Oxford: Oxbow Books.

Zuckerman, S. 2010. "The City, Its Gods Will Return There . . .": Toward an Alternative Interpretation of Hazor's Acropolis in the Late Bronze Age. *Journal of Near Eastern Studies* 69/2: 163–78.

Zwickel, W. 2012. The Change from Egyptian to Philistine Hegemony in South-Western Palestine during the Time of Ramesses III or IV. In *The Ancient Near East in the 12th–10th Centuries BCE: Culture and History. Proceedings of the International Conference Held at the University of Haifa, 2–5 May, 2010*, ed. G. Galil, A. Gilboa, A. M. Maeir, and D. Kahn, 595–601. AOAT 392. Münster: Ugarit-Verlag.